THE CHRISTIAN TASK
IN INDIA

MACMILLAN AND CO., Limited
LONDON · BOMBAY · CALCUTTA · MADRAS
MELBOURNE

THE MACMILLAN COMPANY
NEW YORK · BOSTON · CHICAGO
DALLAS · SAN FRANCISCO

THE MACMILLAN COMPANY
OF CANADA, LIMITED
TORONTO

THE CHRISTIAN TASK
IN INDIA

BY VARIOUS WRITERS

EDITED BY

THE REV. JOHN McKENZIE, M.A.
PRINCIPAL OF WILSON COLLEGE, BOMBAY

WITH AN INTRODUCTION BY

THE MOST REV. THE BISHOP OF CALCUTTA

MACMILLAN AND CO., LIMITED
ST. MARTIN'S STREET, LONDON
1929

COPYRIGHT

PRINTED IN GREAT BRITAIN
BY R. & R. CLARK, LIMITED, EDINBURGH

PREFACE

THE title of this book may suggest an almost impossibly ambitious purpose, for to anyone who believes in Christianity the Christian task in any land must appear to be one of infinite greatness and complexity. The writers have not set out to deal with all the various ends and activities which concern Christian people in regard to India. Their object is the much more limited one of trying to give, primarily with Christian readers in view, an account of some of the most important organized Christian activities which are being carried on in India and of the purposes which underlie them. The writers are Christian men and women who are either actively engaged in, or who at least are familiar with, the phases of life and work about which they write. They are convinced of the supreme importance for India of the Christian message and its practical implications, and they are aware that for the presentation of the Gospel and for the building up of the Church there is need for a great variety of forms of Christian service. They are convinced of the great value of their own special work, not as the only, or necessarily as the most important, form of service, but as a contribution towards the fulfilment of the great common task in which in their different ways they are co-operating. It is hoped that the presentation in this form of some of the most outstanding of the great variety of these forms of service in their relation to the needs of India may help readers to a fuller understanding of the greatness of the task and of the significance of these activities in the Christian movement as a whole.

Throughout the book the Christian position has been taken for granted. Assuming the supreme value for all men of the Christian message, the writers have sought chiefly to explain how it is touching, or how it ought to touch, the life of India. There are many people, even in so-called Christian countries, who do not share this assumption. These people often have their own views of Christian work in lands like India, views which are sometimes favourable and sometimes unfavourable. There are those who have no interest in the specifically spiritual message of Christianity, but who approve of some forms of Christian work on the ground of their social, economic or political value. There are others who pass a more or less wholesale condemnation upon all missionary work, because they consider that it leads to results that are in conflict with their secular purposes. Illustration of this is hardly necessary, but I would say that almost as much harm has been done to the Christian cause by people who have praised missionary work as a tranquillizing political influence or as an auxiliary to trade, as by those who have roundly condemned it as exercising influences that make people more difficult to govern and less amenable to commercial exploitation. Praise and blame of this kind are very largely irrelevant. The Kingdom of God is not a tributary to any of the kingdoms of this world, whether they be political or economic.

This does not mean that the Kingdom of God is so spiritual that it has no touch with the earth. It stands not for the negation of the material and the secular, but for their transformation so that the highest spiritual ends may be fulfilled in them. Participation in the Kingdom of God means, accordingly, not mere spiritual

PREFACE vii

status, but a life in the world which derives its direction and inspiration from the Spirit of Christ. Man's deepest need is for a right relationship to God. And this relationship to God, as the Christian understands it, involves right relationships to the world. This is a point of view which is diametrically opposed to the secularist view. It assumes an entirely different standard of values. We have here taken the Christian standard of values for granted, and have tried to show some of its implications in India. To those who do not accept it this book will make little appeal, but we trust that many who do accept it will be helped to a fuller understanding of the task which lies before not only the Christian Church but all Christian people in India.

A number of chapters have been devoted to Christian activity in relation to some of the most outstanding human needs—needs of which every dweller in India is conscious. It is a familiar fact, which is abundantly illustrated throughout the book, that there are two lines or streams of Christian service. There is the simple ministry to human need which springs from Christian love and sympathy, the " cup of cold water in the name of a disciple ", and there is the service which aims more directly at what we speak of as the extension of the Kingdom of God. They are two streams, but they have one source and one end, and it is impossible to pursue one of them to the exclusion of the other without grave misrepresentation of the Kingdom itself. This does not mean that all Christian service must be performed with an eye to " spiritual " results. It does not mean, to put it crudely, that the Christian doctor and teacher, for example, should be animated in all their work of healing and teaching by the direct purpose of making Christians of those whom they serve. It is to a service far more Christian than this—a service far more divine and at the same time far more human—that our Lord

has called us. His own service of men was in a very real
sense of the word " sacramental ".   His works of love
awakened men's sense of the spiritual not by their
external association with spiritual purposes, but by the
revelation of love which they themselves conveyed. All
the human needs which He met were but parts of the
one great need, the need for God ; and His gracious
acts to the needy and the suffering were performed not
in order to point to a source of supply for other and
deeper needs, but as the expression of a love that goes
out to meet the whole need of man. This is the secret
of all true Christian service, and no work can be fully
Christian in which any kind of " philanthropic "
activity is practised as an external and more or less
adventitious means of securing attention to a "spiritual"
message. The great question concerning these forms
of Christian service is not whether they are producing
results, but whether they are being rendered in the
spirit of Christ. I think that in writing thus I am
interpreting truly the minds of the contributors to this
volume.

We have given a place of central importance to the
Christian Church, because, differing as we do in many
things, we are all convinced of the need that Christian
men and women have for fellowship in worship, thought
and service. We should all say more about the basis of
Christian fellowship than this, but here we have at least
its simple psychological basis. In the letter of invitation
which was sent out to proposed contributors it was
assumed " that we are agreed that the aim of all our
work is to bring the people of India into the fellowship
of the Church of Christ, with all that this means of new
spiritual, ethical and social life ". It was not assumed
that we were all agreed in regard to many questions
concerning the constitution and character of the Church.
As a matter of fact, the reader will find differences in the

ideas of the Church presented by different writers,
ranging from the " Catholic " conception of the Church
to such a conception as that of " the Fellowship of the
Kingdom of God ". There is no doubt in any mind as
to the need for fellowship.

The historical Christian Society has had its great and
glaring weaknesses and faults. Bishop Gore, whose
zeal for the Church no one will doubt, has written :

> The Catholic Church of history has by its superstitions,
> its moral and intellectual weaknesses and its narrownesses
> —especially at certain periods—alienated such a vast body
> of the world's best feeling, that the very idea of the Church
> as the home of the Spirit (" *Extra ecclesiam nulla salus* ")
> excites the sort of resentment which seems to deprive many
> men of the very capacity for fresh inquiry.[1]

We cannot but acknowledge that the Church in
India has her own weaknesses, weaknesses which have
alienated men who ought to have been in the Christian
fellowship. But it is a question which merits serious
consideration whether these weaknesses are inherent
in the ecclesiastical structure, or whether they are
not rather weaknesses which have to be continually
guarded against in any fellowship that is not vague,
temporary and unsubstantial. To quote Bishop Gore
again :

> " Ecclesiastical " ought to mean " brotherly ". It did
> really mean this in the days when it cost men much to
> call themselves Christians. It may come to be so again
> in no distant future, and the Church may regain its ancient
> meaning.[2]

This is what all truly Christian people desire that
the Church should be. Whatever other impression
this book may create in the minds of readers, I think
it will create at least this one, that there is in India a

---

[1] *The Reconstruction of Belief*, p. 646. [2] *Ibid*. p. 648.

body of Christian men and women who are concerned not with the mere victory of one religious institution over others, or even with the victory of one faith over others, but with the bringing to men of the good news of the love of God in Jesus Christ, and with the bringing of those who accept the message into fellowship in worship and in service of one another and of the world. It is through the Church, with all her faults, that the inspiration to the highest Christian service has been mediated, and, whatever view we take of the question of the divine institution of the Church, we shall find it difficult, if not impossible, to separate the thought of the Christian Gospel from that of a Christian Society. In the past it has not been the Christian features of that Society that have given offence to good men, but the un-Christian features, and we need in India, as much as in any other part of the world, to test everything that we would associate with the Church by reference to the mind of Christ.

In the closing chapters attention is directed specifically to the Christian Church in India, and it is fitting that the movement towards unity should be described and explained. At the time of writing the negotiations in South India have reached a stage which gives solid ground for hope that an incorporating union, more comprehensive than any previous union, may be achieved in the near future. If this hope is realized, India may, by God's grace, have the distinction of setting an example that may have the greatest and most far-reaching consequences for the Christian Church throughout the whole world. Whatever may be said in defence of our divisions—and no reasonable person will assert that their outcome has been wholly evil—there can be no doubt that much evil has come from our carrying into India divisions which are largely the result of Western controversies. By this our witness to Christ has been confused, and our service of Him has been weakened. We who are concerned with the development of the Churches which are growing up in non-Christian lands are perhaps more deeply conscious of this than are most people in the West. Yet in both East and West the evils of division are being increasingly felt, and many readers may be helped to a new conception of the significance of the Christian task in India when they realize how the great problem of unity is there being faced.

Writers are responsible only for the views expressed in their own chapters. The editor does not commit himself to agreement with all the views that are contained in these contributions, but he has taken the responsibility of presenting them to the public as being in line with the general purpose of the book.

Thanks are due to all who have co-operated in the preparation of this work, and, in particular, to the Rev. Dr. Macnicol, who has read all the proofs and made many valuable suggestions.

JOHN McKENZIE.

INTRODUCTION

ONE of the earliest names for the religion of Christ was
" The Way ", and for the first three centuries of its
existence it was primarily as a " Way of Life " that it
was presented to the non-Christian world. With the
rapid expansion of the Church after the Edict of Con-
stantine, heresies multiplied, and attention was directed
to the right intellectual expression of the Faith, and the
holding of the correct belief became the hall-mark of a
Christian, rather than the character of his life. I would
not minimize the importance of a true theological foundation for the Christian life, but the secret of the
Christian life is to be found in fellowship with God in
Christ, and that can be realized without any intimate
acquaintance with the theology which justifies faith in
the great truths upon which it rests.

I am sure that in India to-day we need to present the
Christian religion far more as a way of life than we have
done, and as such it must cover the whole of life in all
its diverse activities and relationships. It is thus that
I conceive of the Christian task in India. In essence it
is not different from that which confronts the Church in
every country, but in practice the special conditions of
India must determine the character of the presentation,
and, indeed, provide the stimulus which will evoke an
expression of some aspects of the truth which would
otherwise have remained latent.

The spirit of Christ is the spirit of service, and

missionary fervour has embraced the opportunities of
varied service which poverty of many kinds affords in
this as in other lands. The demand for education,
healing and uplift has given ample scope for presenting
in a practical way the ideals of the Christian life, and
the secret of its power.

This book tells of the way in which those opportunities have been used. The authors, in their several
chapters, treat of those special branches of missionary
activity in which they have themselves been noted
workers. They endeavour to relate their own work to
other parts of the missionary task, and, not shrinking from the duty of criticism, to point out defects in
method, while indicating the direction in which improvement lies.

The book is itself the fruit of that co-operation for
which it pleads, and an argument in its favour ; may
it bring home to every reader the sin of our divisions,
and so hasten the day when the Church shall face its
task in India with an unbroken front.

FOSS CALCUTTA.

CONTENTS

CONTENTS xvii

By P. OOMMAN PHILIP, B.A., Secretary of the National
Christian Council of India, Burma and Ceylon.

By the Rev. WILLIAM PATON, M.A., Secretary of the International Missionary Council; formerly Secretary of the
National Christian Council of India, Burma and Ceylon.

By the Rev. N. MACNICOL, D.Litt., D.D., and P. OOMMAN
PHILIP, B.A.

By the Right Rev. EDWIN JAMES PALMER, D.D., Bishop of
Bombay, with the co-operation of the Rev. J. H. MACLEAN,
B.D., United Free Church of Scotland Mission, Conjeeveram,
and the Rev. F. H. RUSSELL, D.D., United Church of Canada
Mission, Dhar, Central India.

8

CHAPTER I

THE NATURE OF THE TASK

By S. K. DATTA

AN interesting subject of a thesis would be the consideration of the development of the missionary message in
India from the time of Ward's *View of the Hindus*,
published at Serampore over a century ago. Readers
may recollect that a few years later, Raja Ram Mohun
Roy, in the columns of a Calcutta paper, stated that
Christianity had been misinterpreted by its followers.
He wrote under the pseudonym of " Ram Loll "—for
had he not himself issued from the Serampur Press a
pamphlet entitled *The Teachings of Jesus the Guide to
Life and Happiness*? A Christian controversialist in a
public rejoinder to the Raja had closed his letter to the
press with the following words : " Your determined and
inveterate foe in the Lord ". It was difficult in those
distant days to appraise the Christian message to India.
Is it any easier to-day, when the solvents of comparative
religion, science and economic determinism have led to
such fundamental changes in our outlook ? It is easy
to be critical of those early, bigoted, yet devoted, Christian propagators, but it is still easier for us to fail to rely
upon the inherently divine in the Christian message, or
to believe in its efficacy for all men as individuals.

What, then, is the nature of the task in India ? We
are told that the purpose is to make India Christian.

What exactly does this mean ? Since the early nineteenth century various interpretations have been given to this process. In the first place, the task of the Church in India was said to be the substitution of Christianity for the older and indigenous beliefs of the people. In the second place, the task was conceived as one of permeation. In other words, the change was not to be cataclysmic, though the object was the same. It was conceived that indigenous religious ideas would change through the inductive influence of Christianity. In the third place, some have held that the product would be not Christianity, as we conceive it to-day, but something else, the resultant of inter-religious activity in India ; in fact, Christianity itself might begin to learn from other religions, and would also be transformed by this process.

In India there are examples, on a small scale, of substitution. Thus we find it in the old Portuguese dominion of Goa, where the non-Christian religions are now in a minority, so far as numbers are concerned. Churches and monasteries have taken the place of Hindu temples. Yet, it would be a legitimate question to ask whether this substitution has in any way brought Christianity nearer to India. There are many who would doubt it. During the nineteenth century some substantial communities have become Christian ; this is true in what are called the mass-movement areas. The characteristics of these movements is that Christianity is confined to a particular class, and that, ordinarily, these classes are the humblest elements of the population ; that as a result of Christianity these particular communities become unified, on the whole show great religious zeal, and are willing to undertake responsibility for the development of their local churches. These churches have become the centre for a social revolutionary movement among the outcastes, a marked feature of Indian life at the present time. The movement thus come to

birth is directed against the old social order of Hinduism,
which looked upon the lowest as being without the pale of
civilization.   India is reaping a Nemesis for the neglect
of the outcaste, and to-day is beginning to recognize
that these groups are embarrassing her in her political
evolution.   In recent times attention has been called to
their importance by leading British politicians.   Twenty
years ago no responsible British statesman would ever
have conceived that this class was of any political
value.   Very largely this revolution has taken place as
the result of work carried on by the Christian Church.
To appraise its value, for an Indian, may possibly be
difficult.   In the first place, this movement is looked upon
by the Indian nationalist as being anti-national.   In the
second place, Christianity is not the only movement that
has contributed to the welfare of these classes.   Islam
did it under the old Moslem dynasties, witness the
Moslem tenantry of Eastern Bengal.   In South India we
have also a very remarkable movement among a particular caste, who, within the last few years, by their own
unaided efforts, have attempted, and successfully attempted, to bring about a social revolution.   In many
ways this community is further on than any of the other
depressed communities in India.   This uplift movement
was brought about without help from Christian missions,
and certainly the results have justified the efforts made
by these peoples.   The results may be the production of
stronger character by an indigenous leadership than in
a movement which is largely fostered from outside by
foreign missions.

A very fascinating study would be the consideration
of the current literature of India, and especially the
autobiographies of eminent Indians of the last fifty
years.   Such a study, I think, would result in the discovery of the immense place that Christian thought, life
and even phraseology have in modern Indian expression.

From whence have these been obtained ?   It is clear that
the two main sources have been, firstly, schools and colleges, and secondly, the circulation of literature.   Possibly, in a smaller degree, but probably qualitative
even more valuable, has been personal contact wit
Christian men and women.   From the days of Raja Ram
Mohun Roy to Mr. Gandhi, the Sermon on the Mount
has been one of the outstanding sources of spiritual
stimulus to many Indians.   In more recent times even
more impressively than Christian doctrine, the Christian
life has made its influence felt.   It may be that the
Christian message at this juncture will be to give the
modern man and woman something to live by.

Whatever the triumphs of Christianity, which, be it
remembered, have been questioned, yet they are small
and imperfect compared with the claims made in the
name of that religion.   Let us re-examine the situation.
Throughout the latter half of the nineteenth century,
and, indeed, through the first decade of the twentieth, a
mechanical conception of the progress of Christianity,
it would appear, held the ground.   By this theory is
meant the belief that, given sufficient resources of
Christian personnel, institutions and money, it would be
possible to evangelize the world.   This was the age when
the best of missionary literature dealt with figures; maps
were dotted with mission stations, and the prospects of
an advance were calculated.   It rarely occurred to
Christian thinkers to inquire as to what was happening
in the countries to which their efforts were directed.   If
they had done so, they would speedily have discovered
that opposition was steadily developing, which made the
Christian task even more difficult than it ever had been
when it dealt with more or less passive populations.   The
position of Christianity as an imperial religion was being
challenged, and particularly in those countries where the
political power was in the hands of so-called Christian

nations. Has it occurred to anyone to inquire why it is that in India, the Dutch Indies, and, I believe, in French Indo-China, Christianity, as a religion, has failed to be accepted by the influential intellectual classes. This is probably not as true of Japan and China. May the explanation not lie in the fact that Christianity in the first three countries is the ruler's religion, and, as nationalism becomes stronger, Christianity is thrust aside as being the symbol of a governing race? It may be said that Christianity really never has a chance in these countries to be considered on its own merits. Somehow or other, Christianity must divest herself of the imperial purple. Again, Christianity has been challenged on her failure to live up to her own teaching. On the one hand, her propagandists have attacked the Hindu social order because of its illiberality and failure to acknowledge the equality of all men. It is an irony of fate that some modern Christian countries have erected a social and political order from which the Asiatic and other non-European races are for ever debarred. It would appear that a Hindu social order has been transplanted from across the seas, and has taken root in alien soil, among nations whose religious representatives are for ever dinning into the Indian ear the injustice of the caste system.

India, among other Eastern nations, has suffered a rude awakening ; she, too, has attempted to organize herself. Together with these nations she has pinned her faith to a creed in which the main articles are as follows : In the first place, a system of national education, which means that the whole method of educating the country should be inspired with a national purpose. Such a system is bound, in the long run, to become an instrument of intellectual and spiritual tyranny, and with it will go, if carried to its logical conclusions, that intellectual liberty, on which Indians have, in the past, justly prided themselves. In the second place, India, together with other Eastern nations, has developed a profound belief in the efficacy of the modern economic and industrial order. Mr. Gandhi's life and teaching are a protest against the view, held by many modern Indians, that in economic and industrial power lie the means of national salvation. We have arrived at the stage where money has become a power that will attempt to exploit the poor, and all this in the name of nationalism. In the third place, in spite of Mr. Gandhi's protest, the directing classes in India, as in other Eastern countries, have acquired a new faith in the efficacy of force. Is it without significance that China, which in the past has always been regarded as a country with pacific ideals, in whose social order the soldier took a humble place, has recently decided, through her modern political organs, to impose compulsory military service throughout the country ? In India, too, the governing bodies of universities, which are largely composed of Indians, have considered with favour schemes for compulsory military training for all students in their universities. Now, in these situations can Christianity play a part ; has she sufficient moral authority ? If she can rid herself from her Western trappings, only then can she give guidance and help. The task of the Church is far greater than she has ever conceived, but it would appear doubtful at times whether she can give to India, at the present time, direction and guidance.

On the other hand, the right of self-government for any nation is a sacred concern, and Christians should make no reservations, however rights which may accrue to them as members of a governing race or a protected minority are adversely affected. This, however, does not mean that all Christians must give their assent to any particular scheme drawn up by all and sundry political parties ; but for Christians to stand in the way of genuine

and even radical reforms is unworthy of the Christian
profession. But with this assent, the task of Christianity
has only just begun, for upon Christians will lie some of
the responsibility of constantly directing the attention
of the nation builder to higher ends, and, above all, to
spiritual realities. Industrialization and the possession
of economic power often lead to social injustice, and to a
secular view of life, in which men believe in their own
unaided authorship of all good, and human action is untrammelled by the divine. Spiritual ends are forgotten,
and the individual is subordinated to materialistic conceptions of personal profit. Can Christianity continuously utter its protest against these aspects of the new
national life ? Can its followers so live and act in this
new world of India, that men will recognize the direction of God, and the imperative rights of the spiritual
world ? This can only be accomplished if Christians
will humble themselves even as their Master did, by
emptying Himself of all privilege, by taking up the
Cross of self-effacing service, by uttering the gospel of
love, by healing the wounds of strife.

Concretely, however, Christianity operates partially
at any rate through missionary institutions and agency.
How should they envisage their task ? In the first place,
the missionary enterprise is called upon to continue in
many other spheres its efforts of service to the people of
India, possibly not so much by an extension of its work
as by its quality. During the last ten years or more,
constant evidence has been given by the missionary body
of its desire to meet the present situation, and this probably most vitally in its educational activities. In this, as
in other directions, missionaries can become the conduits
through which the best in Europe and America flows
into India in the form of educational ideals and technique
—education in its broadest sense.

Christianity is called upon to emphasize constantly

8 THE CHRISTIAN TASK IN INDIA CH.

the value of the individual, the necessity to free him from oppression of all kinds—economic, social, religious. The welfare of the agricultural labourer, and now of the industrial worker, has claimed attention. Christianity is called upon to summon men to pattern their lives according to the example of Jesus Christ. The essence of Christianity lies in the transforming qualities of a personal relationship of men to its Founder—whether within or without the Christian Church as it is constituted to-day. Of this, men such as Narayan Vaman Tilak have dreamed : " The Lord Jesus Christ is founding Swaraj in men's hearts, hence also in the world of men ; . . . by Swaraj is meant the Kingdom of Heaven, the Rule of God ". But this transformation cannot be accomplished by machinery or by a system. Christianity is an infection which is caught from the example and lives of its followers, carrying on the ordinary tasks of life, as teachers, through their social and family life and spiritual experience.

The task of Christianity is to open its doors to the spiritual experience and life of all those around them who seek to discover God. Christianity has influenced Indian religions, but for the reason that the nexus with the dominant civilization of the world still continues, it has proved irresponsive to the wealth of spiritual experience and religious idealism outside its immediate boundaries. An immense field of discovery lies at the hand of Christian thinkers in India.

The task of Christianity can never be completed ; it is as varied as evolving Indian life itself. Our concern should be whether its capacity to fulfil those tasks is not limited by its alien environment. The missionary system may itself be a handicap, but just here the necessity arises to state what is involved with greater precision. Some appreciation of the problem may be obtained by the analogy of the old " colonial system " in

Europe, which grew up in the eighteenth century, and still continues to exist, although considerably abated in strength, and certainly in public esteem. The colonial system, it is true, had its value ; it evolved order frequently out of chaos, its agents were persons of rectitude, and certainly showed great devotion in carrying out their tasks. Yet the system failed when tried with European peoples, as in the United States of America, in Canada and in other parts of the British Empire, for it was based on the subordination of distant communities to the interests of the metropolitan power. While it would be unjust to assert that the analogy is complete in the realm of Western Christianity, yet there is a certain truth in the contention that Christianity, as introduced to India through the missionary system, has (it may be in spite of itself) exercised a dominating influence of power and authority—this, at any rate, would be the verdict of many a thoughtful Hindu. Where does the solution lie ? It may be stated in these terms : the task of Christianity is to create in India a Church—not a community—whose agents will be a spiritual order of men and women, without distinction of race, who will give to India through their lives and teaching the inexhaustible riches of Christ.

CHAPTER II

THE INTELLIGENTSIA

By J. C. WINSLOW

I

THE expression " the Intelligentsia " is used here to denote that element in the population of India which has received what we think of as a modern education through the medium of English. In this sense it is not synonymous with the educated classes, for there are large numbers of Indians who have received a purely vernacular (and Sanskrit) education, and yet ought certainly to be ranked as educated men and women. For the purposes of this essay the term Intelligentsia will be restricted, whether legitimately or not, to that class which has come under the influences of what may be described comprehensively as " Western thought ", through an education received in schools and colleges where English is the medium of instruction, English literature holds a foremost place in the syllabus of studies, and Western history, science and philosophy also figure prominently in the curriculum.

This class is not confined to the adherents of any one religion. It is recruited from Hindus, Moslems, Christians, Parsees, Jains and Sikhs. It contains women as well as men ; but, except in the case of the Parsees and Christians, the men enormously preponderate. Of this whole class of the Intelligentsia, 75 per

down the long-standing obstacles to its realization. His teaching about the Fatherhood of God would be rejected by many educated Moslems, but would be accepted by most Hindus as in line with their own " bhakti " teaching,[1] though many would add that the conception of a personal God which it implies is one which, legitimate in its own sphere, is transcended in the ascent of man's spirit to the higher conception of the Absolute.

(2) Side by side with this widespread acceptance of Christ's teaching goes a very general reverence for His life and character. Moslems acknowledge Him as one of the great Prophets. Hindus will readily speak of Him as a veritable incarnation of God. In spite of recent attempts to impugn the character of Christ, His life is recognized by very many as the ideal human life. His passion and death make a very deep appeal to the heart of India as the supreme instance of that patient and unswerving holding to truth in the face of all suffering, which Mahatma Gandhi has named Satyagraha.

Dr. Stanley Jones, through his book *The Christ of the Indian Road*, has made widely known the attitude of educated India to Christ, and has given numerous and striking illustrations of the extent to which Hindus everywhere are found willing to accept Him as Guru, or Master. This movement probably reached its height a few years ago under the influence of Mahatma Gandhi in the fervour of the Non-co-operation days, and seems to have somewhat declined of late. But there can be no doubt that very large numbers of educated Indians everywhere are still looking to Christ as their Guru in a sense in which they look to no one else, and now, as always, a certain number of them come forward into full and open allegiance through baptism.

(3) On the other hand, the claim that Christ was, and is, in a *unique* sense divine is not one which the

[1] Union with God by the way of a loving personal devotion.

majority of Hindus, even of those deeply attracted by
His life, would be prepared to accept.[1]   India holds in
reverence all great religious teachers as having come
from God—as being indeed manifestations of the divine
in human form ; and so deep is the appeal that Christ
makes to her that she would set Him side by side with
her own great Prophet, the Buddha.   But the Christian
claim that He, and He only, is God Incarnate, and that
salvation is to be won through faith in Him, and Him
alone, she rejects as exclusive and narrow.   She believes
that all religions are in measure true, that all are ways
by which man may attain to God, and that the essentials
of all the great religions are the same.   To her the
Bhagavad-gītā has teaching as uplifting as the Gospels.
To all Gurus she opens her heart wide, abhorring
intolerance or exclusiveness in the religious sphere.[2]
Thus the Christian claim to possess the one way of
salvation arouses in India an almost instinctive re-
pugnance.

(4) Further, even those who accept Christ as the
one Guru whom they seek to follow have little desire
to enter the Christian Church by baptism.   This is not
only from fear of breaking caste and incurring the per-
secution or social ostracism which this usually brings,
nor merely from what is often the still more daunting
fear of causing heart-rending sorrow to dearly loved
parents.   It is due still more to the sense that the act
of baptism implies, not simply breaking with one's
religious heritage from the past (that any convert
expects to face), but a break with one's whole social
and cultural inheritance also.   It appears to mean joining oneself to a community which is foreign and strange
in all its ways.   For not only is Christianity to the

[1] Moslems would, of course, refuse to acknowledge Him as divine
at all.

[2] This is true only of matters of faith.   In practice, as in regards to
the breaking of caste, Hinduism is as intolerant as any other religion.

Hindu the religion of the alien ruling race, but its
churches are Western and its worship unintelligible,
while its converts for the most part imitate their Western
teachers in habits and ways of life, and thus appear
divorced from the rest of their fellow-countrymen and
from the main stream of the national life.[1] It is not
unnatural, therefore, that a high-caste Hindu, even
though he desires to become a disciple of Christ, should
shrink from the kind of change which that step seems
to him to involve. He believes that faith is a matter
of inner conviction rather than of outward forms, and
that he can be a true Christian without the acceptance
of baptism. There are to-day in India hundreds of
such men who would regard themselves, and speak of
themselves, as unbaptized Christians.

(5) Perhaps we might summarize the characteristic
religious attitude of the educated Hindu to-day by
saying that, whilst he greatly reverences Christ, and
accepts the main principles of His teaching, he is quite
content to remain a Hindu, and feels no difficulty in
interpreting Hinduism for himself in a way that is in
no conflict with Christian teaching. Prof. Radhakrishnan's book, *The Hindu Way of Life*, whilst it has
been freely criticized by Hindus themselves as not being
a true account of the real Hinduism, is an admirable
example of this modern attitude. The neo-Hinduism
of forty or fifty years ago (associated with the names of
Ramkrishna Paramahansa and Swami Vivekananda)
sought to give symbolic and spiritual interpretation to
those elements of orthodox Hinduism which the modern
mind finds objectionable. The neo-Hinduism of to-
day does not trouble to re-interpret these elements. It
ignores them as not forming part of the essential
Hinduism. Even a belief which would generally be

[1] It must be admitted that the Christian students of Bengal are a
happy exception to this rule.

C

thought so vital to Hinduism as that in transmigration
is almost ignored in Professor Radhakrishnan's lectures,
whilst " karma " is treated (without special reference
to previous births) as simply the law of cause and effect
in the moral sphere—" What a man sows that shall
he also reap ".   Clearly we have here a *rapprochement*
to Christianity from the side of Hinduism which no
thoughtful Christian can do otherwise than gladly
welcome.[1]

III

What, then, is the task of the Christian Church in
relation to the Intelligentsia of India in the conditions
we have here summarized ?

It is perhaps hardly necessary in these days to
emphasize that the Church's task is not to carry to
India Western culture or Western civilization.   India
may or may not desire these.   They may or may not
be for her good.   In any case their propagation is not
part of the Church's commission.

It is more important to make clear that the Christian
task is not " proselytizing " in the sense of simply
seeking to win as many adherents as possible to one's
own religion.   There is a widespread conviction
amongst educated Indians (unfortunately not altogether
without some plausible foundation in view of things
which some missionaries have said and done) that the
missionary, even if he be not an emissary of Government,
is at least the counterpart of the British imperialist in
the religious sphere.   His aim, it is thought, is to
increase in every possible way his own prestige and the

[1] I have omitted, for lack of space, any reference to the Shuddhi
and Sangathan movements, which are in some ways the most important
movements within Hinduism at the present time.   They are directed
towards its consolidating and strengthening ; and, though at present in
their aggressive aspect they have specially the Moslems in mind, they
are logically, and might at any moment become actually, opposed in
equal degree to the results of Christian propaganda.

prestige of the Christian Church by winning the largest
possible number of " converts " without any real regard
to their actual conversion.   It is therefore of the utmost
importance that missionaries should make it clear that
respect for personality and for individual conviction
is essential to the Christian attitude, that they care
nothing for accessions to the Christian community un-
accompanied by " change of heart ", and that they
recognize " the futility of an aggression which has
egotism and not the love of Christ and of mankind in
Christ as its centre " (Macnicol).   There are few
educated Hindus or Moslems who would question the
right of any man to change his religious allegiance in
case of a real change of conviction.   We must make it
clear that this is all which we too desire.   Few things
so lower the spiritual life of the Christian Church as the
accession to her ranks of large numbers of purely
nominal Christians.   We can have no interest in working
for this.

   Yet once again, it must be made clear that the
Christian Church is not out for the destruction of
Hinduism or of any other religion as such.   The
Church's campaign is not against any religion, but
against all that is evil in the world, all that stands opposed to the Kingdom of God, wherever found.   This
does not mean that we accept the position, so frequently
taken up by Hindus, that all religions are true.   In
view of the radical divergences that exist between the
different religions in regard to most of their principal
tenets, it is, indeed, amazing that so many people, in
other respects sagacious and thoughtful, can be found
to concur in this superficial judgement.   It would, in
fact, be much truer to say that hardly a single belief
can be found, either in regard to the nature of God or
the duty of man, which is common to all religions.
What is undoubtedly true, and what is perhaps usually

intended by the facile dictum quoted above, is that all
religions contain large elements of truth. Hinduism,
for example, contains within it a rich store of spiritual
treasures, gradually built up through the centuries,
which it would be the veriest vandalism to destroy.
Christ comes "not to destroy but to fulfil".[1] He
comes to bring to completion all the noblest elements in
Hinduism and the other faiths, and in that very process all that is ignoble or unworthy or inadequate
begins to be automatically sloughed off. The enlightened Hindu conscience is itself rejecting much that was
formerly considered orthodox Hinduism, and carrying
on a gradually strengthening campaign against the
evils within its own society. The Christian could desire nothing better. He does not wish for the overthrow
of Hinduism, but for the victory of truth and right.
If these are preached and practised, under whatever
name, he must therein rejoice.

The Church's task, then, is neither to propagate
Western culture, nor to multiply adherents in a spirit of
domination, nor to aim simply at the destruction of
other faiths. It is, as it has always been, to set forth
Christ before the world, and above all, Christ crucified
and risen. The true Christian missionary is out for
one thing, and one only, and that is to share with others
his own supreme treasure, that thing which transforms
his own life with radiance, "the excellency of the
knowledge of Christ Jesus his Lord". To hold back
this, which means all the world to him and countless
others, would be the veriest selfishness. To make it
known becomes the absorbing passion of his life. "Woe
is unto me if I preach not the gospel".

He seeks to present Christ as that which he has

[1] This sentence had reference, as originally spoken, to Judaism. I
believe it may be more widely applied, but I must not be understood
as supposing that it applies to any other religion as fully as to Judaism.

found Him in his own experience to be—the Way to the Father, because He is both the Truth and the Life. He is the Truth. In Him is seen the very image of the likeness of God, according to His own saying, " He that hath seen me hath seen the Father ", and in Him is seen also the very pattern of what true man should be. This revelation in Christ of God's nature, and of man's ideal, culminating and focussed in the Cross of Calvary, results, for those who accept it, in an immense illumination of conscience, both revealing the true hatefulness of sin and also quickening the longing for escape from its shackles. But Christ is also the Life. He is, for the Christian, not only the one supremely triumphant character in human history, but the risen and living Lord, imparting to all who will accept Him His own Spirit, charged with all the unimagined poten- cies of His own victorious life. There is in Him, we believe and know, unlimited power both for escape from the chains of past failure and for sustained moral renewal. We would have all men know and share these riches of Christ. It is this moral re-creation of men, through faith in and obedience to the living Christ, which is the supreme objective in the Christian task.

Now, if our aim be thus envisaged as the invitation to others to share our own most treasured possession— the desire to introduce to others the Christ whose beauty and power have transfigured life for us—it surely becomes not only easy but inevitable that we should combine in that task a flaming and almost intolerant zeal and passion for Christ, with the most generous breadth of sympathy and appreciation to- wards other religions. There have always been in the history of Christian missions two main lines of approach to other faiths. There has been the way of uncom- promising opposition, represented by people like Ter-

tullian in early days, and St. Francis Xavier in India
at a later date, or Pandita Ramabai in our own times.
To such Christians, what is most obvious is the gulf
of difference which separates the light that has come
to them through Christ from the darkness with which
their earlier days were surrounded. They can see little
that is good in other faiths. To them Christ is the
great Uprooter and Rebuilder. The other way is the
way of sympathy, represented in early days by Clement
and the Alexandrian school of Christian teachers
generally, and later, in India, by such men as De Nobili,
or, in our own time, Narayan Vaman Tilak. Such men
delight in stressing the resemblances, rather than the
differences, between Christianity and other religions.
They welcome the lives of good men of other faiths,
and all noble teaching found elsewhere, as rays proceeding from the one divine Logos. To them Christ
is the great Fulfiller, the goal of man's spiritual quest.

If we have correctly described above the nature of
the Christian task, both these ways are seen to have
their place. For in the positive presentation of the
Christ we know and love, we have a unifying principle
enabling us to possess and manifest what Baron von
Hügel considered the supreme desideratum in Christian
propaganda—" conviction without rigorism ". Let us
consider this with special reference to the Intelligentsia
of India.

On the one hand, it is surely plain that, if we are
to present Christ as we know Him to be, then His
whole claim must be set forth before men in all the
sternness of its uncompromising demand. We dare
not whittle away anything from it, for it is only by the
acceptance of His claims in their fullness that the true
riches and strength of the Christian life may be known.
When Stanley Jones asked Mahatma Gandhi to send
some message by him to the Christians of America,

he replied that they should preach the Christian message in all its fullness, compromising nothing and explaining away nothing. It is not stated whether Mahatmaji desired to apply this only to Christ's ethical teaching, but it is certain that it must apply to His personal demands as well—the claims that He makes for utter, unswerving allegiance. If we would have our Hindu brother share with us in the full riches of Christ, we dare not hold back from him the knowledge of that Christ, not merely as one great teacher or prophet among the teachers and prophets of the world, but as the living Saviour, whose Spirit can still change men's lives. We dare not suppress the teaching of the Cross, nor let the Hindu who is attracted towards the spiritual treasures of Christ fail to realize that it is the key of sacrifice which unlocks those treasures—that " we must through much tribulation enter into the Kingdom of God ".

Further, we must make plain in this connection to those who are drawn towards Christ the true signi-ficance of baptism. We must try to clear away the notion that the acceptance of baptism implies the abandonment of one's cultural traditions or social customs, and absorption into a foreign community. We must urge men to go on living even after baptism, if it is in any way possible,[1] in their old homes, chang-ing none of their customs in regard to food and dress and other such external things. We must show how baptism admits men, not to some new community that is strange and foreign in its ways, not to some particular and limited denomination or sect, but to the Church of God, the great Catholic society, in which is stored the universal heritage of Christian faith and living, in which are administered those Sacraments that convey

[1] The loosening of the hold of caste is making this far more possible now than in earlier days.

in special and intimate reality the presence and touch of the living Christ, in which is experienced the blessed and uplifting fellowship of holy men of God, both living and departed. We must teach further how baptism, by its open confession of Christ, saves men from the timid wavering and half-allegiance which paralyse the spiritual life, and gives authority and courage to speak of Christ to others. But, having taught thus, we must never *press* for baptism. The desire and the demand for it must arise spontaneously. We should rather urge delay for full thought and conviction, and careful counting of the cost.

In such ways, then, we must be stern and uncompromising in our presentation of Christ and of the claim that He makes. Then, on the other hand, we must preach Christ the Fulfiller, Christ the tender and gracious Son of Man, welcoming as by natural kinship all that is lovely and of good report, all that is eager and aspiring, all humble devotion, all simple charities. If we possess in any real measure His mind, how can we fail to see and love all the rich and rare treasures in the spiritual heritage of India ? How can we curse where He would bless ? How can we do other than seek to interpret Him to India as the crown of her long spiritual search, and, clearing away all those unessential Western accretions with which we have hindered the true presentation of His message and life, endeavour to set Him forth in ways that the spiritual genius of India will readily understand and welcome ?

Space does not admit of any detailed exposition of this portion of our task. But it includes the obligation laid on the Indian Christian community to make impossible the reproach of denationalization by becoming as truly Indian in its life and outlook as the other great communities of the land. It means the building up of a Christian worship which shall clothe in Indian forms the

II   THE INTELLIGENTSIA   25

liturgical heritage of the Church universal. It involves the abandonment of much that is foreign in the life and methods of work of the Christian Church, and the assimilation of these to those ways which long centuries of Indian tradition have made native to the land. Above all, it must call us to a far more thorough attempt than has yet been made to think out the implications of our Christian faith in relation to Hinduism, to understand better the points of contact and difference, to discover the truest presentation of the Christian message in terms of Indian thought, and, particularly to explore more deeply the riches of that spiritual experience of the great Christian mystics which makes so instinctive and immediate an appeal to the mystical intuition of India.

But deeper and more urgent than all these is the need for a more worthy and attractive type of Christian living. So long as there is disunion and strife within the Christian Church, there can be no effective witness to a secret of unity and love as found in Christ alone. So long as there is racial antipathy and racial prejudice among even practising Christians, there can be no convincing preaching of brotherhood. So long as there are glaring class distinctions, there can be no useful protest against caste. The witness to Christ for which India, and above all, educated India, waits, is the witness of lives of humble and devoted service, exhibiting no trace of superiority or patronage, exhaling only the sweet fragrance of Christian love. In the words of Dean Inge : " What we most need in all our missionary work is a few saints, a few men who are really living such a life as apostles of Christ ought to live, whose lives are a living testimony, not only that they believe what they teach, but that what they teach is the most holy and beautiful creed that could be believed and professed. That surely is the way in which from the very first our Lord both taught Himself and wished His religion to be propagated—by personal influence. . . . That is, I believe, the only way in which Christianity can really be transmitted ; and, as I say, what we really need above all is real saints who will go out full of love and sympathy, without any racial prejudices, who will try to study the lives and beliefs of the people to whom they go, seeing on the whole what is best in them, and so try to bring them to the foot of the Cross." We need not " a few " but many such humble followers of Christ, preaching not themselves but Christ Jesus as Lord, and themselves the servants of India for Jesus' sake. That is the true heart of the Christian evangel, and to that India will never fail to listen. For it is still the spirit of Bethlehem and Calvary, made manifest in human lives, which, in India as in all the world, most deeply stirs and captivates the hearts of men.

CHAPTER III

THE PEOPLE OF THE VILLAGES

By the BISHOP OF DORNAKAL

INDIA is a continent of villages. Ninety per cent of the population is rural, living in villages of 5000 people and under. Over a third of this rural population dwell in hamlets with less than 500 people.

The villages of India are little self-contained republics. Be a village ever so small, it has representatives of all the important castes following the occupations indispensable for village life. It has its village officials, bankers and tradesmen ; its weavers, carpenters and masons ; its potters, barbers and washermen ; its field labourers, leather-workers and sweepers—all of whom are interdependent.

The greatest triumphs of the Christian Church have also been won in rural India. There are four and a half million *Indian* Christians in the land, of whom about 93 per cent are rural. Wherever the religion has won victories and has left its mark on the life of the country and the people, it is where it has struck its roots in villages. Effective and indigenous has the Christian enterprise become where it has touched rural life : feeble and exotic it continues to be where it is merely urban.

Look at the map of India. The areas where the religion of Christ has spread in the villages are exactly

27

the areas where the Christian community is appreciably strong and powerful. The Punjab, the United Provinces, Chota Nagpur, the Telugu districts of the Madras Presidency, Travancore and Cochin, and the Tamil districts of Tinnevelly, Ramnad and Madura are notable examples. Look also at the statistics of missions. Those missions that have thrown their resources in men and money into the work of village evangelism are precisely those that have gathered in a large number of converts. The Presbyterian and the Anglican Missions in the Punjab; the Methodist Episcopal Church in the United Provinces; the American and Canadian Baptists, the Wesleyans, the Lutherans and the Anglicans in the Telugu country; the Syrian Churches, the London Missionary Society and the Church Missionary Society in Travancore; the Anglican Church in Tinnevelly; the Congregational, Presbyterian and Lutheran Societies in the Tamil country—these are the principal agencies that rightly claim to have had a share in the establishment of the Church in India : and these have all concentrated their efforts in rural India.

It is sometimes said that the Church in rural India consists of converts from the outcaste communities, and cannot therefore be of much consequence in the evangelization of the country.[1] This criticism is most unjust and untrue. The great Syrian Christian communities in Travancore and Cochin are rural, but do not consist of outcaste converts ! The well-established churches in South Travancore, Tinnevelly and Madura, can no longer be called mass-movement churches. The rural church in Bihar and Orissa is due to a mass movement, but a movement from among the aboriginal inhabitants of the forests of Chota Nagpur. If the rural church

---

[1] For example, the *Census Report of 1921*, p. 71, vol. i., says : " Of the Christians, the Europeans and Anglo-Indians are town residents; Indian Christians belong largely to the lower classes of the countryside ".

in the Punjab, the United Provinces and the Andhra area are at present largely drawn from communities once outcaste, they ought not to be reckoned so in the second and succeeding generations; and from that stage on, they are bound to be a factor, and an effective factor in the Christianization of rural India. A close study of facts will prove that such wholesale criticism of rural churches is often the result of ignorance on the part of those confined to urban areas.

Close acquaintance with rural churches will, however, convince anyone that these constitute an even more important asset than the town churches for the Kingdom of God in this land. I offer the following considerations.

(1) *It is in rural churches that the Christian religion approximates indigenous conditions.* It has been truly said : " Everywhere the country is homogeneous and native, the town heterogeneous and cosmopolitan ".[1] This is true of the Church too. Surpliced choirs in Gothic edifices, with pews and benches, and organs and harmoniums, appear to be essentials of urban churches. Not so in the villages. The chapel architecture is natural and Indian. The singing is always to indigenous music, often accompanied, too, by Indian musical instruments. The seating and worship is in Indian style —all sit on the floor and worship, either kneeling as in South India, or prostrate upon their faces as in Chota Nagpur. The offertories are given and received in indigenous style — food grains, home-grown vegetables, first-fruits of all garden crops and of all cattle and chickens come to the altar. The spontaneity and naturalness of the worship are often most refreshing and inspiring. By saying this I do not mean to deny that we have yet a great advance to make. We cannot rest satisfied until every village chapel is a house of prayer, and breathes the atmosphere of mystery, worship and

----

[1] *Census of India, 1921,* p. 70.

adoration. The forms of service—whether liturgical or otherwise—are now almost always foreign ; and the ornaments of the church and of the minister are always Western too. In spite of all these, the church in the rural areas is the church that will first make the outward manifestation of our religion truly indigenous.

(2) *It is in rural churches that the evidence of the Christian dynamic is most unmistakable.*

(*a*) Christianity changes the health and life conditions of the village.

This is particularly so at present when the rural Christians are very largely made up of those belonging to ignorant aboriginal or outcaste classes. Impartial observers have repeatedly given their testimony to the change that has come about among the outcastes through the Christian religion.

The Commissioner of the 1921 Census writes thus :

The vast bulk of the Christian community is essentially rural and is exposed to the general conditions which determine progress in the rural areas of India. Christians are free from a good many of the restrictions which hamper the growth of other communities—early marriage and the prohibition of the marriage of widows. The recorded death-rate among Christians is distinctly lower than the Hindus and the Muhammedans. The number of children below five years old per thousand married women compares favourably with that in both those communities.

This is from a student of racial progress. Certainly none but a superficial observer will fail to see that the social and national problems of " Mother India " are solved most effectively where the religion of Christ has had a chance.

Where Christianity goes, education, civilization and habits of cleanliness in body, dress and food, in speech and conduct, are the concomitant results. Mr. E. A. H. Blunt, I.C.S., wrote in his Census Report thus :

The missionaries all these years have been providing the *corpus sanum* (if one thing is noticeable about Indian Christians it is their greater cleanliness in dress and habits), and now they are being rewarded by the appearance of.the *mens sana*. The new convert, maybe, is no way better than his predecessors, but a new generation, the children of the first generation of the converts, is now growing up . . . and this generation is beginning to make its influence felt. The Hindu fellows of these converts have now to acknowledge not only that they are in material ways better off than themselves, but that they are also better men.[1]

The change in the Christian converts inevitably affects the higher castes too. " We dare no longer use foul language : the Christians would not work for us if we did ! " was the testimony of a caste woman to me in a Christian village of fifteen years' standing. Is it exaggeration to state that the regeneration of the Indian village is being effected through the Christian Church ?

(*b*) Through Christianity, too, illiteracy is being chased out of rural India. It is well known that the first thing done for a village which desires to join the Christian Church is to send a resident teacher to instruct the villagers in the Christian faith, and open a school for their children. The teacher and his wife—if he has one—are truly to this village the introducers of light and learning. Be their education ever so little, they are of course far in advance of any in the neighbourhood. This advantage makes them the instruments of rural uplift, and of the regeneration of the village. Through deeds of loving service, through daily teaching in chapel and school, and, above all, through the example of their lives, they bring mental and moral enlightenment to the villager. While the proportion of pupils in the primary schools of India to the general population is 2·5, it is 7·3 for Christians ; and nearly all these Christian primary schools are in rural areas. Literacy is very

[1] *Census of United Provinces, 1911.*

backward in new mass movement areas : and yet even here it is greatly in advance of the non-Christian community. While 226 per 1000 of the Christian Santalis can read, only 3 per 1000 of the non-Christian Santalis are found to come up to this standard. While the number of literate Telugu outcastes is almost nil, 15 per cent of the Christians can read. Bibles, prayer books and lyric books are in evidence in every Christian village. Booklets on Sanitation, Health, Epidemics, etc., are being eagerly bought and devoured by those who erstwhile constituted the most backward and conservative classes in all India.

The Census Superintendent of the Mysore State, himself a Hindu, says :

The enlightening influence of Christianity is patent in the higher standard of comfort of the converts and their sober, disciplined and busy lives. To take education, for instance, we find that among Indian Christians no less than 11,523 persons or 25 per cent are returned as literate, while for the total population of the State, the percentage is only six.[1]

(c) The change, too, is marked in the religious and moral life of the rural population. Hinduism is deplorably defective in ethical teaching. What the Hebrew prophets so unequivocally taught as the two-fold obligations of religion is blurred and lost sight of in the sacred literature of the Indian rishis. " Thou shalt love the Lord thy God with all thy heart, and with all thy soul "—this readily appeals to the Indian devotee. But the " great commandment like unto it "—" Thou shalt love thy neighbour as thyself "—falls on deaf ears. The essence of sin, according to Jewish prophets, was oppression of the poor ; the essence of all true religion and virtue was " to do justly, to love mercy and to walk humbly with thy God ". These are what the Indian philosopher consistently ignored.

[1] *Census of Mysore*, 1911.

Else, the age-long tyranny of caste would have been unknown.

In rural life of old, capital was with the village aristocrat; labour was supplied by outcaste serfs: and no love was lost between these two classes. The average landlord squeezed as much work out of the labourer as he could, and gave his dependents as little wages as possible. The labourers on the other hand gave the landlord as little work as possible, and, by fair means and foul, squeezed as much wages out of him as they could. Under these circumstances, cruelty and injustice on the one side, and dishonesty and deceit on the other, became inseparable features of rural life: and what was worse, religion and society loved to have it so!

It is true that a just and impartial government has done a great deal to mitigate the evil consequences of such a system. But the inner change, a change of heart in either the oppressor or the oppressed, could alone permanently change this vicious circle in which rural life moved.

That is exactly what the Gospel of Christ has attempted to do, and has done so successfully. In some areas, testimony has come that Christians, on account of their integrity, command higher field-wages; that Christian labourers are in demand for transplantation and harvesting, because they do not require close supervision; that Hill Estates would gladly grant Christians extra privileges because they are sober and regular and reliable; that non - Christian Zamindars become friends of their tenants when these embrace the Christian religion; and Christians are treated with respect by the caste people who once despised them as untouchables. Quite recently, we heard of a non-Christian caste man spending as much as Rs.1500 in feeding his Christian serfs when the whole Christian

D

village was burnt down by an accident. Testimony
has come from several fields, that poisoning cattle,
abusive language, drunken brawls, have become unknown since the Christian religion was introduced into
the village. A missionary of the American Baptist
Mission writes thus : " The change in the Christians
is weakening the caste prejudice against Christianity.
Their caste employers are showing them more and
more sympathy, and are positively honouring their
teachers and pastors." Would that such testimonies
were universal ! But the fact that such testimonies
have come at all, shows the untold possibilities of rural
evangelism.

(3) *It is in the villages that the Church is becoming truly self-supporting, self-propagating and self-
governing.*

It is well known that the South India United Church
in South Travancore and the Anglican Church in
Tinnevelly have advanced far in the direction of self-
support. The Wesleyan Mission in South India had
on its rolls 81,000 Christians in the year 1925, who gave
Rs.48,800 for the support of the ministry.[1] The
American Telugu Baptist Mission, with about 82,000
adult converts, reports to have received Rs.47,326 for
the same purpose.[2] The Anglican Church in the
Telugu country, with about 150,000 adherents, receives
from the people about Rs.75,000 for all religious purposes. When we consider that the people who give
these large sums are poor daily wage-earners, one cannot but wonder at the generosity with which these
people contribute towards the support of their religious
ministrations.

The village communities are second to none in their
evangelistic zeal. The South India United Church

[1] *Wesleyan Missions in South India*, 1925.
[2] *Report of the American Baptist Telugu Mission*, 1924.

has particularly developed this in its congregations through what is known as the Evangelistic Campaign. In the Kistna area of the diocese of Dornakal, 4000 people were enrolled as the result of a single week's voluntary evangelistic work by the people. Instances there are of caste people being brought over into the Church by the witness of Christians that have come from outcaste communities. Distribution of literature, too, is a great means of evangelism. Who has not heard of the distribution last year by the Village Christians of the Punjab of hundreds of Scripture portions among the followers of Islam in the North-West Frontier Province ?

And self - government ? Everywhere the people are given some share in the administration of church affairs from the beginning. What the share may be differs in different bodies.[1] In churches of Episcopal and Presbyterian polity the lowest representative body is the Pastorate Committee (or local Church Committee or Quarterly Meeting)—under the presidency of the ordained minister, consisting of representatives of laymen elected from among the communicants of the local church. Several such Pastorates (or churches or circuits) are usually grouped in a District (or Deanery or Circle) under the chairmanship of an experienced missionary (Deanery or Circle Chairman), with all the ministers sitting on it. Several such Districts (or Deaneries or Circles) combine in a Church Council (or Diocesan Council or Synod). In the smaller as well as the larger Councils the congregation gets adequate representation. These bodies usually administer the Indian Church Fund, consisting of the Indian contributions as well as grants made by Missionary Societies. They are also often responsible for

[1] See a very full description of the organization in the S.I.U.C. in *In and Around Madras*, 1927.

village primary schools, and have the power of select-
ing and appointing lay workers and village teachers.
They also make preliminary enquiries into cases for
Church discipline and restoration.   In some areas,
and especially in Episcopal Churches, no sentence of
excommunication is pronounced before an *ad hoc
panchayat* enquires into the facts of every case, and the
District Committee weighs the evidence and apportions
blame.

In Anglican dioceses, where diocesanization has
been carried out, the entire responsibility for all branches
of work is centred in the Church and its representative assembly.   For instance, the Society for the
Propagation of the Gospel makes a block grant to the
diocese which is administered entirely by the chosen
representatives of the Diocesan Standing Committee.
The allowances of missionaries, grants to Church
Councils, to higher education, to women's work, to
evangelistic work and medical work are all determined
by the Administrative Committee.   What is called
Devolution is here complete—from the Mission to the
Church.   Such real advance in self-government has
only been made possible in rural mass-movement areas
by the faith and statesmanship of the missionary
societies and their representatives in the field.

If the work in rural India is so effective and hopeful,
it has also its problems.   First and foremost comes :

(1) *The Problem of Education.*—At a very generous
estimate, about 15 per cent only of the rural Christians
are literate : a fairly large proportion of these are under
training for " mission service ".   While missions have
been ready to open schools in all villages, the net result
in the literacy of the rural community is far from satisfactory.   In the Anglican diocese of Dornakal, there are

1500 village schools with about 17,000 Christian pupils enrolled. Of this number, 87 per cent are in the first two standards ; 96 per cent are in the first three standards. In a report of the Wesleyan Mission in Hyderabad, out of 6147 children, 5650, *i.e.* 91 per cent of the total, are reported to be in the infant and first classes. This state of affairs is more or less universal.

One reason for this inadequate response has certainly been our educational policy. Missions have in the past undertaken the elementary education of the Christian children, not in the interests of the people but in the interests of the mission itself ; that is, not primarily for the uplift of the people, but primarily for the manufacture of " mission workers ". Hence the scope of the education was restricted ; a literary education was all that was given ; the ambition of the pupils was limited ; they only aimed at becoming village schoolmasters and schoolmistresses ; the equipment of the village teacher was scanty, and his usefulness was therefore limited too. In very many cases he neither knew how to serve the village community nor did he care for village life.

Thanks to the Fraser Commission on village education, experiments are now being made in most rural missions to rectify these evils. Vocational schools and industrial schools are included in all programmes of advance. The institutions, however, suffer for lack of men and money. Rural India cries for reconstruction. Friends of rural India are in demand, with special knowledge of things vital to rural life. A new type of village school, a new type of village teacher and a new type of training school are the crying needs of the hour. The missionary societies that have established rural churches have to-day the unprecedented opportunity of making these churches the instruments of rural uplift and regeneration. May they be equal to the call !

(2) *The Problem of Self-support.*—For missions sup-

porting rural work and mass movements, self-support is
an anxious problem.   It is evident from missionary
speeches and reports that there prevails a feeling of
impatience at the increasing cost of all rural work.
Educational work, it is argued, becomes self-supporting
with the increase of pupils ; government grants and
fees increase in proportion.   Not so with rural work.
The more the church expands, the more is the cost of its
enlarged plant.

Let us at once admit that this estimate of rural work
is just.   The task of winning rural converts and building
them up in Church life so that they may be evangelists to
their countrymen is indeed costly ; especially when the
church is made up of the most poverty-stricken in the
land.   When missions do not make converts, the budget
remains stationary ; and when the converts are in large
numbers, the liabilities increase.   That being the case,
missions should make up their minds as to what they
want.   Do they wish to be organizations for merely
proclaiming the Gospel and spreading the knowledge of
Christ widely over the land, or do they wish to establish
the Church of Christ in city and village, and make the
Church the chief means of spreading that knowledge
effectively in the land ?   This latter task *does* cost money.

While all this is true, the criticism against the costli-
ness of rural work still deserves the most careful consideration of those engaged in it.   Has not the time
come when vigorous experiments ought to be made to
make village work independent of outside support,
standing on its own resources ?   The following are
suggested :

Serious attempts should be made from the initial
stages to make the converts build their own places of
worship, and their own village schools.   All Oriental
nations have a passion for temple-building.   Indian
Christians are not free from it.   This passion should

be fostered and the people ought to be encouraged to build a place of worship—plain or ornamental, cheap or expensive—something which they can call their own.

ii. Indigenous methods of offering to God should be inculcated. Harvest festivals, *melas*, *tirunalas*, offerings in kind, first-fruits, rice or flour collections should be encouraged. " Thou shalt appear before the Lord thy God in the place where He has chosen "; " Thou shalt not appear before the Lord empty "; these are words addressed to an Eastern nation.

iii. Indianization directly advances self-support. The indigenous leader knows how to reach the people's pockets ; he knows methods that will appeal to them ; his people realize he has no inexhaustible funds at his command—and they respond.

iv. An unpaid voluntary ministry for the Church should be systematically developed. Men with independent means should be encouraged to give of their service freely to the Church. Voluntary clergy, voluntary lay evangelists, voluntary lay catechists and the like need to be courageously instituted. The paid system, universally in vogue in missions, is not native to the country ; and it must be discouraged. Our new vocational schools ought to aid in this direction. The ambition to serve the Lord " without charge " must be inculcated in boys who learn a trade, so that when they go back to their villages they may honorarily undertake the responsibility for the local congregations. Village elders, too, ought to be encouraged to learn to read and to teach, so that they may lead the worship and instruction in the village of which they are the natural leaders.

The ordination of such village elders and honorary workers commissioning them to administer the sacraments has been vigorously advocated by the Rev. Roland Allen in his well-known books on mission

policy.[1] Doubts have been expressed as to the practic-
ability of these proposals for rural India where illiteracy
dominates.   But Mr. Allen's main contention need not
be set aside simply because of the abnormal conditions
at the initial stages of mass movements.   The dis-
couragement of the paid agency and the encouragement of the voluntary ministry ought to be the vigorous
aim of all rural missions.

v. The separation of the village school from congregational work is another much-needed reform.

The great bulk of mission agency now consists of
teacher-evangelists, who are responsible both for the
village school and the village congregation.   The
separation of these two functions might necessitate the
closing of many inefficient little schools.   It might also
stop the employment of men to conduct the daily and
Sunday services in each village chapel.   But both these
consequences would be wholly beneficial.   The former
would result in fewer but efficient and well-attended
schools, and throw the burden of the education of the
masses more upon the State; the latter would develop
voluntary lay leadership.

These are only a few suggestions.   The acceptance
of some of these proposals would undoubtedly mean a
radical alteration of mission policy.   But they are worth
the earnest consideration of mission and church leaders
all over the country.   By these means an indigenous and
independent Indian Church can be built in India.

(3) *The Problem of the Spiritual Life.*—The Church
cannot be built up apart from the Christian life of its
individual members.   The Christian life of the individual
cannot ripen and fructify apart from the Church.   If
the Church in rural India is to be an effective witness for

---

[1] *Missionary Methods — St. Paul's or Ours ?   The Spontaneous
Expansion of the Church.*   Both published by the World Dominion Press,
1 Tudor Street, E.C.4.

the Lord, attention must be paid to the spiritual condition of the individual and the Church. At bottom, the problems of the rural church are spiritual problems. Given a passionate devotion to the Lord and a love that constrains men and women to bear witness for Him, self-support, self-government and self-extension become easy problems to solve. How can this be done ?

i. *By the Ministry of the Word.*—" The entrance of Thy Word giveth Light " ; and the foundation of all spiritual life is the knowledge of God's will and purposes as revealed in the Scriptures, in our Lord Jesus Christ and in the Church. The important rule in all rural work is Teach, TEACH, TEACH. Daily services, carefully planned lectionary, the use of song, verse and plays as means of instruction, distribution of literature— all these are indispensable means of increasing in the people knowledge of divine things.

ii. *By the Ministry of the Sacraments.*—We believe that the sacraments are gifts of the Lord to His Church. The sacrament of Holy Baptism is the sacrament of entrance into the sacred Fellowship and the sacrament of the Lord's Supper that of intimate communion with the Lord and with one another. The Apostolic Church " broke bread " daily during the early days of the Church and later it was their custom to come together to break bread each Lord's Day. How can we expect our Christians to grow strong in their devotion to the Lord, if we deprive them of the sacrament which, by universal recognition, is the sacrament of holy communion ? It is, however, a fact that a large proportion of baptized Christians do not have a chance of coming to this oftener than once in two or three months. The breaking of bread in each church every Lord's Day is impossible as long as we confine the celebration to a highly trained pastor who often has ten to twenty separate and distant village congregations to minister to. And yet the Indian people are sacramentarian by temperament and religious training. We know in experience of nothing that inspires devotion, touches the emotions and strengthens the will of the village folk as the reverent and intelligent observance of the sacrament of the Lord's Supper.

iii. *By the Ministry of Prophets.*—Every British Christian knows the value to the life of the Church of great preachers like Moody, Meyer, Spurgeon, Shepherd and Gore. The Church in India has not produced many prophets of this type One important service that the churches in the home-lands can render to the Church in India is the sending of such " Missions of Help " to impart spiritual gifts to the people. Moreover, days of fasting, prayer and intercession supply occasions which appeal to the Indian religious genius and are productive of spiritual results.

iv. *By the Ordinary Ministry of the Church.*—The missionary, the Moderator, the President or the Bishop cannot very effectively reach the village congregation. Higher ideals of life and service can come to the village only through the village teacher and pastor. What the Church in the West can do is so to train the village teacher and the village pastor that they in their turn will influence the villagers. The most helpful contribution that the Western Churches can at present render to the Church in India is to send out their best men and women for the task of training the Christian young, and training the workers and the clergy. Will the Western Churches and Societies respond to this call ?

CHAPTER IV

THE WOMEN OF INDIA

By Alice B. Van Doren

THE relationship existing between the Christian message and certain trends and developments among India's women is a thing not easy to define. Throughout India, as through nearly every country of the Orient, has swept during the last decade a swift and irresistible urge, snatching women from the ways of age-long custom and setting their feet upon paths of new adventure. This " Women's Movement " has given to educated women a new freedom of thought and an entrance into professional and political life and social service. The educated Indian woman, from being a mere unit in the family or caste, has suddenly entered upon the estate of an individual, with powers of self-choice and self-determination, with all the opportunities and all the dangers of individualistic life opening before her.

How far these new conditions are due to the impact of Christian thought upon Indian life is a question hard to answer. The ardent missionary is prone to claim all reform and all progress as the natural fruits of his message. To the nationally minded Indian, whether man or woman, such claims and proprietary labels are extremely offensive. The Indian reformer searches the Vedas, the Epics and all the classic literature of India

43

to prove that the seeds of progress lay buried in the soil of his own Motherland. The truth is that in such situations the social fabric is too closely interwoven to be successfully unravelled. Religion, national tradition, racial characteristics, and the urge of modern world movements all enter into the warp and woof of the new life.

Let us first ask, " What was Jesus' message to women ? " On this subject, as on other social questions such as war, slavery and Roman imperialism, we find Him making no definite pronouncements but keeping to the one revolutionary principle of the intrinsic worth of every child of God, a worth affected by neither race nor sex nor condition of servitude. In His personal dealings with women, Jesus treated them as He did men—that is, as human beings worthy of His respect and love. When we turn to the Epistles and their interpretation of the teachings of Jesus, we strike a lower level. We find St. Peter and St. Paul hedging women round with many confusing restrictions not applied to men—restrictions as to dress, as to relations in the home, as to silence and subjection in the Church. Only occasionally did St. Paul rise to the universalism of Jesus' message and proclaim that in Him " there is neither male nor female ".

This then was the original Christian message to women which has interpenetrated the traditions of Greek and Roman culture and the hereditary attitudes of Celt, Anglo-Saxon and Norseman. Out of this fusion has been born the new day of woman's opportunity. Just how much of it is due to the influence of the Christian message, even in so-called " Christian countries ", it is hard to say. One thing at least can be asserted with confidence : it has combined with freedom, moral restraint and unselfish service. As has been said by one woman writer, in speaking of the freedom of the women of pre-Christian Greece and Rome :

Women seemed unable to combine freedom and moral
dignity. It is a dangerous thing to weaken the domestic
and self-sacrificing traditions of women if there is no strong
religious devotion to replace them ; and the emancipation
of women may be disastrous to themselves and to their race
if it is uncontrolled by the unselfish enthusiasm and stringent
morality of Christianity.[1]

" Life abundant " and the self-forgetfulness of " one
that serveth " are the rare combination of qualities that
Jesus gives.

Having thus briefly considered the nature of Christ's
message to women, let us next look at the national and
social characteristics of the womanhood of India.
Though of that " infinite variety " of which Shakespeare
sings, there is yet among Indian women a certain likeness, impossible to analyse, intangible, elusive, yet real.
Perhaps in likeness and diversity their characteristics
may be compared to the *sari*—that almost universal
feature of the Indian costume. Merely a straight piece
of cloth from three to nine yards in length, unsewn,
unpinned, it yet lends itself to infinite variations. Of
silk or of homespun ; the white of the Travancore
Syrian, or the reds and yellows of Tinnevelly, or the
gold embroideries of Benares ; worn here over the right
shoulder, there over the left ; knotted from shoulder to
shoulder as in Coorg and the Southern hills ; drooping
in long lines as among the Parsees ; girt snugly from
ankle to hip as in the *kashta* fashion of the Marathas ;
covering the head as in the North, or exposing it as in
the South ; for widow or bride, for beggar or Rani, it
is through all these variations the typical dress of the
Indian woman—always suitable, always graceful, always
recognizable.

In Indian womanhood there are certain character-

[1] Miss Eleanor McDougall, *International Review of Missions*, July
1912, p. 440.

istics which, like the lines of the *sari*, keep their identity even amid great diversity of environment. All women of the Hindu community from the Himalayas to Cape Comorin, from palace to hut, have their ideals formed upon the women of the Indian Epics. The Hindu Scriptures far exceed those of the Hebrews in their wealth of women characters. Deborah, Ruth and Esther pale into comparative insignificance beside the " Golden Company " of India's women led by Savitri and Shaibya. These are the tales upon which Indian girls are nourished. Mrs. Sarojini Naidu says of herself : [1]

I am no more than the symbol of the woman in the villages, not the citizen, not the interpreter in accordance with outside vision of our inward things. I am she to whom Sita, Savitri, Damayanti and Draupadi have left as a legacy to be handed to generations after generations, of that devotion, courage, fortitude, love, wisdom and sacrifice which were the very pivot of Indian culture. Every woman who sits on the floor of a lowly hut or on an ivory throne of a marble palace, is the custodian of that tradition.

It is upon these passive virtues, " devotion, fortitude, love, sacrifice ", that India's ideals of woman's character have been built. To them are now being added the active virtues dear to the more masculine woman of the West. It is the part of the Christian message to infuse into this new union of opposite qualities the selfless passion of Christ who strove and suffered not for family or clan but for the world. If Indian women can purify education, politics and social service by the spirit of devotion which they have shown in home life, and can transfer to the Motherland the homage paid to the husband, then India's future will be assured. India may show to the world a new type of womanhood, offspring of the union between the spirit of Jesus Christ

[1] The Kamala Lectures, Calcutta, Jan. 23, 1928.

and the inherited spiritual culture of the East. Such a woman was Pandita Ramabai. Her qualities we need not analyse, saying " This was Christian " and " That was of her Hindu heritage ".   Suffice it to look upon the unified beauty of her character and say : " Thus shall it be with Indian women who are the Bhaktas of the Cross ".

From the Christian message, it is but a natural transition to turn toward the Christian task.   In regard to this new current of thought and feeling, what is to be the attitude of the Western woman who comes to India as a disciple of Christ ?

To ignore such an awakening would be futile.   In point of numbers but a negligible minority, yet in the matter of influence this company of intelligentsia is a power enormously to be reckoned with.   Many of these women are radiating centres of light and energy.

That the movement contains within itself a certain amount of contradiction—that some of its hypotheses have so far failed to be thought through—is not to be denied.   That is the inevitable mark of youth and im-maturity.   Women who so whole-heartedly exalt the ideal of Sita and Damayanti—the ideal of utter abnega-tion, whereby the wife lives only in and for her husband —just as earnestly join in the war-cry of feminism, claiming absolute equality with man, and in certain cases, superiority to him.   Is it a foolish contradiction, and hard to understand ?   Not if the observer realizes that in the hearts of India's women there have met and mingled the two opposing tides of nationalism and feminism—the one exalting all that belongs to India's past, the other claiming all that the life of to-day has bestowed upon the woman of the West.   Not without eddies and cross-currents and even whirlpools can those waters mingle.   Is it to be wondered at if, in their rush and surge, a logical view of life is for a time submerge

What, then, is to be our relationship with this corporate body of the new womanhood of India ?   At times one wonders whether there is to be any relationship at all ; whether in this Swadeshi movement there is any place for foreigners.   Usually, however, we find that we are wanted, but wanted on India's own terms, the terms not of leadership but of co-operation ; the condition of willingness to learn as well as ability to teach.

As a concrete example we may instance the Women's Conferences on Educational Reform which are now meeting annually in every Indian province as well as in some centre representing India as a whole ; also the Women's Day which followed the 1927 Congress ; as well as the Graduates' Unions and Women's Councils which exist in Indian cities.   In these the leadership is in Indian hands, and in many cases it is of admirable quality.   Indian women believe that they know India's needs as no foreigner can hope to. Any Western woman who enters one of these groups with the intention, however altruistic, of leading the group according to her ideas, or of dominating the situation, will soon find herself unwanted.   One, however, who comes in a spirit of co-operation, willing to learn, anxious to look through Indian eyes, able to accept graciously a subordinate place and to work shoulder to shoulder with her Indian sisters will find for herself a welcome that grows on acquaintance.

In smaller towns and more backward areas, there are yet places where leadership is required for a time. But the Western woman who assumes such leadership should do so with the clear realization that she is but a *locum tenens*, that the measure of her success is to be found in the speed with which she can make herself unnecessary ; that her objective is not to do things perfectly herself but to work through others whose ideas of perfection are different from her own : to

" decrease " that others may " increase ". There are
to-day many pieces of constructive social work in which
Christian women may co-operate with non-Christians,
showing the spirit of Christ not so much by the spoken
word as by deed and spirit. Such opportunities are to
be found in health centres and baby welcomes ; in the
observance of Health Week ; in welfare work in industrial centres ; in ladies' recreation clubs ; in missions
to the depressed classes. In all these the Westerner
is welcomed for her experience and organizing ability,
provided only that she be free from the attitude of
superiority and desire for domination.

In every such attempt, one of the first requisites is
a sympathetic acquaintance with Indian customs and
ideals. The writer recently listened to an address by a
European woman in which the making of *beef tea* was
urged as one of the first essentials of an Indian girl's
practical education. Even where such crass ignorance
of national customs is not exhibited, too often well-
meaning attempts are rendered useless by the lack of
information and imagination—inability to see life from
the Oriental standpoint, and a resulting attitude of impatience when things are " different ".

Let us pass from relationship with the group to
contact with the individual. If the former is to be
indicated by the word co-operation, friendship will
describe the ideal of the latter. The dictum of St.
Paul that " Love never faileth " still holds good, and
friendship can still open doors that respond to the turn
of no other key. But such friendship to be real must be
a mutual experience, offered with no tinge of superiority
on the part of the foreigner, rather sought humbly with
the realization that she has much to receive as well as
to give. Many earnest and eager women spend years
in India, in some way just missing this boon of friendship, sometimes mourning for it when it is too late and

E

in other cases never realizing how much richer life might have been.   Recently a woman missionary, after years of unselfish service, was heard to remark that during all her life in India she had not found a single intimate Indian friend.

We may ask how such international or inter-racial friendships may be formed.   Friendship is a thing too elusive to be bound by rules or promoted by directions ; it is a spontaneous and creative thing, a growth of the spirit, a gift from God.   Yet there are certain situations conducive to the growth of friendship, as there are others that repress it.   These conditions we need to know ; but most of all we must realize its preciousness and search for it as for hid treasure.   Just because differences of race and language and culture make its attainment more difficult, by so much more do we need to strive for that whose difficulty only enhances its value.

Of the many situations that give opportunity for the growth of friendship one may first mention that of working together.   The co-operation mentioned above is one of the surest ways to know people and to gain a background of common knowledge and interest.   Even the dullest committee gives a chance to get acquainted with those sitting around the office table.   The give and take of discussion, and, still more, the sharing of the responsibilities of a health campaign or of the running of a social club, open doors that may lead to real understanding, if only followed up.

Hospitality is another door too little used.   Liberal Hindus of to-day are increasingly willing to lay aside caste exclusiveness, to accept invitations to a Christian home, and to reciprocate by offering hospitality in their own.   Orthodox ladies may not advance beyond biscuit and bottled waters ; others will capitulate to the extent of sandwiches, cakes and tea; still others will join in a vegetarian dinner.   One knows certain missionary

bungalows that might be characterized as " Homes of
the Open Door", where representatives of all creeds and
races are welcome and at home ; but homes of this
character are all too few.

There is also the other side to hospitality—the willingness to receive as well as give. For the newcomer in
India, few things are more important than the ability
to eat, and eat with pleasure, Indian food. This ability
conditions any real entrance into Indian home life.
Hospitality is one of the fine traditions of India. It is
only as Europeans become able to accept and enjoy it,
that we may enter into those intimate relationships that
come from the sharing of one another's life.

Another gate to friendship is the willingness to accept
criticism. Educated Indians, women as well as men,
especially those who have been in the West, are full
of bitterness against Western exclusiveness, Western
imperialism, Western interpretations of Christianity.
" You have brought us a Christ wearing a hat and
trousers ; we want to see him in a turban and *dhotee* ",
said an " Oxford returned " woman the other day. For
such, friendship with a European is difficult until they
have rid their minds of these repressions. What seems
to the alarmed hearer a friendship-destroying flood of
attacks and criticisms may be in reality only clearing
the way for frank understanding. The ability to listen
to such an attack, not so much patiently as sportingly,
in a spirit of give and take, is often a long step toward
real friendship.

There is close relationship between friendship and
the message of Christ. Among nationally-minded
women, one may almost dare to say it is the only entrance. It is a truism to repeat the oft-quoted aphorism
that educated India loves Christ but hates Christianity ;
yet it is a fact that can never become trite to one who
feels its constant impact. Thinking Indians, women as

well as men, find their stumbling-block in the racial
exclusiveness and unconscious " Imperialism " of so-
called Christians. Only a life that lives out the spirit of
Jesus can open hearts to receive the spoken message.
Even then, along with the sincere desire to share
Christian experience, there must exist friendship for
friendship's sake—not a pretence at friendship that
exists for propaganda. A Western girl once said of an
ardent Christian worker, " You know she doesn't really
care for me ; she only wants to save my soul ". Indian
women are far too intuitive to be deceived by a hollow
mask of pretence, by sounding brass or tinkling cymbal.
In the twentieth century, as in the first, it is only love
that never faileth.

But great as are the opportunities for work and
friendship among India's educated women, they must
not be allowed to obscure that pathetic "multitude whom
no man can number ", the girls and women of the
villages, especially of those villages which lie under the
curse of untouchability.

Among the sixty millions of India's depressed classes,
one-half are of course women and girls, and it is to
them, perhaps, above all others, that the hearts of
Christian women must turn in love and pity. Surely
Jesus Himself, He who " had compassion on the multitudes ", would have turned first to these least among all
His brethren. To know of their needs it is unnecessary
to refer to Western writers. One needs only to read the
appeals of Mahatma Gandhi, who himself yearns over
the lot of these downtrodden folk, and prays that in his
next incarnation he may himself be born among them,
to know and share their sufferings to the uttermost.
Undoubtedly the most cheering feature of the situation
in regard to these people is the fact that to-day Indians
and Europeans, non-Christians and Christians are working for their uplift.

The special burden laid upon the Christian woman in India is her responsibility toward her lowly sisters of the Christian community, numbering between one and two millions, drawn largely from mass-movement areas, dwellers in tiny mud-built hamlets scattered up and down the length and breadth of the Indian continent. Along with fathers, husbands and brothers they came for baptism and received it. Christianity seemed to them a way up and out—the only way. Rightly or wrongly, churches and missions received them, and now, again rightly or wrongly, the responsibility is ours. Whether it is ever right to gather into the Christian Church more of the ignorant and helpless than can be nurtured and cared for, is a moot question in mission policy. It has been done, and cannot be undone. Yet these masses came at their own request, and once refused, might never seek again. Too often, however, for them the way has led neither up nor out, and with them in many cases it is still " as it was in the beginning ". Where numbers have been smaller, and intensive work, educational, evangelistic and economic, has been done over a period of years, these humble folk have shown marvellous capacity for development.

It is the women of these partially Christianized villages whose needs we must consider, for it is largely on the mothers of families that the future of the community depends. A British Government official who has done a remarkable piece of intensive rural work says of the comparative needs of men and women :

In order to spread the elementary principles of health and hygiene in as many villages as possible and to uplift the people with the greatest possible speed, it is necessary to concentrate on improving the ideas of the women on these subjects rather than the men. The women will pass the ideas on naturally to their children and will spread them far more than men, as they are personally and vitally interested in them.[1]

Of the many needs of such women, we may here mention four with the hope of viewing in relation to these needs the help that the Christian message may bring.

There is first the problem of ignorance, including that of illiteracy. Illiteracy is always a terrific handicap, but in cultured communities its evils may be mitigated by an education without books, handed down through oral tradition, inherited custom and the general cultural heritage. Hindus often claim that their womenfolk, though illiterate, are not uneducated, and there is a modicum of truth in the statement. With the outcastes this is not true. Shut out from culture as well as from literacy, born in a community with no cultural traditions, the " depressed " woman is ignorant indeed. Taught in early childhood the work of the village—to sweep, to carry water, to collect cow dung and herd cattle ; later to cook the crude and scanty meal and to toil in the fields ; then to bear a large number of children, many of whom die in infancy—this is her life, not far removed from that of the bullock and buffalo that share her house and her labour.

Education, then, is the first need of the village woman —but education of what sort ? Not " literacy " unless, as someone has said, there is something to be literate for. Why spend years in learning an intricate Indian character when in all the village there is never a newspaper and scarcely a book ? Why learn to write when one has not even the price of a postage stamp ? Too often the villager calls his daughter back from school, judging rightly that education is of " no use ", spoiling the girl for village existence and fitting her for nothing better. It is because of these conditions that some of the ablest

[1] F. L. Brayne, I.C.S., *Village Uplift in India*, p. 84.

minds in India, both Indian and foreign, are spending themselves in the search for a new type of rural education in which literacy will be a means and not an end, from which the village girl may learn the things that will make her an intelligent home-maker, a thrifty housewife, a mother who can train her children after her, a citizen who can make the village a clean and healthy place to live in. Village women want education, but of a new sort.

The second great handicap is that of poverty—a poverty so terrible that in a country less fertile and a climate less kindly, life itself would be impossible. Ignorance and poverty form the proverbial vicious circle, each reinforcing the other. As we are looking at the woman's side of life, it is not necessary here to enter into questions of land acquisition and methods of field cultivation. We shall see rather what ways are open to the village woman to conserve or augment the family income, for without sufficient food for daily needs no village can be expected to rise socially or spiritually. Some few saints may find God through voluntary fasting ; but ordinary men and women do not develop spirituality on an involuntarily empty stomach.

Certainly a village girl should be taught in school the use of every square foot of available ground for the planting of fruit trees and vegetables ; the conservation and use of common fertilizers ; the building of thorn fences to protect gardens ; the raising of improved breeds of poultry, and of the goat, which has been called " the poor man's cow " ; among the better-to-do, the care of cows and buffaloes. These things, taught not in theory but with demonstration and practice, would do much to raise the amount of family income.

Even among women who work in the fields, there are months of leisure in the dry season, which are too often also months of idleness. It is during these seasons that women may practise those " cottage industries " which in some cases have a marketable value, and even where that is not possible may provide for the family, in some cases saving unavoidable expenditure, and in others giving comforts and even necessities that would otherwise be done without. It is here that we meet and welcome Mahatma Gandhi's cult of the *charka* or spinning-wheel. Though spinning brings in not more than one or two annas a day per spinner, that very pittance may lift a family above the starvation line. It has possibilities, too, for household use. Home-spun thread may be turned into home-woven cloth ; and in the off season, instead of idleness that quickly degenerates into gossip and quarrelling, we may see the family new-clothed in garments that, though coarse, are clean and whole. Sewing, too, should be added to the accomplishments of every rural schoolgirl. A woman who is able to spin, to weave, to sew and, in some sections, to raise her own cotton will be somewhat in the position of the self-sufficient housewife of the West in the days preceding the Industrial Revolution.

But spinning, while it perhaps stands first, is not the only possible subsidiary industry. Mat-weaving, broom-making, coarse basketry, rope-twisting, pottery and similar occupations belong to different communities and different parts of the country. One of the tasks of the new rural education is to encourage them and kindred indigenous industries that will add to the comfort and efficiency of the home or provide an additional bit for the family income.

Unhygienic living—in other words, dirt—is the third curse of the village woman. The Christian message must exalt the body as the temple of God, to be kept clean and healthy in order to be worthy of His indwelling. Personal cleanliness, the formation of clean habits in children and the care of the house are among the lessons that the village girl must learn through the rural school—not through memorizing paragraphs from a text-book, but through actual doing, until habits are formed. Still more difficult is the teaching of the collective cleanliness that applies to the streets and commons of a village, only to be done through the corporate work of a school or of girl guides. Along with all this must come the teaching of the close relationship that exists between dirt and disease on the one hand, between cleanliness and health on the other. The use of simple but effectual methods of sanitation ; ways of keeping food and water uncontaminated ; the prevention of epidemics ; the feeding of children and sick people—all these are yet to be worked out as an integral part of the education of village girls from the standpoint not of Western but of Indian life. Until this is done, no one can feel that the Christian message for India has been adequately expressed.

No scheme of rural uplift can be complete unless religion is also taken into account. The body cannot be exalted and the soul left behind. Village women know nothing of the tenets of the Higher Hinduism ; religion for them is Animism, pure and simple—the placating of the dread spirits that inhabit earth and air. The large part played by fear in the life of these women cannot be realized until one has come close enough to learn it through personal experience. Even Christians of the second and third generation, girls who have spent years in a Christian school, have not wholly escaped from the all-enveloping terrors that infest the night— that people the *neem* tree, the well and the cemetery with unearthly dread. Among village women, the casting out of fear—the fear that hath torment—is one of the great parts of the Christian message. Among women of better education, science will play its part ; among these ignorant folk courage can only be communicated through religious teaching that shows God as a loving Father, far stronger than any spirit of evil, and both able and willing to protect His children.

But when the half-gods go, something greater must arrive. To be delivered from superstition is not enough; in its place must come another fear, not of demons but of sin. New and holier sanctions must take the place of those that are outworn. As to other parts of the Christian message, much can be given through the parables, which deal with the homely everyday situations of rural life familiar to the village girl. Story and drama and song will help to explain Christ's life and teaching and death through familiar mediums.

An increasing number of highly educated Indian women are hearing the call of the villages. It must be Indian and European working together who will solve the problem of the new type of education for the girls of the rural community.

In connection with the education of depressed class girls, two problems of a somewhat different nature arise. That the majority of village girls should be trained in the village, for village life, may be taken as an axiom of rural education. Among such, however, are found occasional individuals of outstanding ability, with sufficient natural intelligence to carry them through the ordinary boarding-school, while some are fit for high school, and a very few for college. The recent development of intelligence-testing in India has made it easier to identify such gifted children. When discovered, what policy is to be followed in regard to them? To refuse the chance of higher education to girls so gifted is a denial of all the principles of democracy, and a refusal to develop for the community its natural leaders—the only possible " bridge " that may serve to connect the backward classes with the world of opportunity. Yet the difficulties involved are many. Higher education is a question not merely of mental ability, but also of physical stamina, cultural adaptability and moral restraint. The strain and the risk are great—as great as the spiritual distance from a Pariah hut to the halls of a university. Can a girl who has been removed from the former to the latter again find a natural level in the life of her family ? Can she raise them to her height, or must she sink back to their depth, or will she go on her separate way, cut off from the ties of home ? One practical solution to the problem is that great care must be taken to see that from such communities boys and girls should be given equal opportunities. This will make it possible for a girl to marry a man of her own class, yet one who has had advantages similar to her own. Homes formed by such marriages will afford leadership among men and women alike and will do much in setting standards for the rest of the community.

This leads to consideration of a second problem, that of the danger of Europeanization. Girls of this class, as has been said, have little or nothing of Hindu tradition behind them. Their cultural heritage is practically nil. Hinduism would in the past have none of them. Their only chance of liberation has come to them through Christianity—a Christianity usually mediated to them through the European missionary. It is not strange that such girls and women have failed to distinguish between Christianity and Western forms of civilization— that they have been all too ready to copy the missionary teacher in the use of English dress, English ways of living, even English names. In all fairness also it should be admitted that missionaries have not been without fault. In some cases at least the European head of a school has been too little conversant with the higher side of Indian life and too ready to consider as best the ways she has herself been accustomed to Whatever the cause, the result is the same—a deplorable split between the Christian community, especially that of depressed class origin, and *Indian* India. It is in schools where the gifted girls of this community gather that the remedy must be sought. Indian Christian teachers who envisage the broader meanings of Nationalism and women from the West who have learned to admire and love all that is highest in Indian life must work together to establish the new tradition ; to form even from the depressed classes a younger generation of Christian women who will look to India rather than to the West for their ideals of life and culture ; who will count themselves one with their non-Christian sisters in all strivings after a new and purified India ; who will become to their own people interpreters of the Oriental Christ.

We have considered the Christian message first in connection with India's favoured women of the privileged classes, and then in relation to those of the great outcaste community of the villages. We shall now try to investigate the needs of a third group, smaller than the second, composed of women who have entered the ranks of organized industry.

Although not more than 10 per cent of the population is as yet industrialized, yet with even that small percentage of her people thus engaged, India already ranks as one of the eight great industrial nations of the world, and as such has her seat in the International Labour Conference at Geneva.[1] Women as well as men are drawn by the lure of higher wages, and are employed in all of the great centres. Cotton mills in Bombay, Gujarat, the Central Provinces and Madras ; jute mills in Bengal ; tea gardens in Assam, Ceylon, Darjeeling and the South India hills ; the great steel and iron

---

[1] For facts and suggestions concerning women in industry, the writer is indebted chiefly to Miss Tara N. Tilak, Head of the Social Workers' Training Class, Bombay.

factories of Jamshedpur ; and the coal-mines of Bengal, are some of the industries that have attracted women workers. One peculiar feature of Indian industrial life is the seasonal nature of employment and the phenomenal proportion of labour turn-over. For the sake of larger wages, especially in times of scarcity and unemployment, numbers of the peasantry migrate from the land to some industrial city such as Bombay or Cawnpore. When sufficient money has been earned to tide over the emergency, they return to their ancestral holdings. The system has certain advantages for the worker, as he is not permanently separated from rural life. Disadvantages, however, are at least two : families are broken up for long periods, their separation often leading to a serious lowering of moral standards ; and the impermanent nature of residence in the factory town makes workers less keen to secure proper housing and more ready to put up with insanitary and even indecent living conditions. To show that such conditions are not unavoidable, one has only to mention the " Model Village " in process of construction near the Nagpur Cotton Mills, and the pride which permanent workers are taking in building their own homes.

For women employed in industry there are several dangers which should be noted. There is first of all neglect of home and children. A woman who works eleven hours a day and sixty a week can scarcely see her home by daylight, except on the one weekly holiday. Unless a *crèche* is furnished by the mill, and a school by mill or municipality, the children must be left to the care of a relative or neighbour, too often to that of an older sister, perhaps only nine or ten herself. A second danger is to health, primarily to that of the mother and through her to the children she bears. A woman doctor in the Nagpur Mills told the writer of women who carry a day of eighteen or nineteen hours, rising at three in the morning for housework and cooking, spending the day in the mills, and working again in the house until ten at night. The third danger is to morals and religion. In the village, however low the state of life, there are customs and taboos and " public opinion " of a sort. There are local religious observances, however crude and elementary. When a family breaks up even temporarily and members migrate to a city such as Bombay, these sanctions slacken. For the peasant, almost any city is located " East of Suez ". Cinemas of the worst type, liquor shops and organized prostitution, ever hungry for new recruits, threaten the morals of women as well as men.

There are certain needed reforms in industry which would provide great relief for employed women. There is at least one industry from which women workers should be definitely excluded, viz. underground work in the coal-mines. Such exclusion is now under serious consideration. The question is as to what other occupations may be offered in its place. Suddenly to throw out of work the 35,000 women now employed below ground would bring many families face to face with starvation.

In the main industries, one of the first needs is the reduction of hours of labour for women workers, thus safeguarding the health of mother and children, and giving some chance for the supervision of the home. Equally pressing is the need for improved housing. The great *chawls* or tenements of Bombay are pre-eminently bad. In the industrial areas of the city the density of population rises to between three and four hundred persons per acre. Sixty-six per cent of these people live in one-room tenements—rooms usually about sixteen feet by ten. When rooms are larger, they are occupied by four, five or even six families. In other cities conditions are somewhat better than in Bombay, but there

are many areas where they are distinctly bad. Even
where to the casual observer houses seem an improvement over the mud huts of the village, one must remember that in rural areas the peasantry are at least in touch
with the soil, with abundance of fresh air and wide
spaces always at their command. For those on the
land, the long hours of toil are spent out of doors in
sun and wind, with intervals of rest, and with work
carried on at a leisurely pace. In the factories all this
is exchanged for confinement, close air, deafening noise
and the rapid pace of machine production. It needs
extremely good housing conditions to offset these losses,
especially in the case of women.

In the mills themselves, various improvements are
needed. Women workers should have retiring rooms
set apart for them where they may eat, rest and chat
during the noonday interval. In all mills women
doctors should be employed, both to give preliminary
physical examination to new workers, and to provide
medical advice and aid whenever needed. This is especially urgent in India, where social custom prevents many
women from availing themselves of a man's services.
Compulsory rest for some weeks before and after confinement, and maternity benefit, are also reforms greatly
needed.

For the children of workers every mill should provide
a *crèche*, simply fitted with swinging cradles of the usual
Indian type, and provided with competent and trust-
worthy *ayahs*, working under the supervision of a
woman doctor. For older children, schools should be
provided by the mills unless the municipality already
has free and compulsory education. The Buckingham
Mills in Madras furnish a splendid example of what mill-
owners can do for the education both of young children
and for half-time workers.

In regard to meeting these needs of industrialized

women, there are certain definite opportunities that lie before the Christian womanhood of India. There is first of all the duty of helping to form a stern and un-relenting public opinion as to the duty of mill-owners and shareholders toward labour. The disabilities of working women, their needs and practical methods of improvement, need to be held constantly before the public. This can be done through the Press, through lectures and addresses and through personal influence.

A second method is found in the training of educated Indian women to carry on welfare work among their needy sisters. Such a class now exists in Bombay under the joint management of the Y.W C.A., the Women's University Settlement, the United Free Church Mission and the American Marathi Mission. It is working under the leadership of Miss Tara Tilak, who received her training at the Selly Oak Colleges, Birmingham. One of the interesting features of this class is found in the number of non-Christian young women from well-to-do homes who are taking this course with the purpose of themselves entering lines of social service in Bombay. In the future there will be a need for great increase in such facilities for training.

But aside from professionally trained social workers, there is and always will be a need for volunteer helpers —women of ordinary education who will be willing to give of their leisure time to help the cause of social betterment. Of this need, Miss Tilak says :

The Churches should take a real interest in the local social problems, thus creating an understanding of the need, not exclusive and limited to the group of Church members, but all-embracing, concerning the problems of the whole of the city. They should engage themselves in definite, active, and, if possible, independent work for social welfare. There is plenty of scope for such work for women in any industrial city. It is not only educational but individual work that is needed among women who are deep in the mire of ignorance, misery, and stagnation of life. Such work ought to be done by Church women—maybe just a handful —who would devote to it all their time and energy, backed up by their Churches with sympathy and help. To make possible such an effort, preferably Indian and self-supporting, co-operation of the various Churches should be sought. What India needs to-day above everything else is women who will dare and do in the name and strength of God. Such women will be able to uplift the women of India. Indian Christian women ought to venture forth opening up new ways and channels of service to their sisters. Women of the Christian Church must also seek close co-operation with non-Christians, not only by working alongside them, but letting them work along with us in the great task of bringing about the rule of love and goodwill for all men.

This paper makes no claims to completeness. It has scarcely mentioned the older ways of bringing the message of Christ to India's women—the ways of medical help, of house-to-house teaching of the Bible, of many forms of school and college training. This omission has been due to no desire to discount these methods, many of which have stood the test of long periods of successful use. Rather there has been the feeling that since these methods are well known to all who have any knowledge of the Christian mission, it would be wiser in this paper to draw attention to certain attempts to relate the message of Christ to situations that have more lately developed in the strange and confusing " modern " India of to-day.

F

CHAPTER V

THE EDUCATION OF THE ILLITERATE

By Ethel A. Gordon

" ONE-SIXTH of the human race lives in the villages of India." " Ninety-two per cent of these villagers are illiterate." [1] These two statements give us some idea of the problem facing all, whether Christian or not, in India who care for the progress of the human race. Who to-day, when all the peoples of the earth have been brought into much closer touch with one another by the development of the means of communication, can doubt the importance of the existence of these illiterate masses for the world as a whole, as potential producers of far greater wealth than heretofore, when they are educated and trained ? Raise the standard of life of these people and their purchasing power, and it will mean increased employment in mills and factories all the world over. Raise the standard of life in regard to hygiene and sanitation, and it will mean removing some of the most serious sources of infectious diseases for the world. Educate these people in Christian living, and it will mean the upbuilding of the Body of Christ among a people whose religious heritage will enrich the whole Church of Christ in the world. The problem then is of first-rate importance for all who are concerned with the progress of the Kingdom of God in the world.

[1] Olcott, *Village Schools in India*, p. 1.

66

It will be well to indicate the nature of the problem by sketching very briefly conditions as they obtain to-day in the villages in India, for the problem of illiteracy (by which, I take it, we mean more than mere inability to read and write) is essentially a village problem; though we must not omit to consider the increasingly large numbers of mill and factory workers in the large industrial centres whose efficiency and therefore whose earning power and standard of life can only be raised by suitable education and training.

The chief factor in the village problem is the bitter struggle for mere existence. The land in many cases cannot support the population ; it is subdivided by the laws of inheritance so that profitable farming becomes wellnigh impossible ; farmers are bound by traditional methods to an extent that makes improvement very difficult and slow ; most families are heavily indebted— incurring debt for seed grain and common necessities before the harvest is due, but more often for expenses (dictated by caste rules and tradition) on weddings, funerals and other social occasions, or on litigation. Any savings there may be are invested unproductively in jewellery and ornaments. Poverty is one cause of the low vitality of the average villager, which leads to a lowering of the power of resistance to disease. Ignorance of the simplest and most elementary rules of hygiene and sanitation is also a predisposing cause of disease and ill-health. Bad housing and dirty water supplies are additional factors making for insanitary conditions of life. Health pamphlets are of little avail, as no one can read them ; and superstition, bred of ignorance, makes the villager a prey to fears which lead him to the grossest and most foolish practices in regard to disease. While poverty means not enough food for health and strength, ignorance means that no effort is made to secure variety and no attention is paid to nutritive value. A great deal of research work needs to be done on the subject of Indian food values in order to discover for the villager the best value he can get out of his food. In certain areas it will be necessary to induce the people to eat other grains, in addition to rice and their other staple products, in order to secure a balanced diet and so maintain health and efficiency. An additional result of filthy and insanitary conditions is the incidence of malaria, hook-worm, dysentery and other similar diseases.

In dealing with conditions as they are we cannot overlook the large part taken in village life by the women of the community. The custom of early marriage is undoubtedly one cause of the high death-rate, certainly in the case of children and women, and to some extent is also the cause of impaired vitality. Traditional treatment of child-birth brings many evils in its train. In the village the women, in addition to all the work of the home, which includes grinding of grain in hand-mills, do a great deal of field work. All the making of cow-dung cakes for fuel falls to their share. As a result the children are neglected and grow up unwashed and uncared for—their eyes often being ruined by neglect. Early marriage means usually that a girl has no opportunity to learn much before she is married, and is too busy afterwards with family and household cares. And the women are the key to this part of the problem.

In order to spread the elementary principles of health and hygiene in as many villages as possible and to uplift the people with the greatest possible speed, it is necessary to concentrate on improving the ideas of the women on these subjects rather than of the men. The women will pass the ideas on naturally to their children and will spread them far more than men, as they are personally and vitally interested in them.[1]

[1] Brayne, *Village Uplift in India*, p. 84.

The hope of rural India is the girls—give them a fair chance and you will turn the village into a paradise.[1]

In the matter of the education of girls, however, we have got to break down much prejudice and conservative tradition before any advance can be made.

No outline of rural conditions is complete which does not take into consideration the ever-present possibility (at least in some districts) of famine conditions. (In Jatisgaon there were only nine good agricultural seasons in twenty-four years.)[2]   In certain sections of the country, irrigation has proved impossible.   This ever-recurring menace accounts surely to some extent for the lack of initiative and seeming idleness of most villagers.   What is the use of better ploughs and more manure, of selected seed and well-bred cattle, when the rain may not come and the labour will be without fruit—the seed will be wasted in the ground and there will not be fodder for the cattle ?   Add to this the traditional religious teaching that all material existence is "maya" or illusion, and it is hard to see how a man— whose vitality is already impaired by poverty and disease—can be expected to rise above present conditions and put vigour and energy into his daily work and have a mind open to new ideas and suggestions.   The hope, it may be said, lies in the children.   Yes, but we have to remember that poverty compels the parents to make use of the child's power to earn just as soon as his labour is worth anything.   " Probably from one-quarter to one-half of the children in most of the villages of India add to the family income during part of the year." [3]   Child labour in the villages is one of the many hindrances to effective village schools.   Until some form of compulsory attendance is introduced a

[1] Brayne, *op. cit.* p. 92.
[2] Mann, *Land and Labour*, ii., quoted by Olcott, *op. cit.* p. 14.
[3] Olcott, *op. cit.* p. 31.

large amount of the money spent on village education
is wasted, as 39 per cent (which is a low estimate) of
those who pass through the village schools relapse into
illiteracy. " To bring out more clearly the defects (of
the voluntary system) it is necessary to remind ourselves
that India is essentially a land of small villages ; it is
in these small villages, inhabited mainly by castes and
classes opposed to education, that the battle for literacy
has mainly to be waged and that the wasteful methods
of the present system are most clearly seen." [1] " The
economic provision of effective education for the masses
must be on a compulsory basis." [2]

Before we pass on to consider ways and means of
combating the obstacles to a sound system of village
education let us look for a moment at the conditions
obtaining in the large industrial centres. The vast
majority of the labouring classes are illiterate and un-
trained. Skilled labour is difficult to get and in consequence output per head is much below that in Western
industrial centres. It follows that the standard of life
is low, and poverty and ignorance here, too, take toll of
life in impaired vitality and impaired power of resistance to disease. The ignorance and conservatism
of the uneducated workman is delaying industrial progress in India, and labour conditions can only improve
as the labouring classes are trained and educated to a
higher standard of working efficiency and of life. In
the towns there are educational facilities, but far more
needs to be done in making these available for the
children of mill-workers and in adapting curricula to
their needs. A notable example of the kind of work
that is needed is that done in the Buckingham and
Carnatic Mills Joint School, Madras. Night schools,
welfare work and schemes of adult education all need
to be developed in the large industrial centres.

[1] Mayhew, *The Education of India*, p. 235.   [2] *Ibid.* p. 238.

From the foregoing brief sketch of conditions as they obtain to-day in the villages of India, it is brought home very clearly that the problem of illiteracy is both an educational problem and an economic one. Improve farming methods and thereby the economic condition of the people, and it will be possible for the farmer to send his children to school; without better education and a more open-minded and receptive attitude on the part of the farming community, agriculture cannot be improved. We must plainly attack the problem from both sides.

One of the most successful methods of promoting the economic welfare of the people is that of co-operative credit societies and co-operative societies for buying goods and selling produce, and for other common projects. There is a very intimate connection between co-operation and the improvement of agriculture. Too much stress can hardly be laid on this point.

Some of the good results of the different kinds of co-operation are: 28 per cent of the members in the Punjab are entirely free from debt; litigation and extravagance are diminishing; land is being redeemed; cattle are stronger; drink is lessened; the sense of common citizenship is being created and education is being fostered.[1]

The extent to which village education is dependent on economic improvement is well illustrated in *Village Uplift in India* by F. L. Brayne—a Punjab district official who has had remarkable success during the last few years in improving conditions of rural life in his district. His first remedy was to increase produce by good methods of farming, and he can now report that 1500 girls are attending boys' schools, and that in a province where Moslem influence is strong! "Our object is not to make rich but to make happy. We only try to remove poverty, as poverty brings disease, misery,

[1] Olcott, *op. cit.* p. 35.

suffering and unhappiness." [1]   In addition to a basis of
improved economic conditions, is the paramount necessity of so relating village education to village life that the
teacher and the school may play that part in rural life
which we are entitled to expect from them.   What is the
aim of village education ?   Hitherto it has seemed that
one main aim has been to enable the bright boy to
escape from the village and to fit himself for lucrative
employment, which did not involve soiling his hands, in
the town.   " Rural education has not yet become the
uplifting force in village life that it should be, and
immediate steps must be taken to bring it into line, so
that attendance at school will not only drive the lad on
to the land instead of, as at present, off it, but will
stimulate him to put things right in his home and
village." [2]   " The problem seems to me to be to devise
a system of education which will stimulate the educated
not to flee from but to uplift village life, to strive for self-
improvement instead of merely running away to the
towns." [3]   The true aim of a system of rural education
is well expressed by Sanderson of Oundle—

Rural education demands that schools should be brought
into harmony with the community life and should take part
in the industrial and economic life. I would suggest that
we must not keep the life of a school too much separated
from the working life of the community. When boys and
girls go home, even to the humblest home, parents should
find that some part of the school life is associated with their
own life and work. This principle should modify the kind
of work done in schools, so that when boys leave school
they should have already taken part in the work which they
go out to do.

These are wise words and we do well to ponder them.
The effective organization of a school system on these
lines is, however, no easy matter. It requires the most

[1] Brayne, *op. cit.* p. 3.   [2] *Ibid.* p. 72.   [3] *Ibid.* pp. 120 ff.

careful study of conditions obtaining in each district or
each area to be served by the schools in question, for
without such detailed study the work of the school
cannot be planned as part of the life of the community,
nor can the school serve the community adequately.
The life interests of the community must be the guiding
principles at the back of the educational system. Here
we need much greater co-operation in village life than
has been known hitherto. Communities have lived
separate lives and there has been no real understanding
of the identity of their interests. Caste and community
distinctions have been emphasized at the expense of
really identical interests, for what is good for the labourer
is in the long run best for the landlord too.

Our ideal village school then will base its curriculum
on village interests and the children will learn by doing.
The vocational work will not be separated from the
literary work, and the aim of both will be the betterment
of village conditions. It is a truism to say that we learn
by doing, and yet in how many schools in India to-day
is the curriculum built up on this principle ? Does a
village boy learn counting as a skill necessary to the
accomplishment of some aim in which he is interested ?
Does he learn hygiene because he is interested in acquir-
ing the knowledge needed to stamp out malaria in his
section of the village ? The ideal which is inspiring
most of the experimental work which is being done in
India to-day is that of relating education to life—
an ideal necessary not only for the village school, but
for all grades of education. This does not mean the
neglect of those subjects and interests which " feed the
mind ".

The responsibility of the Christian Church and the
various missionary societies for very large numbers of
illiterate village people in what are called " mass-movement areas " made it necessary for them to try to evolve

a more satisfactory system of village schools than was possible with the average village teacher, who had more often than not no professional training, and whose whole conception of teaching was confined to forcing the three R's down the throats of unwilling children. Naturally the village school did not flourish—in the parents' eyes it served no useful end except as a *crèche* for the younger children who could not profitably be engaged herding cattle and goats. The vast proportion of the pupils in the village schools are in classes I. and II., and learn very little. It is difficult to get exact figures, but probably over 50 per cent of boys leave school at the end of the second year or earlier. Of the total number of children entering school less than one-tenth complete the four years necessary for the production of mere literacy in a child. A large part of the problem centres round the poverty of the present literary curriculum and the dearth of well qualified teachers. "One-teacher schools" are the rule rather than the exception. The difficulty of employing women teachers especially for the lower classes is a factor hindering progress. It is an acknowledged fact that women are better teachers of young children than men. Neither the parents nor the village community are interested in the work of the school. (It is to be remembered that in the mass-movement areas the Christian community is in general drawn from the outcaste classes.) The responsibility of those missionary societies by whose activities large numbers of these outcaste people had been baptized for the training of these people involved such far-reaching questions that a group of them together appointed an Educational Commission in 1919 to study the situation and to advise as to the best means for the improvement of village education. Stimulated by the report of the Commission, a great impetus was given to the study of the whole problem, and during the last few years the work of missions in this field has been of outstanding importance for the whole of Indian education.

Probably the most important work has been done at Moga in the Punjab under the auspices of the American Presbyterian Mission. The pioneer work done in the Moga school has given an impetus to research and experiment all over the country. Here we have a rural community middle school of the type described in a definition adopted by an all-India Conference on Rural Education which was held under the auspices of the National Christian Council of India in December 1922, in order to follow up and devise means for carrying into effect the recommendations of the village Education Commission.

A rural community middle school is a school which seeks to use the activities and valuable interests of the village as means for educating rural boys and girls for more abundant living and service in their communities. All the work of these schools, including the vocational or practical work, should be closely related to the pupils' village environment and should grow out of it. The vocational work should not be a separate entity, but should be an integral part of the curriculum, enriching it and having as its aim (along with the other work of the school) the bettering of present village conditions.

A curriculum framed on these principles and worked on the project method has been successfully used at Moga, where, also, teachers for village schools are trained along these lines. Agriculture is the main vocation taught, but subsidiary village industries such as basket-making, rope-making, tailoring and smiths' work also form part of the practical work which is used as a means of education. " Self-help " is a prominent feature of the institution, each boy being paid for the actual value of the work he does—whether it be in the form of profits from his field or garden plot or from trade work, or for general work about the school.   In this way the boys learn to respect manual work and also to value the education they are receiving.   While the work at Moga is more advanced and better consolidated than that done any-where else, the example set there has been followed *mutatis mutandis* all over the country.   A new interest and a new impetus have been given to the study of rural conditions and to experiments in discovering the best type of education for village life.   A great deal of experimental work in education is being carried on in Western countries, and missions have a considerable number of persons qualified by experience and training to do this work in India.   Also missions (under the grant-in-aid system) are being given very considerable freedom to experiment with new methods, provided that there is some reasonable assurance that this work is likely to be followed up.   All over the country we have at present men and women who are thinking out, and experimenting with, new ideas.   The greater part of this work is being done in what are called the district boarding-schools, which are being transformed into real community middle schools, and we find many working on most progressive lines.   It must be noted here—what is true of all mission educational work—that far more, and generally far better, work is being done for Christian girls than for boys.   This is an important point to which we shall return later.   One important fact to remember is that, while the training of women Christian teachers is still to a very large extent in the hands of Christian bodies, that of Christian men is not, to anything like the same extent.   The reforms initiated in these central schools have not yet got out to the village schools to any-thing like the extent we could wish.   The reason is that the work done in the middle schools has not yet produced its full results,—we have not yet got a supply of young men who have passed through these schools.   Without

figures one cannot dogmatize, but one suspects that an
adequate share of the mission budget does not go to this
vital work of educating and training our village Christian
population. When we remember that nearly 90 per
cent of the people live in the villages, it is surely apparent
that the upbuilding of a strong Church in the rural areas
is an essential factor for the progress of the Kingdom of
God in India. Nor have we at all found the best ways
of adequately and constructively supervising the schools
in the villages. Specially trained and qualified men are
needed for this work, which is both exacting and difficult.

One of the real difficulties facing those who are promoting rural community middle schools is the provision
of opportunity for those who are intellectually capable
of profiting by advanced literary education, to get it,
while at the same time the rural atmosphere of the school
is maintained. The teaching of English almost invariably
turns boys' thoughts to the towns. The difficulty is a
very real and very difficult one, for a good grounding
in English is necessary for advanced studies later on, and
the sooner it is begun the better. One wonders whether,
at the expense of perhaps adding a year to a boy's
school course, selected boys from rural schools could
not be given intensive work in English to make up for
beginning the subject late. In areas where for economic
reasons (famine conditions and poverty of the land,
etc.) it is necessary for a proportion, at any rate, of village
people to migrate to the towns, such an intensive course
in English at the end of the middle school course would
be of great use in giving boys a mastery of colloquial
English and so enabling them to get work as apprentices
in railway and other workshops. Probably there is
already considerable practical knowledge of the best
ways of teaching English, but it needs to be co-ordinated
and made available. In determining the curriculum to
be followed in a community middle school, careful study

of local conditions needs first to be made, and we have to be constantly on our guard against a stereotyped curriculum.   Life conditions are rapidly changing, and we must see that school conditions do not stand still.

The relation of the school to the community is of the utmost importance.   At Bolpur the work of the rural reconstruction department in connection with Dr. Tagore's school has been valuable.   " When 80 per cent of the population of the surrounding villages was down with malaria after the rainy season of 1923, the village of Modhpur was wholly free, due to the simple measures taken by their own troop of scouts ".[1] This is simply an instance of how a school can serve the community.   Where agricultural teaching of the best kind is provided, the school can serve as a centre for agricultural experiment and improvement for the whole district.   One example may be given.   All over a certain district there has been remarkable improvement in the breed of fowls as a result of the work done by a Christian industrial and agricultural school.

Two factors go towards insuring success in the development of these schools.   It is essential that the right man be chosen to initiate the work—be he Indian or foreign—and to secure this, co-operation with other missions may be necessary.   Often one mission has the plant and the school, and another the man, and no effort must be spared to bring the two together, though the writer knows well how difficult it often is.   In all cases, too, the interest, help and co-operation of Government should be sought, and it is usually found that these are forthcoming.   Indeed, in more than one province, the Government Educational authorities are learning to rely on Christian agencies for the initiation of schemes of this kind—for naturally their ways of work can be made more elastic than those of a whole Government system,

[1] Quoted by Olcott, *op. cit.* p. 43.

and they acknowledge gratefully the constructive thinking and planning which Christian agencies are doing. It
is obvious that the Christian mission in India can never
overtake the whole field of rural education, but it can
render outstanding service to the country by inaugurat-
ing and carrying on schools where the latest knowledge
and research from the West are made available for the
solution of this most difficult of all India's problems—
the education of the illiterate masses—on the solution
of which to a large extent depends her attainment of her
rightful position among the nations of the world.   There
is always a conflict, when resources are limited, between
those who advocate intensive work of the best kind and
work less effectively done but spread over a wider area.
We should like to urge that missions and Churches set
themselves together to establish at least one model school
of the type outlined in each important language area.
Such a school would be an example for others and would
set a standard to which others could aim.   It would also
serve the most important function of a laboratory for
research and experimentation.   Through the National
Christian Council, the work of such schools could be
co-ordinated and the results made available to others
working in the same line.

The greatest need in the villages is the provision of
the right kind of teacher—men and women whose real
interests lie in the villages and whose outlook is wide
enough to get beyond the limits of work in the actual
class room.   It would seem to the writer that in the
provision of teachers of the right kind for this work lies
to-day one of the greatest opportunities the Christian
Church in India has ever had.   Attached to each model
rural community school should be a teacher training
centre.   Here also should be the headquarters of the
village school supervisor, for all these institutions must
work in close co-operation.   The teachers in training

must have experience of real work in villages. Their
whole outlook must be set towards the villages.   Their
practical work should be under the actual conditions
obtaining in the district in which they are to work, and
the material for their laboratory studies in the central
training institution must be drawn from village work;
and they should, later, when teachers out in the field,
be free to bring their problems and difficulties for
advice and help to those working in the training school.
In a well co-ordinated scheme the village school super-
visors would be in close touch with the work at the
training centre, so that they could be the intermediaries
between the training centre and the village schools. Part
of the progress made would depend on the opportunities
given to the teachers to return for short courses of
instruction at frequent intervals, when the help given
would be related to the actual difficulties they had been
experiencing. One of the main services the central
institution in such a scheme could perform would be
the scientific study of the best ways and means of
teaching the various school subjects under Indian village
conditions.   For example, much investigation has been
undertaken in regard to the ways of teaching hand-
writing in the West, so that the best results may be
obtained with the least possible drudgery and weariness
to the pupil. Similar work needs to be done for each
of the many different Indian scripts. The problem
of language work in the early stages, where children
come from an area in which many dialects are used,
but where the main vernacular only (and necessarily) is
taught in schools, needs scientific investigation. Here
we have the bilingual problem in its earliest stages, just
as we meet it again when English becomes the medium
of instruction, and a child's life is divided into two com-
partments—home life and religious activities being conducted in his own mother tongue, while school work and

other interests are carried on in a foreign language. Here, surely, is a field for expert investigation in order to discover how best to adapt instruction and utilize the child's whole life interest in the educational process. Compare the wealth of folklore available as fairy stories, nursery rhymes, etc., with which childhood in the West is enriched.   Similar material is available in India, but it needs to be collected, prepared and made usable. This offers a wide field of the most fascinating research, the results of which would do more, perhaps, than anything else to enrich the present curriculum on its literary side and make a child's early education a part of his real life. We would plead for the expert study of these and other subjects, and this would seem a field where co-operation between missionaries from the West with the requisite training and Indian educationalists with their knowledge of the country could be very fruitful.

The provision of suitable literature for the maintenance of literacy might well be a part of the work of the training centre.   Work of this kind could be undertaken as a " project " by students in the training classes. That would tend to maintain their interest in this side of their work after they were back in the village as teachers.

A serious caution must be entered here.   No training school must be too large.   Nothing in the way of organization and expert management can replace the value of the close and intimate touch which those who train teachers should have with their students.   In the end, what counts in a teacher is a consecrated personality, and that tender growth needs the greatest nurture and care and the stimulus which contact with other personalities alone can bring.   This holds especially, I think, in a Christian institution, where stress is laid on the religious nature of education.

G

Religious training in the village school must be carried on in close touch with the local Church and Sunday School organization, and the right village master will know how to secure the co-operation of the whole village community.

Conditions in village India are rapidly changing, and as schools under local authorities are opened the place of the Christian village school becomes precarious. The more need, therefore, that Christian agencies should seek to provide teachers inspired by the Christian ideal of service. But the Church in India will do well, for many years to come, it seems to me, to provide Christian schools for their village people, so that a strong Church may be built up. The advent of the motor bus, with the corollary of more and better roads, may, perhaps, make it possible to provide more women teachers in the villages. These might live together in a larger centre, and go out to villages day by day for their work. If the uplift of the village depends on the uplift of its women, nothing could do more for the cause than the provision of well-trained capable women teachers, and the sooner conditions in the villages are such that women can be successfully employed as teachers, the sooner will a new day dawn for our village communities.

As education spreads, efforts will need to be made to induce children to attend larger central schools, where it will be economically possible to employ a larger and better qualified staff. Experiments have been made in this direction ; where these have been successful, success has been due to constant supervision and visiting in the villages concerned. " Travelling schools ", such as have been used with success in the Southern States of the U.S.A., might well be given a trial in India.

Another large and important part of the problem of illiteracy must be tackled under the head of adult education. Perhaps no more encouraging example of what can

be done in this line is to be found than the work of the
Folk High Schools of Denmark.   These were founded
by Grundtvig, whose

whole work for the enlightenment of the common people
was based upon his faith in the original nobility of mankind.
He did not approach his countrymen as one who would
condescend to give them crumbs from the tables of science,
art and culture ; he wished to share everything with the
people, to live in common with them, and to nourish himself from the same sources that were accessible to the lowliest.[1]

Evidence goes to show that the attitude of the Danish
farmer to-day, whose work has won the admiration of
the world, is largely due to the work of the Folk High
Schools initiated by Grundtvig and his associates.
" Behind the new and swift reorganization of one of the
most conservative and individualistic of industries were
brains, leadership and unselfish public spirit."   The
Folk High Schools had inspired their pupils, and
" awakened in them a yearning for knowledge and a
desire to work ".   This development took place alongside of a great national movement, which resulted
in a conflict between Danish and German culture.   Is
India on the eve of similar enterprises ? And what share
can the Christian mission take in the awakening of
her masses ?   Character, says Goethe, makes character, and the Church in India must send forth men
inspired, as Grundtvig was, to live and to share in all
village life, and to seek to raise it, so that " the adult
sons of the plain people " may be able to " discuss the
common concerns of the people ".   His schools were
intended to be a means of developing folk-life in all its
fullness.   Caste-ridden India has far to travel before such
an aim can be accomplished, but the signs are not want-
ing that an awakening is at hand.   The Church must

[1] *The Folk High Schools of Denmark and the Development of a
Farming Community*, pp. 81 f.

set herself to send forth men and women ready for this sacrificial service, and the preparation lies largely in the work being done to-day in our village schools, whose importance cannot therefore be minimized.   Churches and missions must set themselves to provide for this work in the future in a way that has not been done in the past, devoting to it their best in service and in personnel.

CHAPTER VI

HIGHER EDUCATION

By John McKenzie

MISSIONARIES have always been teachers, but at no time in the history of missions has so large a place been given to definitely educational work as during the past hundred years. Intellectual and spiritual illumination belong closely together, and in India during the past century there has been developed a public educational system in which Christian education has found a natural place. It has never been the policy of either the Government of India or of the Provincial Governments to undertake the education of the whole community. The Governments have their own institutions, but these are, by comparison, few, and the great mass of the educational work which is being done in India is done by private bodies. The policy which still prevails was set forth in the famous Education Despatch of 1854, a despatch sent by the Court of Directors of the East India Company to the Governor-General. It provided, among other things, for the giving of grants-in-aid to educational institutions under private management, if they submitted themselves to Government inspection, and were found to be efficient. Government itself was pledged to religious neutrality, and no religious instruction could be given in its institutions, but private bodies were left free to teach religion. Further, in accordance with the policy of the Despatch,

85

the first universities were established in India. These were of the " affiliating " type, the actual work of teaching being done in affiliated colleges, and encouragement was given to private bodies to maintain colleges, with the same freedom in regard to religious teaching as in the schools.

There is now in India a very large number of missionary educational institutions, recognized by Government and receiving grants-in-aid. Among these there are between 250 and 300 high schools, and about forty colleges affiliated to universities. Of these Colleges about thirty teach up to the standard of the university degrees in Arts, and several prepare students for degrees in Science also. There are few missions of any size which do not have at least one high school under their care, and a large number of missions have some share in college work.

There is no branch of missionary work which has been subjected to so much criticism as educational work, or regarding which so many questions have been raised. There are in particular those who think of the preaching of the Word as the chief instrument for the extension of the Kingdom of God, and many of these have found it difficult to understand why missionaries should give so much time and energy to what is sometimes spoken of as " secular education ". These objections and questions are not new. They are as old as missionary education itself. Duff had to meet them in his day, and quotations from his speeches will show the lines along which he met them. In a speech delivered before the General Assembly of the Church of Scotland in 1835, he said :

Let me again crave the attention of this venerable court to the grand peculiarity, that if in India you only impart ordinary useful knowledge, you thereby demolish what by its people is regarded as sacred. A course of instruction

that professes to convey truth of any kind thus becomes a
species of religious education in such a land—all education
being there regarded as religious or theological. Every
branch of sound general knowledge which you inculcate
becomes the destroyer of some corresponding part in the
Hindu system.[1]

On another occasion he compared the work of the
evangelistic missionary with his own, in these words :

While you engage in directly separating as many precious
atoms from the mass as the stubborn resistance to ordinary
appliances can admit, we shall, with the blessing of God,
devote our time and strength to the preparing of a mine
and the setting of a train which shall one day explode and
tear up the whole from its lowest depths.[2]

Lastly, his biographer gives Duff's statement of his
policy in regard to the positive teaching of the Christian
religion :

Whatever scheme of instruction he might adopt must
involve the necessity of reading some portion of the Bible
daily by every class that could read it, and of expounding
it to such as could not, with a view to enlightening their
understandings, spiritually impressing the heart and quickening the conscience, while the teacher prayed, at the same time,
that the truth might be brought home, by the grace of the
Spirit, for the real conversion to God of at least some of
them. As he read the Scripture and the history of the
Church, he did not expect that all or the majority of these
Bengali youths would certainly be thus turned. . . . But
he did expect that, if the Bible were thus faithfully taught
or preached, some at least would be turned from their idols
to serve the living God.[3]

There are several interesting points in these statements. One of the most interesting is Duff's confidence
in the value of Western education in itself. He was a
supporter of the Anglicists in their controversy with the

[1] Smith, *The Life of Alexander Duff*, p. 132.
[2] *Ibid.* p. 57.   [3] *Ibid.* pp. 57 f.

Orientalists, and he contributed to the decision which was given in 1835 in favour of the former, not only by his advocacy but by the practical embodiment of his ideas in his own institution. The first of the four resolutions in which this decision was promulgated was as follows :

His Lordship in Council (Lord William Bentinck) is of opinion that the great object of the British Government ought to be the promotion of European literature and science among the natives of India, and that all the funds appropriated for the purposes of education would be best employed on English education alone.

This was entirely in line with Duff's views. His motives were in part identical with those of Macaulay, the chief author of the scheme. The one was more concerned with the diffusion of Western culture and civilization ; the other with the diffusion of Christianity. But Duff, in common with many others in these days, considered Christianity and Western civilization to be bound up together to a degree that will probably surprise most people to-day. Wilson of Bombay, who began work in India about the same time as Duff, had not the same unqualified confidence in the beneficial effects of Western education. He was acutely aware of the dangers of Western learning without religion, and he had a wider knowledge and a juster appreciation of what was best in Indian civilization and culture than Duff had. He too founded a college where the medium of instruction was English, but he attached far more importance to the vernaculars, and to the study of the ancient languages and culture of India, than Duff did.

Closely connected with this is Duff's insistence on the need of destroying the Hindu system. We must not make too much of words and phrases apart from their context. Duff was never a mere destroyer. He made it clear at all times that his mission to the people

of India was the positive presentation of the Gospel of
Christ.   But both he and many other missionaries in
the early days were convinced that this meant the
destroying of the old system, root and branch.   Regarding Duff's own standpoint, it must be remembered that
he had not an intimate acquaintance with Hindu
philosophical thought, and that it was the cruder manifestations of Hinduism that obtruded themselves on his
notice.   I think one will find a considerable difference
in the attitude of men like Wilson, who were familiar
with Hindu life and thought in all their aspects.   They
too used the language of destruction more than it is
used now, but in a more guarded way.   Wilson was
out for the destruction of superstition and idolatry
with all their concomitant evils.   He by no means held
that Christianity was the fulfilment of Hinduism in the
way in which some have held this in recent times.
But he discriminated between the worth of different
elements in Hindu thought and life, and on the plane
of what he conceived to be true and good in their own
system he met the people of India with his presentation
of the Christian Gospel.

There is a third thing which strikes one in the
passages which I have quoted from Duff.   In all his
work he had the very definite aim of winning converts
to the Christian faith.   Now every Christian educator
has a definitely religious purpose in his work.   He
conceives his end to be not merely the imparting of a
certain amount of useful information to his pupils, nor
even the development of a number of latent powers
which reside in them, but the development of a personality which is through and through Christian—a
personality in which all powers and purposes receive
meaning and direction in relation to an understanding
and experience of God which are mediated by Jesus
Christ.   When education is so conceived it is an

enormously big and complicated thing. It would be
sheer impertinence for me to suggest that Duff was
unaware of the greatness or complexity of the task.
His is perhaps the greatest name in the history of
education in modern India. Yet there are things
which we see more clearly now than Duff did.

Education has not proved to be the powerful means
for the winning of converts which he believed it would
be, and which in measure he found it to be. I say
in measure, for the number of his converts was not
large. He wrote in 1844 regarding the conversions in
the educational institutions in Calcutta, Madras and
Bombay: " The number has been comparatively small.
But the amount of general influence excited thereby
must not be estimated according to the number." As
years went on the number grew, but it never was large,
and the use of education as a missionary method continued to be justified not on the ground of the number
but on that of the quality of the converts. Those who
know anything of the history of the families in India
to-day which owe their origin to converts of these days
will realize how great a contribution Duff made to the
upbuilding of the Church in India. But educational
work did not continue to produce the steady stream of
converts which it might have been expected to produce.
There is no religious system in the world which is more
misunderstood in the West than Hinduism. People
have often thought of it as rigid and inflexible, whereas
it has a remarkable capacity for adjusting itself to new
situations and new ideas. It is wonderfully hospitable,
under conditions, to new truths and new practices.
Under the shade of its ample boughs there is shelter for
the greatest variety of cults and cultures. And Hinduism proceeded to adjust itself to the conditions which
an aggressive Christianity had produced. It is no part
of my plan here to trace the course of the movements

which began within Hinduism during the nineteenth century, or to show their relations to Christianity by way of dependence or of reaction. But this much has to be said, that it became increasingly easy and natural for those whose spirits had been led to higher religious and ethical aspiration to seek a home not in the Christian Church but in one of the new indigenous societies. It was not only the flow of converts to the Christian Church that was seriously checked ; Hinduism was proved to be not a mass of rock that might be mined and blown up, but a living plant with many roots, that was capable of eluding the art of the sapper and miner.

This was the situation in the early sixties when there came to India another of the great educational missionaries of modern times, Dr. William Miller of Madras. He exercised for over forty years an influence in South India more widespread and deep than almost any other modern missionary. He early became aware of the complexity and difficulty of the situation with which he had to deal, but throughout his long life he was inspired by a faith in God, and in God's purpose to establish His Kingdom on the earth, that led him to take long views of his task, and to pursue it with a patience that did not always commend itself to those who had not fully understood the significance of our Lord's word, " The Kingdom of Heaven cometh not with observation ". He was impressed by the barriers that kept the great mass of the Mohammedan and Hindu population from being effectively influenced by Christianity, and he realised that education was the most important means by which the mass could be leavened and permeated. In a note communicated to the Edinburgh Missionary Conference of 1910 regarding the ideals animating Scottish missionary education, he wrote :

It is a mistake to suppose that the making of individual converts was at any time the only, or even the main, aim of these schools and colleges. Undoubtedly, conversions based on matured conviction and settled purpose were warmly welcomed, not only on account of the converts themselves, but even more on account of the influence they might exert on the inner life of the nation. It was hoped that, by the effect of Christian education on this inner life, the proclamation of the Gospel and other missionary methods might become far more effective on those hitherto inaccessible to every form of Christian influence.[1]

This did not mean any weakening of the Christian appeal. Nor did it mean any weakening of the sense of the inestimable value to the individual of a personal experience of Jesus Christ But it did mean a clearer recognition of the fact that there are obstacles to the spread of Christianity that are inherent in the whole structure of Indian thought and practice. If this social and intellectual structure were simply wrong and wicked, then the business of the Christian teacher would be to say to the non-Christian " Come ye out from among them and be ye separate ". But being an inheritance into which he comes, so that it is almost as much a part of himself as his own physical frame, and separation from it can in most cases be accomplished only by what approximates to an act of violence, it presents a problem which cannot be so summarily dismissed. There have been some, even within the Christian Church, who in the light of the response of multitudes of the more enlightened of non-Christian Indians to certain of the great elements in the Christian message, while still remaining within their own communities, have been led to regard it as the special function of Christianity not to bring the people of India into its own organization but to purify and enrich their own systems. Over against these there have been those who have been able to conceive no Christian work as worthy of the name which does not lead directly to the making of converts. And among

[1] *World Missionary Conference Reports*, vol. iii., p. 443.

the Indian people themselves there are many who
welcome the work of the educational missionary as
making a great contribution to the cultural, moral and
spiritual welfare of their land, who nevertheless look
upon all efforts to proselytize as unworthy.   And both
among Indian people and among Christian people in the
West there is a great deal of uncertainty and a certain
amount of suspicion in regard to the whole enterprise of
Christian education.

What I am writing here is addressed primarily to
Christian people who are concerned with the extension
of the Kingdom of God. Many of them would be
astonished if they came to realize how comparatively
small are the sections of Indian society in which
Christianity has come to be known so as to be understood.   It has been among the untouchable classes that
the largest and, measured by number of converts, most
fruitful activity has been carried on.   Apart from these
the lives and the minds of the mass of the people have
been comparatively little touched.   The agriculturists
and the artisans, who form the backbone of the population, have been very largely outside the sphere of missionary influence, and what Christian influence has been
exerted upon them has come mainly through educational,
medical, and in recent times, economic channels.   If
among the upper classes a more powerful Christian
leaven is working, it is due chiefly to Christian education and Christian literature.   The importance of this
influence it would be impossible to exaggerate.

It is not, as has sometimes been vulgarly supposed,
that a school or a college has served as a centre to which
by its extrinsic attractions certain classes of young people
might be drawn, and where, once gathered, they might
receive instruction in a system of religion which has no
integral relationship to the other subjects in the curriculum.   Christian education rests on a far more solid

basis.   On its intellectual side it rests on the conviction that all truth is God's truth, and that all truth receives its full illumination only in the light of Him who is the Truth.   Or to look at it from another point of view, it rests on the conviction that truth is a unity, and that religious truth cannot without serious misrepresentation be taught except in its relationship to all other truth. When we look at the matter in this way, we realise that to give a Christian education does not mean in the first instance, at any rate, the striking of the evangelistic note whenever opportunity offers in the conduct of any or every class.   It means the helping of the student to a Christian understanding of the world, from whatever angle he views it.

    This is a process ; it is not something that can be accomplished " sudden, in a minute ".   For we have to deal not simply with the mind of the individual student, but with the mind of a race, which has had its forms of thought shaped and confirmed through millennia of reflection and meditation.   It is not inveterate obstinacy that keeps the students of India from accepting the Christian view of God and the world when it is presented to them ; it is the fact that they have been born into, and live and move and have their being in, a system of thought which in its great philosophical formulations is as coherent as any system that has been conceived. Further, it is not only a system of thought ; it is the intellectual basis of a culture which has been more persistent than any of the cultures of the West, and to which the Indians of the present day feel a loyalty which must command the respect of everyone possessed of intelligence and sympathy.   We have been made very familiar with the evils of Hinduism, with the grotesque-ness of some phases of its thought and life.   That there is much that is grotesque and evil in it, no one who knows anything of it will attempt to deny.   But the enlightened people of India claim that any religious or social system must be judged, not by what is worst in it, but by what is best, and by the capacities which are inherent in it. And many claim that, judged by that standard, Hinduism is not only a system that can satisfy the needs of the people of India, but that it is superior to all other systems. In pressing this claim they have the emotional support that comes from the sense that they are the heirs to a great and ancient heritage, which the upstart peoples who dominate the world have failed to appraise at its true value.

Those who have found in Jesus Christ " the light of all their seeing " will come to such a people with no pride of race or culture or material power, and with no contemptuous scorn of the ideals by which the people live. But they will come bringing the best that they have to give in the way both of intellectual and of spiritual gifts. They will seek in all their teaching and in all their intercourse with their pupils and students to build up rather than to break down, helping them to develop true thoughts about God and about life, and helping them to form and to pursue ideals for life that are rooted in these thoughts. If ever missionaries had ground for imagining that a primary part of their function was to break down the ancient system, this ground has largely gone. There are influences at work to-day that are doing the work of breaking down far more insidiously and far more ruthlessly than the missionaries of any religion can do it. Western education is doing it, where it is an education divorced from religion, or where, as in some cases, it is an education hostile to religion. The greatest enemy of Christianity in India to-day is not to be found in the religions of the land, but in influences secularistic and materialistic that have come from the West to India through many channels and not least through that of education. They are insidious, because they touch first not the social structure or even the forms of religious ritual, but the intellect and the heart, and they are ruthless, because in their final consequences they destroy the noblest elements in the life of a people.

It is in such a *milieu* that Christian educational work is being carried on in India, and I believe it is in the spirit which I have indicated that it is being done by most educational missionaries. There is in it a sphere of almost unparalleled opportunity, for the Christian teacher may exercise an influence of the deepest and strongest kind on the minds of his students. He can count in his work on the goodwill of the community, and on their appreciation not only of the intellectual, but of the spiritual service which he renders. For the people of India are conscious of the need of the spiritual element in education, and they deplore the absence of it in so many of their institutions. The belief that is current in some quarters that there is widespread hostility to Christian education is based on the fact that in some provinces there has been a strong movement to secure that attendance at religious instruction in schools and colleges be made voluntary. That this does not rest upon hostility to Christian education as such, or to the study of the Bible, is proved by the fact that where a " Conscience Clause " has been accepted, either voluntarily or in accordance with the terms of an Act of the Legislature, there is practically unanimous testimony that there has been no slackening of religious interest The antagonism has not been to religious teaching, but to the spirit that insists on attendance as a condition of admission to an institution.

What is actually being accomplished by the Christian high schools and colleges of India ? Are they justifying their existence as centres of spiritual influence ? These are questions which are often asked by Christian people in the West who are interested in the establishment of

the Kingdom of God in the world. I shall try to answer
these questions.

1. Christian educational institutions have been exercising an enormous influence, intellectually, morally
and spiritually, on the lives of those who have studied
in them, and through them, on the life of the whole
community. It is an influence that has led to comparatively few accessions to the Christian Church, but,
nevertheless, it is an influence that is Christian, and that
is fraught with great significance for the religious life
of India and of the world. It is manifest in many ways,
but I believe what is most significant is the fact that the
eyes of increasing numbers of educated men and women
are being turned to Jesus Christ. They are finding in
Him not merely a great ethical teacher and social reformer, but a great guide in the deep things of the spirit,
and a great illuminator of the ways of God in the world.
There are many who go beyond this, and who are prepared to use almost all the language of Christian faith
and devotion regarding Him, but who do not believe
that the Christian Church has any necessary and essential place in the Christian life.[1] Those who know anything of Hindu religious life must recognize in this great
gain. When one thinks of India as the most religious
of all lands, and yet as a land in which the religious
aspirations of the people have so often failed to find
the highest fulfilment, it is a great thing that many
should have found in Jesus Christ their ideal. They
are on the march, and God is their leader, and we need
not be too anxious to hurry the pace.

On the practical side this quickening of the spirit
has led to a multitude of activities for the service of
society. Movements for social reform, for the removal
of hindrances to the moral life, and for the combating

[1] For evidence of this, see *e.g.* Dr. Stanley Jones's *The Christ of the Indian Road.*

of sickness, ignorance and poverty, owe a large part of their inspiration to this source. There certainly have been other influences at work, but the Christian influence has been the most powerful. And this Christian influence has come through various channels, but there has been no other channel which has had anything like the importance of Christian educational institutions.

2. They have also rendered a great service in helping to break down racial and national barriers. I do not refer to what some people in the West have supposed to be one of their chief merits—making the people more amenable to foreign rule. If they actually had this influence, it would still remain to be considered whether or not it was a distinctively Christian service. Curiously enough, they have sometimes been praised by another class of people on the ground of their influence in stimulating the desire for independence. There is this element of truth in both points of view, that Christianity has always both stimulated the desire for liberty and fostered the spirit which is called in the New Testament ἐπιείκεια—sweet reasonableness. But the barriers of which I speak are not those narrowly political ones. They are the barriers of a narrow racialism that manifests itself in the glorification of all that belongs to one's own race and people, and in hostility to all that is foreign, simply because it is foreign. They are barriers that in some degree limit the vision and inhibit the sympathies of almost all of us. The evil of racialism is one of the most terrible of the evils under which the world groans to-day. It would be an evidence of sheer ineptitude if one were to assert that it rests on sentiment, ignoring the deep economic, political and other forces that have contributed to the maintenance of the sentiment. It would be folly also to suppose that a mere flood of emotion is capable of lifting the minds of the peoples of the world above the bogs and shoals in which so many

of them lie. But it may be asserted that there is no
influence available to men which can compare with
the Spirit of Christ in freeing the minds of men from
the spirit of narrow racialism and nationalism.[1]   His
message of deliverance to men as men, without distinction of race or condition, has furnished a motive that
has not only led men to seek a fellowship with their
fellowmen in which these distinctions are transcended,
but that has led them in the spirit of love and goodwill
to work for the removal of the causes which have led to
division.

One of the most remarkable things in the mind of
modern India is the way in which it has been turned to
Jesus Christ as the great teacher and exemplifier of
human brotherhood. It is true that Indian people have
only too often, and with a large measure of justice,
pointed to the disparity between the spirit of our Lord
and that of His professed disciples, charging them with
the desire merely to swell the membership of a sect, and
with failure to realize in their own lives the spirit of
Him whose Name they have taken. But the fact remains that, however weak may have been the witness
and example of Christian people, the Spirit of our Lord
has been creating a new conscience among the educated
classes in India. Multitudes are now ashamed of the
racial and communal divisions which have done so much
to disfigure the life of India. Evils like untouchability
and Hindu-Moslem hostility lie heavily on many consciences, and many men and women are spending themselves in labours for their removal. More than that there
is evidence even in quarters where nationalist feeling

---

[1] Nothing was more impressive in the discussions at the meeting
of the International Missionary Council in Jerusalem in March and
April 1928 than the spirit of the Christian men and women from the
East and Africa, deeply conscious of unjustifiable racial inequalities
and active in their labours for their removal, yet delivered from bitterness
by the Spirit of Christ.

runs high, and the desire for complete political freedom
is strong, of a disposition to make a sharp distinction
between the political and the personal and social.
During the period of greatest " non-co-operation "
activity, one continually heard testimonies to the personal courtesy and even kindliness which many of the
non-co-operators showed to those whom they termed
" members of the ruling race ".

We cannot attribute the growth of this spirit solely
to the influence of Christian education. Mahatma
Gandhi, who was not educated in a Christian college,
has done more than any other individual to direct the
mind of India to the teaching of Jesus Christ. But he
worked on ground which was prepared by long years
of Christian teaching in missionary institutions. Knowledge which many possessed without realization of its
profound significance for their own lives became to
them almost a new thing. We must not exaggerate the
extent to which this has taken place, but there is no
doubt whatsoever that there is a great and a growing
sense of the need for brotherhood between man and
man, irrespective of race and social status. There is
also a growing recognition of the fact that a religion that
is simply national or sectional stands condemned. It
is a healthy sign that many Hindu bodies are seeking
to throw open the gates of Hinduism to people of all
races, for this means a weakening of the association of
religion with nationality and race. Along with this
there is a growing tolerance being manifested towards
those who seek entrance to the Christian Church, where
conversion is a definitely spiritual thing. We have still
a very long way to go, and there are many facts that
might be cited in disproof of these statements, but anyone who has been in close touch with enlightened Hindu
opinion will recognize that these tendencies are there.

3. There is a third service that Christian educational

institutions have been rendering to India, and that is in the education of those who have been born into the Christian Church. This is a service the importance of which it is almost impossible to overestimate. The fact that a person is born and brought up in a Christian home is not a guarantee that all the Christian graces will be found in him, whether he be an Englishman or an Indian. The average Indian Christian youth has far greater difficulties to face, economically, intellectually, ethically and spiritually, than the average European youth. There is practically universal recognition among missionaries and Christian leaders of the supreme importance of Christian education for this class of people. It is in Christian institutions, where they have been taught by, and had the companionship of, Christian teachers that most of the leading Indian Christians have received the influences that have been most determinative in the formation of their minds and characters.

Further, it has been of great benefit that in these institutions Christian young men and women should have been educated alongside members of other religious communities. There have been some who have advocated the abandonment of the policy of educating non-Christians in missionary schools and colleges, and the concentration of all our effort on Christians. These proposals have not found widespread support, and I believe them to be entirely unsound. I shall not here go into all the arguments against them, but would only point out that it has been of the greatest advantage to both Christians and non-Christians that they should be educated together. On the one hand, it would be in the highest degree detrimental to the Christian community if its members were segregated for purposes of education. They are being prepared for a life which must be lived in the wider community, and it would be

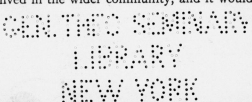

a poor preparation for that life if in their formative years they were withdrawn from association with all but their own co-religionists. On the other hand, Christian students have something to contribute to the common life of an institution. I have known Christian students who, by the consistency of their Christian character, exercised a great influence upon their non-Christian fellow-students. And there is not only the influence that individual exerts on individual ; there is the wider influence which may be exerted in the way of breaking down unreasoning prejudice. The Christian has too much been regarded as a foreigner, and not always entirely without justification. In Christian institutions, especially in Christian colleges, Christians and non-Christians have often come to discover the deep community of interests and of loyalties in which they share. If the Christian cannot respond to the often-repeated call to members of all communities that they should be Indians first, and then Hindus or Mussulmans or Christians, he can show and he has been showing that by being a faithful follower of Jesus Christ he can be, in all the things that count, a true Indian.

In this chapter attention has been concentrated on the spiritual motive and the spiritual results of Christian educational work. Its more strictly intellectual side has not been discussed with any fullness. Regarding this I would only say that if all truth be God's truth, then we can offer to the students of India only the best that it is in our power to give.

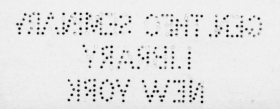

CHAPTER VII

CHRISTIAN LITERATURE: ITS AIM AND OPPORTUNITY

By NICOL MACNICOL

I

IN the task that God has committed to His children of transforming the world into the place of His Kingdom, the sphere of His holy rule, it is our business to make use of every instrument by which men's souls are shaped. And as He Himself to that end sent among men His Word, giving to it many forms and fashions, and finally the perfect form and fashion of His Son, so we have to give what shapes of power and of charm we can to the portrayal of that Word as we discover for ourselves its beauty. Art and poetry and literature present the forms through which this Word becomes flesh to us, and walks our streets and speaks to our ears. Books by men, as well as acts of men and lives of men, can be incarnations of the divine revelation that will speak to us and go on speaking long after the living voice is silent. This is obvious, of course, and a commonplace that everyone admits and passes by, but it needs a new attention on the part of those who are deeply concerned that the divine Kingdom shall be established speedily—that is, in God's good time—upon earth. For this avenue into men's souls is becoming every day increasingly open to our traffic all the world over. Its importance for other ends is being increasingly recognized, and for other ends it is being increasingly and powerfully used. We have to see that it is increasingly and powerfully used for the ends of the Kingdom of God.

Advertisement in the case of the man of business, propaganda in the case of the politician—these are weapons the value and effectiveness of which have been realized in recent years as never before and which are being used now as they were never used before. They may often be poisonous and destructive weapons, messengers of lies, but they need not be so. Its unscrupulous employment during the late war has made us often understand the word propaganda as signifying mere lying and nothing else. But of its power, whether for evil or for good, we were then made vividly aware, and the lesson thus learned is being put to use now as never before in the government of states. Modern psychological study has confirmed what the war revealed. The power that governments through education and all the various avenues of suggestion can exercise so as to create patriotism or indeed to shape men's natures to almost any form they wish is now recognized and acted upon by the rulers of all lands. If these facts are being made use of for selfish, national ends, how much more are we called upon to make the fullest use of them for the end of the achievement for the world of God's purpose, of the establishment of His supernatural, divine dominion! Thus it appears that the present time calls for a new examination of the value in the missionary world enterprise—and especially so in the case of a land such as India possessing a long literary tradition—of Christian literature, and for renewed endeavour to make the fullest use of it.

II

But does India afford such an opportunity ? Has this land, after all, a literary aptitude and interest ? In a recent notorious book we find this assertion : " In the Philippines and in India alike, little or no current literature exists available or of interest to the masses." [1] It might be sufficient in reply to this allegation to say that there were in 1910–11 2751 printing presses in India, that during that year 1578 books were published in English and over 10,000 in the vernaculars, and that there is no reason to suppose that the figures for the years since then have become less. But that would furnish a very inadequate account of the influence of literature in India. In no country is the power that an ancient literature still exerts upon the thought and life of a people greater than that in India of the Sanskrit language and its sacred literature. But even if we set that fact aside, it is only ignorance of the lives of the Indian people that can leave anyone unaware of the profound influence that is exercised day by day through the medium of the vernaculars not only by the ancient sages, but by the poet-saints of a later past. Vernacular translations of the *Rāmāyana* and the *Bhāgavata* are read and are familiar in the homes of many of the people. The songs of the saints are intimately known to multitudes, and are sung by the wayfarer as he goes from village to market, and by the workers as they work. In the city of Poona—the city with which the writer is most familiar—at several centres groups gather daily in the evening round a *guru*, who reads to them from one of their most treasured Marathi poems and expounds its religious message. The writer watched recently one such company as their gathering dispersed, and noticed how many shaven widows there were among

[1] Miss Mayo's *Mother India*, p. 178.

them, how many that manifestly needed comfort.
Another group elsewhere in the city consists of working
people, clerks and artisans, who go there, we may
suppose, to obtain strength for each day's duties and
temptations.   Similar evidence could be adduced from
the regions of all the great vernaculars, indicating how
widespread and how deep is the influence of their
literature.   " There is hardly a rustic in a Bengal
village ", writes Mr. Dinesh Chandra Sen,[1] " who does
not sing to himself some favourite tune, as, after his
weary day of labour, he lays down his tools to retire
to rest."   So it is also with the Tamil hymns which are
memorized by Tamil children as Christian children
memorize the psalms.[2]   And similarly the *Rāmāyan* of
Tulsi Dās is constantly read and studied all over the
wide area where Hindi is spoken, and has in consequence
" been the most potent factor in making Vaishnavism
the accepted cult of the vast majority of Hindus in
North India to-day ".[3]   As one passes from province
to province and marks the forces that mould and sway
the people's hearts, the same tale is told everywhere of
how the poet-saints of a past day speak to the people
still, and " rule them from their urns ".   " Pious women
in Gujarat ", writes a Gujarati scholar, " sing the songs
of Mirā Bai and feel that they are nearer heaven than
earth when Mirā's music is on their tongues.   Young
women sing them at home and in public choruses, for
Mirā's ideal is held to be the ideal for all women."[4]
What W. B. Yeats wrote of Rabindranath Tagore's
poems was true already when he wrote of the songs of
many another poet of the past, whether the language
be Marathi or Punjabi or Kanarese or Telugu or any
other among the languages of India, each of which has

[1] *Bengali Language and Literature*, p. 711.
[2] *Hymns of Tamil Saiva Saints*, p. 1.
[3] *Hindi Literature*, F. Keay, p. 57.
[4] Quoted in my *Making of Modern India*, p. 165.

a literature of which its people may be proud. " As the generations pass," he wrote of this latest-born of the singers of Bengal, " travellers will hum them on the highway and men rowing upon rivers." [1]

And whether the writers wrote centuries ago or whether they write to-day, their main theme is always religion. More than one-third of the books published in 1910 deal with this subject, which has always been the supreme object of India's concern. If these things are true and if literature and religion have been thus yoked together for centuries in the experience of this people, then how manifestly it is demanded of us that we should prepare this way of the Lord and make straight the highway trodden so long by psalmists and by sages, that along it the King of Sages, the Rājarshi, Himself at last may come.

III

In claiming for literature so great a place in the evangelization of India we may well believe that in the circumstances of this land its power will be greater there than it has been elsewhere. But we know how much books have done in all lands—and certainly in Scotland —to build into the character of the people nobility and strength. Throughout the whole history of Christianity, its progress and expansion and the deepening of its power over men have been marked by the appearance of great emancipating books, by means of which men's chains have been broken and the darkness that has kept them enslaved has been scattered. Such a book was of course in the first place the Bible itself—and such it remains. Wherever it goes and men read it with the eyes of the soul, they start up, as Christian did with the book in his hand, and begin to run. Trans-

---

[1] Rabindranath Tagore's *Gitanjali*, p. xii.

forming forces are set in motion. So it was when
Luther read the Epistle to the Galatians ; chains fell
from him as he read. So it was again when John
Bunyan read Luther's commentary on Galatians. How
many have been helped to freedom by what these three
men wrote out of their hearts—Paul and Luther and
John Bunyan. Another book, kindled in a dark hour,
that carried light also to Luther and has carried it since
through him to many another, is the *Theologia Ger-
manica* ; and again there are Augustine's *Confessions*
and the *Imitation*, books that through the dark nights
of human experience shine on like stars, bringing peace
and consolation and strength. These, and so many
others like them, are universal books, to which it is of
no significance that one author lived in Africa and
another in Germany, that one was a monk in his cloister
and another a tinker in Bedford. They bear witness
to the super-nationalism of the Christian religion, to
the fact that it is the common possession of humanity,
and, as such, they overthrow prejudice and win the
way for our Christian message into the deep places of
the universal heart of man.

These are instances such as recur at once to us all
and could be multiplied a hundredfold, bearing witness
to the power that books, charged with the undying
Spirit of Christ Jesus, have accomplished and are still
accomplishing. That what these books have done for
other peoples they can do for India, lighting it on the
road to God, we surely cannot doubt. That is why we
rejoice in the work of the British and Foreign Bible
Society in making it impossible for anyone who desires
at all to read the Bible to leave his desire unsatisfied.
In English and in every vernacular it is at hand and
can be obtained.

But this is not enough. Even the Bible may be so
read (" the veil is upon their hearts ") that its beauty has

no charm. Mr. Gandhi tells us how he set out to read the Bible through, beginning with Genesis. But he did not persist long. " I disliked reading the book of Numbers," he says.[1] We cannot claim that even the Bible is always its own interpreter. A guide is needed. This book becomes a means of grace within, and in association with, the Church, the community of the loyal, by whose experience it was created as God spoke to them, and by whose experience it is interpreted. For it is in the Church, in the hearts of living and loving men and women, that the Spirit of God abides and works. And great spiritual books are crystallizations of the mind of the Church. The creative springs of the Spirit of God are to be found in the Bible, for there we have the record of God's revelation of Himself when out of the dust of the earth He created His Church and breathed into her nostrils the breath of life. To that creative act books of religion are secondary and on a far lower level of inspiration. They may, however, be embodiments of the mind of the Church, and when they are so they become interpreters of God's purpose, making His path plain to us, when His path is so high and so strange our dim eyes could never discover it unaided. If even Mr. Gandhi lost his way among the Hebrew Scriptures and failed accordingly to discover, and to bow before the lofty revelation of a holy God, how much more are guides needed for men and women less gifted with spiritual insight, and especially so when they are, like him, Indians, so far removed in the fashion of their thinking from the prophets of Israel. There are few among us who do not need " an interpreter, one among a thousand ", that is, let us say, one who conveys and imparts to us the wisdom of the Church of the Ages, and also opens our eyes to see what otherwise we would pass blindly by. If this is true of people of all races, it is

[1] *My Experiments with Truth*, p. 168.

especially true of the inheritors of the ancient Aryan culture, whose thoughts of God and of salvation have been for centuries turned in another direction than that from which God, as the Hebrew prophets saw and taught, comes most fully to His children. The mind of India has to be made over again, as well as its heart and will renewed, and that that may be done, that the very climate of their thinking may be changed, not the Bible alone is needed, but " schoolmasters " of many kinds and many gifts, who will lead them to the Bible and enable them to possess its treasures.

IV

To change the climate of a people's thinking is no easy task—especially when their thinking is so ancient and so profound as that of India—and, if we are to achieve it, we must mobilize all the forces of our thought and purpose. This difficult task—" with men it is impossible "—is, however, the very task to which as messengers of God we have been called. The common, selfish, sensual soul of man has to be, by the power of Christ, reborn from above, and has to be given a new atmosphere to breathe, new food to feed upon. The Hindu ideal of negation, of flight and escape, has to be exchanged for the Christian idea of victory by means of a strength supplied. That, on the one hand, has to be made possible ; and, on the other, secularism, material- ism, worldliness, the common enemies that lurk within every soul have to be overcome. The roots from which Christianity springs may be suggested by such a saying as that of the Hebrew prophet, " What doth the Lord require of thee but to do justly, to love mercy and to walk humbly with thy God?" Hinduism, on the other hand, breathes a very different spirit and goes about to create a personality, a self that looks in a wholly opposite direction : " This Self is *Nay, Nay* ; not to be grasped, for He is not grasped ; not to be broken, for He is not broken ; unclinging, for He clings not ; He is not bound, He trembles not ; He takes no hurt.   One (who knows this) is overcome neither by having done evil for His sake nor by having done good for His sake ; he overcomes both ; work done and work not done grieve him not." [1]

Here is a complete contrast of ideals, and he who comes to Christ from such a Hinduism must " burn what he had adored and adore what he had burned ". Along with that exchange there must go in the case of most a change from the dominion of the secular to the dominion of the spiritual.   " We are selfish men ", whether we call ourselves Hindu or Mohammedan or Christian.   The downward drag of our gross cravings controls us, and " getting and spending " we lay our whole lives waste.   This evil spirit is abroad everywhere, lying athwart such a spirit and tradition as that of Hinduism and making the task of India's regeneration infinitely difficult.   A situation such as this demands the mobilization of all the forces of the Church, and if we neglect the aid of those books which tell of those things by which men truly live and of how they so lived, we are guilty of grievous negligence.

These, then, are two hostile forces that stand on guard against the entrance and possession of the Indian heart by Christ Jesus—an alien philosophy of life, whether it be the creation of Hinduism or Mohammedanism or any other deep-rooted tradition, and at the same time, a secular and selfish way of life, an infection of evil, everywhere present and certainly no less so in India to-day than elsewhere.   It is not enough for us to get past the former enemy : we have still the harder task to accomplish of slaying his companion ere we can enter the

[1] *Brihadaranyaka Upanishad*, IV., iv. 23.

Indian stronghold.   Giant Pagan may seem in the case
of many individuals to have grown toothless and
decrepit, but the other Giant may be, in the case of
these very persons, all the more alive.   Agnosticism and
indifference are no satisfactory exchange for Hindu or
Moslem orthodoxy, and the influences that tend to
destroy the old beliefs are active on every side in India
as in other lands.   If Christian books are not in evidence
others are, and carry on their work of destruction.
" The works of the Rationalist Press Association ",
writes Mr. V. Kin Maung, a Buddhist and a representative of Burma in the Indian Legislative Assembly,
" find ready readers among Burman Buddhists.   Such
books as Grant Allen's *The Evolution of the Idea of God*,
Ingersoll's *Lectures and Essays*, Thomas Paine's *The
Age of Reason*, may be quoted as forming the bulk of
the works that Burmans browse over."   What is true
of Burma is true of every province of India.   Destructive
influences are abroad upon every side, and if Hinduism
crumbles and Mohammedanism changes, the result is
seldom in either case that those who have abandoned
these creeds have found a better.   They are for the most
part anchorless and rudderless upon the high seas.
These old religions gave them some guidance in their
lives : they taught that life had some meaning and aim.
For them now it is often mere frustration and futility.

V

How have books helped the Indian Christian Church
to overcome these hostile forces and to possess itself of
the hope that is in Christ and of the strength that He
gives ?   There is no medium by which an evangel can
be so surely carried into the heart as that of song, and
there have been no more effective messengers of the
Christian faith to India than those of her children who

have been able to set that faith to music. This has been found to be the case again and again, even within Hinduism, when someone has arisen with a message that, as one of their old poets [1] says, " lays hold of the heart ". When that is so it has sometimes appeared even to the non-Christian seeker that the longing for union with God is not impossible of fulfilment, and then, as Tukārām, the Maratha poet-saint, can claim :

They are made one with Brahma with a song.[2]

How much more will a song that tells of Christ and of Christian experience lead men to that goal. Thus it has proved; and among the Marathas, Narayan Vaman Tilak, and among the Tamils, H. A. Krishna Pillai, and among the Telugus, a third hymn writer, have exercised an influence by the medium of poetry that has been of the highest value to the Christian Church. Of these, Tilak was the most finely gifted as a poet, and he was able not only to give to his fellow-Christians of the Maratha country hymns that lend wings to their souls, but to win a wide hearing for his Christian message among his cultured non-Christian fellow-countrymen. As one of his admirers, who was not a Christian, expresses it, he " brought poetry down from heaven to this world ",[3] and bringing poetry thus near to men he brought Christ near to them also. H. A. Krishna Pillai seems by his poetic gifts to have won a similar position among those who speak Tamil. What his poems have done to win a way past the prejudices of South Indian orthodoxy is made plain by Miss Amy Carmichael in a little sketch of the poet which she has written :

He has left books [she says] which we can give to the most critical Hindu, knowing that so far as the choice of

[1] Tulsi Dās.
[2] *Psalms of Maratha Saints*, p. 81.
[3] Principal Patwardhan of the Fergusson College, Poona, in the *Indian Interpreter*, October 1919.

I

language is concerned it will not repel him, but will put the message before him intelligently and winningly. Not long ago a Christian schoolmaster was travelling by train in the same compartment as a Brahman. He asked the Brahman if he had ever heard of Christianity. For answer the Brahman retired to the farther end of the carriage. The Christian waited, then asked, " Do you care for poetry ? " If there is one word which charms and draws a cultured Hindu it is the word poetry. The Brahman's eyes glistened. The Christian began to chant stanzas from our poet's *Pilgrim's Progress*. The poem follows Indian rules of art ; to the trained ear the fall of its cadence is quite perfect. The Brahman listened, won to listen at first by the beauty of the poem. Sin, redemption, Christ's life and death, clear teaching about the way of salvation, outpourings of love and devotion—still the Brahman listened. At last, after long chanting, broken by words of explanation here and there, the Christian stopped. " That is Christianity," he said. The Brahman was disarmed. For the first time he had listened to " the wooing note ".[1]

The Telugu hymn writer already referred to has perhaps no claim to rank alongside of these two. The task he has discharged is a humbler one, if one scarcely less important for the Christian people of the Andhra country in South India. He has given them hymns which teach them as they sing the old stories of the heroes of Israel and make those heroes live again as friends and patterns. It may be that what he accomplished was not on a much higher poetic level than what the unknown negro singers did for those who learned from them to sing, " Turn back Pharaoh's chariot ", or to see with the eyes of their imagination how

> Martha and Mary's just gone 'long,
> To ring those charming bells,

the bells of " free grace and dying love ". But in the case both of the American negro and of the outcast

[1] *H. A. Krishna Pillai.* By Amy Carmichael. Madras C.L.S.

Mala of South India the service rendered in bringing down into the common lives of men and women the grace of God and His power to deliver men is a service that is infinitely precious.

Nothing that we can do can create poets in India or anywhere. That is beyond our scope. But in the Gospel of Christ we possess the material of poetry, and our part is to broadcast as widely as possible the music that inevitably finds expression, crude though that expression may be, whenever God draws to Himself a human soul. Hinduism, in its higher flights, is, as one of its sons has called it, " a stringless lute ", and in so far as that is true of it, one can say that it lacks the essentials of religion. Every faith that is an evangel, that brings to men God and hope and salvation must have within it, as its very being and life, what Kabir calls " the music of the forgetting of sorrows ". The hymn book of the Christian Church reveals its secret and lifts, wherever there are burdened hearts, the burden from those hearts. If that be so, we must seek diligently that every vernacular in India shall have such a store-house of comfort, such a guide to peace, as St. Bernard gave to Clairvaux in the Middle Ages, and Charles Wesley to England in the eighteenth century, and Narayan Vaman Tilak to the Marathi-speaking people only yesterday.

VI

But though there must be " golden hours " in the experience of every Christian Church, when she leaves earth behind and mounts to God by the stairway of song, yet the greater part of human life has to be spent upon the plains, among the common duties and demands that meet us every day. We need grace that shall enable us to " slog on ", to walk and not faint. For our prosaic lives we need the help of prose no less than of poetry ; we need books to instruct our reason and to develop our intelligence as well as to inspire and uplift our souls. " The great end of learning ", says the Chinese sage Mencius, " is to seek for the lost mind." If that is to be accomplished there must be books that will train the mind to think, and lead the people onward by the way that brings them home to truth and God. There is no book outside of the Bible that has done this for so many people of every race and colour as has the *Pilgrim's Progress*, yet not even this Christian classic is available in all the chief languages of India. And when one turns to the Bible itself and asks what aids to its deeper understanding are available for those who do not know English, the reply is pitifully disappointing. A few years ago a census was taken of books in the various vernaculars, by means of which the message of the Bible could be made the people's own possession. The replies received were monotonously similar— " inadequate ", " meagre ", " scarcely any ". And yet the provinces of which this report is made contain from 300,000 to a million Christians each. It is true that far too few of these Christians can read, and so it may be asked, What need is there to provide books for them ? In the Telugu area, for example, the estimate, made in 1920, of the number of Indian Christians who could read, was 50,000 out of a total of 500,000 ; and as a general average over all it is considered that one-sixth of the Christians may be literate.

To acquiesce in such a condition of things as that would be to despair of the coming of the Kingdom of God. A Church whose faith is not rooted in understanding, and which is not able to give a reason for the hope that is in her, is a Church built upon sand. When the rain descends and the floods come, such a Church will inevitably fall, as the Church of North Africa fell before the blast of the Moslem invasions. Someone recently speaking in Shanghai on this subject quoted a saying of General Booth to the effect that reading the Bible was like eating fish—the meat had to be separated from the bones. It is not surprising that an illiterate Bhil Christian should discover that the prophecies of Daniel were shortly to be fulfilled, and that the beginning would be in the Bhil hills, or that a group of the same simple people, toiling unaided through the books of Moses, should find the message of the Bible to be that they must cease to eat hare and pig.[1]

How could this be otherwise ? How could it be but that an illiterate Bhil, who has only now discovered Christ among the shadows of his ancient hills, should stumble and go astray in the new world which Christ has opened to him, if he has not someone to guide him ? " Blind one am I, and thou that art my staff, where hidest thou ? " It is a Maratha woman of the thirteenth century that utters that cry for guidance, and, uttering it, speaks for the whole of groping humanity. It amazes one how the instinct of the soul leads them so often straight to the essential things, but still the " lost mind " needs to be led back into the way of truth, and it must have books for its instruction. There is little profit in learning to read if there are not books to read. Education and that which education feeds upon must advance together in this land. The Punjab is one of the provinces in which at the present time progress in education is most marked. Between 1921 and 1926 the percentage of boys under instruction to the total population increased from 4·77 to 9·32. We may safely conjecture that if that is the case of the general population, the increase has not been less among the Christians. There undoubtedly is throughout the whole country a quickening of interest in the education of the rural population,

[1] Rev. J. W. Runciman in United Free Church *Record* for March 1928.

and a desire to remove from India the stigma of its
ignorance and backwardness. But what will this change
profit India if they acquire literacy and have nothing
upon which to feed their awakened minds ? We may
be sure that, in response to the demand, some sort of
supply will be forthcoming, but will it be of a kind to
elevate or to degrade ? Fiction of a kind is multiplying
in every vernacular, but it is often a fiction of the least
desirable type. Literacy will be a curse to India instead
of a blessing if those who desire to feed their awakened
minds must feed them upon garbage. We must give
them what is better than that, and something at the
same time that will interest them and draw them on
with a further desire to explore the unknown land of
knowledge. Mr. Jenkins, a Deputy Commissioner in
the Punjab, writes of the books available in village
libraries for the encouragement of the increasing number
of readers in that province : " The literature that I have
myself seen (Red Cross tracts, etc.) is very well in its
way, but would hardly tempt one to literacy even on
a desert island ".[1] We have no right to leave the
Christian people of India to whom we have opened the
gates of knowledge, either to poison their souls with what
is evil and degrading or to starve their souls on husks.
All over the land we may say, " the hungry sheep look
up and are not fed ".

VII

In the case of those people who can read English, it
may be suggested that there is less need of the preparation of special literature for them in that language.
This would, however, be a hasty conclusion. It is true
that India is in a peculiarly fortunate position, in that,
to an extent that is not the case in China or Japan, her

[1] *Report on the Progress of Education in the Punjab*, 1926–27, p. 4.

educated people are acquainted with English, and can find in that language whatever kind of book they may require. There are many in India who are not Christians, and to whom the vernacular translations of the Bible are wholly unattractive in their style, but who know familiarly the New Testament or the Psalms. The whole range of Christian literature is at their disposal as well, whether they desire to be helped nearer to the Unknown God or to find guidance on His ways with men. There are many who carry with them for their soul's strengthening the *Imitation*, and who are specially attracted by Christian books of devotion, such as Brother Lawrence's *Practice of the Presence of God*, and Madam Guyon's *Method of Prayer*. Each book on the Christian life or on Christian doctrine that stirs interest in the West finds many readers in India. Within the last few months the writer has talked with Indians who had recently read Otto's *Das Heilige* (in German), *By an Unknown Disciple*, Papini's *Story of Christ*, and Middleton Murry's *Life of Jesus*. The fact that this is so is a feature of the situation in India that is in many ways full of encouragement. Those who are able to buy such books, and who can separate the precious from the vile in the tidal wave of printed matter that beats continually upon the shores of India, are indeed fortunate. But, on the other hand, there are many who cannot afford to purchase books so costly, and there are many who do not buy what we would wish them to buy. There is no high tariff to keep the poisonous literature of the West from finding its way into India to pollute and to destroy.

A recent writer on India has described how in the bookstalls of Calcutta young Indian students " brood over files of fly-blown Russian pamphlets ".[1] She was describing what only existed in her anti-Bolshevist

---

[1] Miss Mayo's *Mother India*, p. 13.

imagination. They are much more likely to be seen brooding over the cheap and unwholesome fiction that is pouring in a continuous flood upon this country. But the one way to guard any individual or any people from bad books is to create in them an appetite for good books. We can give them a cheap literature that is not also nasty. There is a great opportunity for the creation in the various vernaculars of a wholesome literature that boys and girls can love and rejoice in. A suggestion has just come to the writer from America, that the children of America might provide a whole series of books for the children of India from among the books that give them so much pleasure There could be no more appropriate or more charming method of creating ties of friendship between the youth of the East and of the West. A common partnership in books that are a precious possession will help more than any other kind of partnership to create understanding and sympathy. Books that make us smile together and weep together, and, still more, that make us pray together, build bridges between the races that shall endure. Such books reveal to us those elements in us that are universal.

There are other reasons why we need books in English for India, as well as books in the vernaculars. Though all the publishing houses of Britain and America are ready to supply their wares—for a price— to India, India needs English books that shall be specially written to meet her needs and to fit her conditions. For example, there has arisen of recent years quite a considerable literature, by means of which foreign missionaries and Indian Christian scholars seek to interpret Indian thought and Indian religion to the educated Indian people, and, at the same time, to relate these religions, in their highest aspects, to the Christian faith. This is an important service, valuable alike in bringing the Christian into sympathy with non-Christian

thought and aspiration, and in presenting Christianity
to India in terms that India is able to understand.
There should arise in India groups of Indian Christians
who by careful and sympathetic study of their own
Christian faith in the light of their Indian heritage shall
be able to plant the universal message of Christ deep
in the deep soil of the Indian soul.   It is a dream that
one sometimes dreams in India, that as this land has
already proved the mother or the foster-mother of so
many faiths, so in days to come she may prove to be
not as the theosophist would have it, the headquarters
of the Ancient Wisdom of the past, but the headquarters
of the Wisdom that cometh from above, the interpreter
and mediator through which the Lord Jesus Christ
shall be revealed and recognized as the World's Desire.

VIII

It is fully agreed to-day by all who observe the
changing attitudes and aspects of the minds of men,
that henceforth the main task of conveying the message
of Christ to such lands as India and China and Japan
must be entrusted to those who can do so in the deepest
sense, in the very speech and accent of these peoples,
with the tones and inflection, as it were, of their own
tradition.   New barriers are being set up, more intangible, more difficult to get past than those which
have faced us in the past.   Some of the old roads of
approach are closing or are being hedged about with
conditions, whose aim is to exclude the foreign foe, the
exploiter, the wolf in sheep's clothing, who has evil
designs upon the country's national inheritance.   We
must willingly submit to these restrictions and respect
this sensitiveness.   We have too often given grounds
for suspicion.   We come to the people of India not
as invaders and destroyers, but as messengers of a truth

which is already theirs, which their fathers dreamt of centuries ago and which they desire to-day.

In these circumstances the value of literature as a channel by which this universal message may find its way unimpeded and unresented into the Indian heart becomes obvious. There is no compulsion upon any-one to buy or read a book. " Truth embodied in a tale " enters in at lowly doors and can be welcomed or shut out as men please.   It exercises no compulsion ; it uses no deception ; it need arouse no prejudice.   And at a time when the Church's own witness is recognized as the most convincing testimony, that testimony can be conveyed only less convincingly in printed books than in lives lived before our eyes.   The life lives on and still speaks when we read its record. Books like St. Augustine's *Confessions* and John Bunyan's *Grace Abounding* are immortal witnesses that will speak to the hearts of men as long as men's hearts desire God.   And so the story of Pandita Ramabai and her little autobiographic fragment, *A Testimony*, are of the utmost preciousness in the history of Christianity in India.   Such a witness to the eternal truth of the Christian message and to its vitalizing power remains indelible to all time, carved in a medium more lasting than brass.   Books that have the life of the Spirit in them are rivers that flow on through the centuries, and " everything liveth whithersoever the river cometh ".

As has already been said, India is a land where books from the most ancient days have had a great place and where they can be sure still of an eager welcome. A missionary lady who lived and worked for many years among the village people of the Telugu country in South India describes a society of women that gathered to hear their own ancient *Rāmāyan* read to them, but they listened listlessly.   The savour had gone from the sacred epic and it found no echo in their hearts. In another *Samaj*[1] of a similar kind, one of themselves, a Hindu, gave them, the same lady tells us, a lecture on the life and death of Jesus. In the room where they sat and listened hungrily, " a little lamp burned before a gaudy print representing Saraswati ", the goddess of knowledge, that knowledge for which their hungry souls were pining. " It made me realize ", adds their Christian friend, as she watched them with a deep sympathy, " how they hunger for the same mental and spiritual food for which I turn to many authors. The Christian literature of centuries is ready to my hand to help me on ; but what is ready to theirs? "[2] Surely that little lamp burning dimly before Saraswati makes a silent appeal to us. The smoking flax He shall not quench.

[1] Society.
[2] Miss Christlieb's *An Uphill Road in India*, p. 248.

CHAPTER VIII

THE MINISTRY OF HEALING

By R. H. GOHEEN

THIS arm or department of missions deals with the restoration of physical ills and defects. To it is entrusted the care of the sick and the prevention of disease.

So universal an experience is illness that the adequate provision for its treatment is an enormous task. Even more important, modern thinking convinces us, is the prevention of disease. This conception, however, by reason of its modernity has not yet borne full fruit even in its home in the West. India is slowly awakening to this idea. It will be the great adventure of the future; large enough to demand the activities, the organizations, the expenditures of a world war. Would that the day had come when men would be satisfied to expend their activities in so splendid an enterprise : in Conservation, not Destruction ! When will this idea grasp and rule the human mind and the civic will ?

How rare the individual who has required the assistance of no doctor, no nurse, no sympathetic and capable friend, that he might learn to breathe upon entering into the world. Even so, who has escaped all the contagious diseases of childhood ? Who later has married and raised a family without requiring any medical aid ? And finally, who has entered upon the pathway to death without seeking or longing for a steadying hand ?

Our civilization to-day is annihilating distance, drawing individuals, communities and nations together. What is good can and will be shared more commonly, and definite benefits will accrue.   What is bad must also be shared.   Diseases of the human race, as well as of cattle and cotton, will benefit by improved communications.   These are commonplace facts indeed.

Populations are increasing to such an extent that in course of time the world may be called upon to support twice as many people as it does to-day. Mother India is adding annually to the number of her children.   Prevalent "tropical" diseases have done much to prevent these increases—plague, cholera, malaria, dysentery, smallpox, leprosy, hydrophobia and kala azar.   When other diseases more common to the world as a whole are mentioned — tuberculosis, cancer, influenza, pneumonia, heart diseases, venereal diseases, etc.—it is found that in these also poor India is not behind in her quotas.   Maternal and infant mortalities when compared with the West are appalling.

The sanitation of the 800,000 villages of the motherland, as well as of her towns and cities, is a problem of staggering proportions.   It is found difficult to persuade qualified doctors to reside and to practise in the villages.   It will be even more difficult to render, through improved sanitation, their presence and aid less imperative.

Personal hygiene must be inculcated that will enable the people of the land to live free from intestinal parasites and other ills, and to improve food, clothing and housing.   The doctor cannot shift all of the responsibility for this inculcation upon the teacher   He must at least see that the teacher is taught.

Intermarriage among small communities, due to caste, creed and custom, results too often in weakness of body and mind.   Mendel's law cannot be disregarded.

The sins of the fathers are visited upon the children unto the third and fourth generation—as revealed long before Mendel's day. Insanity and mental deficiencies of all grades account for much suffering and economic loss here as elsewhere in the world.

Responsibilities enough, these, even if some may have been overlooked or insufficiently stressed. Who is to assume them all ? The State has the most important part to play—the State, inspired, guided and aided by its enlightened citizens, and, in its present incapacity, by all those who are willing and able to help, above all by the Christian Church. The weapons of attack upon these great problems must be many and varied.

I. Hospitals for the care of the seriously ill ; dispensaries for those troubled by minor ailments ; leprosaria ; sanatoria ; sanitaria ; insane asylums ; institutions for the blind and for deaf mutes ; isolation plague hospitals in endemic areas or where an epidemic rages ; infant and maternal welfare centres—these are the institutions required to care for the sick. Medical colleges of higher and lower grades ; training schools for dispensers, for nurses, for midwives—these are the institutions required to supply the workers needed. Laboratories for the preparation of vaccines and specific sera ; pharmaceutical stores ; manufactories for instruments and hospital stores —these are the institutions required to supply the agencies for treatment.

To focus briefly on but one feature—dispensaries. In America, one reads, 8 million patients annually are being treated free in dispensaries. As the population is about 115 millions, this means one out of every $14\frac{3}{8}$ people, or roughly 7 per cent. Granting that this percentage may represent the poor in America who are found to deserve free treatment, what would be the similar requirements for India ? The answer can only be surmised. The most conservative economist would

not say less than 15 per cent.[1] The analogous number
for free treatment would then be over 47 million persons
per annum. But disease is more prevalent, more destructive—by reason of that large group of tropical
scourges mentioned above—east of Suez than west.

II. Prevention of disease requires specially trained
health officers, and the means at their command to
enforce their ideas, to wit, a large staff of visiting
nurses ; an army of public vaccinators ; employees
who will catch rats, clean drains, fumigate houses, kill
snakes, shoot tigers, destroy mosquitoes, sand-flies and
flies, disinfect wells, tanks and streams, dispose of night
soil and garbage—where is one to stop for breath ?
Sanitary engineers and their staffs must drain hundreds
of square miles of swamps ; provide pure, abundant
water supplies, and arrange for the sewage disposal of

[1] The Rev. James Kellock of Wilson College, Bombay, very kindly
made a study of this question for the writer. From *The Wealth of
India*, by Joshi and Wadia, it is seen that the average annual income
per head for British India has risen since the war to about Rs.70 or
Rs.75 (say Rs.6 a month). In Prof. Stanley Jevons' Memorandum
for the Indian Currency Commission of 1919, in which he worked out
the cost of the diet for an average family of a man, his wife and two
children, it appears that if the labourer spent his whole wages on food
he would only be able to purchase for himself and his family 81 per cent
of the diet prescribed for prisoners in the jails. He would have nothing
to spend on clothing, house rent, and other necessities required by
even the poorest.

It is found that families residing in cities have a much larger income
than the foregoing, ranging—according to *India in 1923–1924*—from
Rs.52 : 4 : 6 a month, for the average working-class family in Bombay,
to Rs.115 a month, as determined by Mr. Kellock's investigation of
the incomes of fifty Christian families in Bombay.

Dr. Mann in *Land and Labour in a Deccan Village, Study No. 2*,
p. 158, says, " An average year seems to leave the village under-fed,
more in debt than ever, and apparently less capable than ever of obtaining
with the present population and the present methods of cultivation, a
real economic independence ".

By comparison, Dr. J. A. Ferrell, Director for the U.S. International
Health Board of the Rockefeller Foundation, who writes in the *Jour.
Amer. Med. Assoc.* for July 9, 1927, may be cited as to the *per capita*
yearly income for America. In the States of New York and California
this exceeds Rs.3300 ($1200), while even in the poorer states of the
South it is as much as Rs.725 (or ten times that of British India).

villages and towns as well as of cities ; scrutinize and supervise schools, temples, theatres and other public buildings. Facilities for instructing the public through its current vernacular literature, through primary and secondary text books, through specially prepared charts and posters, through lantern lectures and cinemas, must not be neglected. A properly constituted department of health will investigate, furthermore, the food values of grains and vegetables ; will prevent the adulteration of milk and other foods ; will regulate the preparation and use of poisonous drugs ; will eliminate the use of the flesh of diseased animals ; will determine the qualifications for the practice of medicine, nursing and dispensing ; will prevent the sale of patent medicines of an unknown or a harmful nature ; will control or seek to abolish brothels ; will take measures to check epidemics and to eradicate the foci of the serious endemic diseases ; will control immigration ; will regulate the publication of articles and advertisements that might mislead the public concerning the care of the health or the cure of disease ; will provide research laboratories for the study of disease.

Lest the list seem too formidable for our encouragement, let us remember that not a few of these activities have already been undertaken by one Governmental Department or another, by the Red Cross, by mission or other organizations. But, as we shall see later, missions in the past have not stood high in the list. The reasons will appear.

The foregoing sections may serve as a preface. They indicate the need for and scope of medical work. Why should missions concern themselves with this need and what would they expect to accomplish in this realm ?

The Christian Medical Association of India has issued a statement which is in part an answer to these questions, and this may be quoted as embodying the

considered opinion of a large body of Christian doctors
in India :

It is our conviction that the ministry of healing is an
essential part of the work of the Christian Church whose
mission it is to represent God as revealed in Jesus Christ.
We observe that Christ's own testimony concerning His
mission was that He came to do the will of the One who
sent Him and to accomplish His work. We must believe
then that the ministry of healing the body is an expression of
the attitude and mind of God toward man and has its source
in the compassion and love of God. It is our conviction that
the Christian should concern himself with the care of the
sick, apart from whether others are carrying on this work or
not. From this conviction it becomes our duty to develop
Christian medical work as part of the essential work of the
Church in India, and to consider how this may best be done.
The recognition of the ministry of healing, as an essential
part of the work of God through the Church, involves the
thought that the service thus rendered is a natural and vital
expression of the spirit of Christ. This can be engaged in
by men and women imbued with the spirit of Christ, Who
served men for love of them and Who, as evidence of His
Messiahship, drew attention to the work He was doing :
" The blind receive their sight, the lame walk, the lepers
are cleansed, the deaf hear, the dead are raised up and the
poor have the Gospel preached unto them ".

The statement requires re-reading more than once
before its profound significance, its several implications
can be grasped. Thoroughly scriptural in its major
premiss and unquestionable, it is in the minor premiss
that one is made to pause. Here is a new thought.
To many it comes as a new light. New duties are
assigned to every Christian in India, that, in the West,
if they have been understood, have hardly been stressed
widely or largely practised. Now, it is true that in
America, for example, many churches nominally, at
least, conduct hospitals. Most of the large cities have
their Presbyterian hospitals. St. Luke, St. Mary, St.

K

Thomas and other saints have their names attached to the hospitals of Methodist and Catholic and other churches. Catholic nursing sisters are rendering highly appreciated service in a large majority of the city and private hospitals. It is true that many of the public or city hospitals are supported by the donations of charitable people, Christian philanthropists providing the largest quota. But it is equally true that the average Church member has escaped from the feeling of much definite and personal responsibility. He or she may, and often does, visit the sick in the immediate neighbourhood. Kindly human nature deserves the major credit for that. The local church may observe " Hospital Sunday " with a special collection annually, but beyond that very little official thought is given to every individual's privilege and duty to help to carry on this phase of our Lord's ministry as an outstanding phase.

Building on newer foundations in India, with the incentive of relatively greater medical needs, India's Church must be shown her spiritual responsibility and encouraged to accept the unique opportunity that this conception discloses. Every Christian cannot, need not, be a doctor or a nurse. Every Christian can, in small ways and large, render assistance in the battle against disease, in the adequate care of the afflicted.

The Christian Medical Association of India that has brought forward this revelation may now be introduced. It is the child—that has outgrown its parent—of the old Medical Missionary Association. The latter organization was formed at the general Missionary Congress in Madras in 1900 as a union of medical missionaries. The Association's next General Conference met in Bombay in 1908, but until 1925 only one other general conference was held. Divisional or sectional branches, to correspond roughly with the Provinces of India, had been established, and some of these had held annual meetings. A quarterly publication, *Medical Missions in India*, had been the official organ of the Association almost since its founding.

The word Devolution, a word often in the mouths of Christian educationalists since the World War, finally penetrated the tympanum of the average, busy medical missionary. Did devolution concern him? At the General Conference in Calcutta in 1925, it was found that it did, and so the new and larger Association was formed. According to its constitution not only medical missionaries may become members but—" The membership of the Association shall be open to all Christian medical men and women who hold a recognized, registrable qualification or its equivalent, and who are in full sympathy with the main object, namely, the establishment of the Kingdom of Christ in India ". This, as is seen, admits private practitioners, Government officers, Indians and Westerners alike. With this organization the Association falls into line with the principles of the National Christian Council, and has been accepted by the latter as its medical department.

The new Association at once appointed a Committee on Survey, Efficiency and Co-operation. This Committee of five members met in time with the secretaries of the National Christian Council. Important questions had to be faced. One of the most fundamental needs felt was for a definition of policy. Miss B. C. Oliver, M.B., Ch.B., Chairman of the Committee, had taken pains to gather statements of policy from various Mission Boards. The one [1] most suggestive and clear-cut was found to read as follows :

Medical work is not merely a key to open the door into non-Christian communities, but an integral part of the missionary enterprise.

[1] That of the Board of Foreign Missions of the Presbyterian Church in the U.S.A.

(*a*) Generically, the aim of medical missions is an integral part of the aim common to all forms of missionary work, that is, to lead people to Christ and to organize them into churches and train them to self-propagation, self-support and self-government.

(*b*) Specifically, the aim is : (1) The relief of suffering ; (2) Training a national Christian medical profession; (3) Removal of superstition regarding causes of disease ; (4) Preventive medicine—public health ; (5) To do these things in the name and spirit of Christ so as to strengthen the evangelistic work.

While everything possible should be done to alleviate suffering and save life, at the same time the physician and nurse should aim to multiply their powers through the training of doctors and nurses, thereby establishing in the country an indigenous Christian medical profession. The accomplishment of this purpose requires medical schools and hospitals, training schools for nurses, the creation of medical literature, and facilities for training in medical research and in the promotion of public health.

The duty of medical missionaries is not limited to the treatment of diseases that have developed. They are the health and sanitation officers of their respective stations with responsibilities for the prevention of disease.

The medical care of the missionaries and the institutions under their control is one of their chief responsibilities, and this service properly rendered can be utilized to increase greatly the efficiency and prolong the service of the entire missionary body.

Social service by the medical staff should also be advantageously used for the removal of ignorance, poverty and vice, and undoubtedly is one of the most effective methods of evangelization.

Both physician and nurse ought continually to manifest fervent loyalty to the Lord Jesus Christ in order that His spirit may permeate the entire work and that the seed sown in loving service may yield a rich harvest of souls.

To summarize the aims of medical missions :

1. Every Christian in India is to be shown his privilege and duty to further the work which Christ

Himself did, to care for the sick under the compelling love and compassion of God.

2. This enormous task—even if it could be or was being overtaken by appropriate Government departments, private efforts or by other charitable organizations—does not rid Christian missions of their responsibility and their privilege to aid in the care of India's afflicted. This is a definite challenge.

3. Institutions, such as hospitals, dispensaries, asylums, sanatoria, baby-folds, blind schools, *et alia*, must be provided and maintained wherever most needed. Private practitioners must be encouraged and aided in their work. The prevention of disease must be studied and developed in every possible way.

4. Helpful co-operation is to be achieved with similar Governmental agencies, with private or organized charities, infusing into them all a lofty and loving altruism. Co-operation with the educational, evangelistic and social-service branches of missions must be developed to the greatest usefulness.

Let us now look at the historical origins of medical missions. Among the older missions in their earlier days, there was frequently recognized the crying need for medical aid, especially in out-lying towns and in isolated districts. The true Christian doctor's heart seldom fails to respond to a call for help anywhere. Thus it was that Dr. John Thomas, who came to India first as a ship's surgeon in 1783, later joined the English Baptist Missionary Society and returned as Carey's colleague in 1793. He itinerated and translated part of the New Testament into Bengali. In 1819 Dr. John Scudder entered the meagre lists of missionaries, working first in Ceylon and later settling in the Madras Presidency to establish the Arcot Mission that is still partly manned by his descendants. In 1838 the now far-famed medical work at Neyyoor in South Travancore was started as a dispensary by Mr. M. A. Ramsay, a layman of the London Missionary Society. Neyyoor is hardly more than a hamlet, very near to the tip of India and not easy of access. The Rev. C. Leitch, M.R.C.S.,Ed., appointed in 1852, was the first medical missionary. At the opposite end of the land, Dr. Elmslie began work for the C.M.S. in Kashmir, then accessible by a trail and not by the road so easily traversed by motor-cars to-day. The Moravians pushed on 240 miles further to Leh in Ladakh, still only accessible by a trail, and their chief institution has been a hospital   A departure is to be noted in that not missionary societies but military officers started the Afghan Mission in Peshawar in 1853, captained by Sir Herbert Edwardes The C.M.S. Hospital there now uses as its staff chapel the upper room of an old Moghul *burj* or tower, that carries the scars of many sieges. More recently, since 1889, have come into being the large medical centres of the interior—Miraj, Ludhiana and Vellore, all now conducting flourishing medical schools. The enormous clinic at Ranaghat in Bengal was started by a retired collector of the Indian Civil Service. It was later taken over by the Church Missionary Society, and solid buildings are gradually replacing the original huts. In Nagpur, Guntur, Madras, Poona and elsewhere, women of vision, energy and ability have built up substantial hospitals for their respective missionary societies. In fact, the hospitals conducted by women for women and children outnumber those conducted by men by nearly three to one. There are also a few con-ducted by women as general hospitals—for men, women and children. It was a woman, Dr. Hart, who started the widely-known Tuberculosis Sanatorium at Arogya-varam, now a union institution. This sanatorium is the largest and best in India. In only one or two places, such as at the C.M.S. hospital at Bannu,

N.W.F., are there both men and women medical missionaries on the same hospital staff. (In this connection it is to be understood that missionary nurses are not counted as medical missionaries.)

Work for lepers was an early activity of missions in which laymen found that they could take part. To Wellesley C. Bailey belongs the honour of having started in 1874 the Mission to Lepers. The first institutions were asylums only. It has been a feature of this century largely that they are gradually being transformed into hospitals. The term leprosarium is being used to denote the change. It took a long time for the Empire to awaken to the importance of the leprosy problem. Even so, its interest has thus far borne but scanty fruit. Missions are still the most important agency in this field in India.

Something may be said regarding the methods of work followed in medical missions.

(a) A *Dispensary* is usually the starting-point in the development of a medical mission. Every mission hospital conducts at least one dispensary for the treatment of " out-patients ". It may have several, or many, as in the case of the Medical Mission in South Travancore, with its hospital at Neyyoor and its seventeen branch dispensaries. In the dispensary there may be accommodation for a few " in-patients ", and if the number of beds provided exceeds ten, the designation " hospital " is applied. Regular hours are allotted for the examination and treatment of patients. There may be a charge made to all who apply, but usually this is sufficient to cover only a fraction of the cost of the medicines supplied. This is true of the majority of mission dispensaries. Such a dispensary, then, may be classed as " charitable " but not " free ". However, there are many mission dispensaries that give entirely free treatment. In a few others only voluntary offerings are accepted. In a few others self-support is attained from the charges made. No general rule for charges for all of India would be satisfactory. The ability of the clientele to pay is the best criterion for a given place, but it is certain that large numbers in every locality deserve free treatment (perhaps 15 per cent of the total population, as suggested before). In the list of the Christian Medical Association there are 192 mission dispensaries, but there are probably some 50 others not listed. A recent inquiry has elicited replies from 113, of which 21 were closed. These 92 dispensaries treated in one year 435,829 new and 588,625 returning patients, 635,652, or about 60 per cent, having been given free treatment.

Medicines are usually given for one or two days at a time ; to those coming from a distance, for four, six or eight days.

In dispensaries good opportunities are afforded for presenting the Gospel message. Here are gathered people of all ages and many strata. They have leisure for the time being to listen. They have come voluntarily. Many will buy Scripture portions or accept tracts. In some dispensaries the card bearing the patient's name and serial number contains also a Bible verse or message. He keeps this card for future presentation. In a few dispensaries the patient is expected to buy a Gospel, and his serial number is written on the fly-leaf. Thousands of Gospels are thus distributed.

Leaflets on the nature of the disease from which he suffers, with appropriate instructions, are given to patients in a few mission dispensaries. The Jumna Mission dispensaries in Allahabad have set a good example in this line. More general use could be made of this valuable method. In connection with the dispensaries just named, this opportunity is taken to mention the co-operation which Dr. Forman has obtained

from charitably-minded non-Christian Indian doctors.
A dentist, two gentleman doctors and a lady doctor
thus give their services free in the daily clinics held in
one of these dispensaries.

The " Roadside Dispensary " is one that needs explanation. It was first at Vellore, one understands, that
a weekly run out along a road to a distance of some
eighteen miles was made in a motor-car. This was
started and has been kept up for twelve years or more
by Dr. Ida Scudder. An assistant and students go
along. Stops are made under trees near villages every
few miles, where patients will gather for treatment.
Rain or shine this trip is made, and, lately, at the terminal
town a dispensary building has been instituted, where
a medical assistant is stationed, and where she conducts
a daily dispensary. In a single trip occupying a full
day from 75 to 150 patients may be seen and treated.
Even lepers congregate under the trees, and are given
their injections. While returning, the car is available for
patients who need and will accept hospital treatment.

(b) *Hospitals* are required for the more seriously ill.
There are many diseases that will not yield promptly
or at all to simple remedies. Prolonged efficient nursing
may be required, as in typhoid fever, or surgery may
be necessary, as in the case of most tumours. Mid-
wifery also is best undertaken in hospitals, even when
in the homes sanitation and hygiene are above reproach.
In fact, in all but the simpler ailments, where *vis medi-
catrix naturae* can be trusted, treatment in a hospital
is the safest course.

To be efficient a hospital requires a certain standard
modicum of buildings, equipment and staffing. It
must be, above all other buildings, sanitary throughout. An operating theatre with marble floors and tiled
walls cannot carry all the responsibility ; the wards,
rooms, lavatories and even verandahs must be capable of

being kept clean, free from germs as well as dust. This indicates substantial buildings with washable floors and, preferably, non-absorptive walls. Ventilation and lighting are important. Electric lighting and piped water are rightly regarded in these days as essentials. A convenient arrangement of all the component rooms, rendering them easy of access, is most desirable to facilitate nursing. The provisions for serving food must be carefully arranged for. In most mission hospitals the relatives of patients, for the most part, provide the food. They may prepare it in the numerous hospital kitchens, which is preferable, or bring it from their own homes or other domiciles in the town. The hospital, however, must usually have at least one cook—a high-caste Hindu will be the best solution—to serve the indigent or those patients who are unattended by relatives. Many an Indian patient is found to need sufficient and proper food quite as much as, or more than, medicines. The dieting of patients is a very important department.

Along with other important equipment, the furniture and instruments for all kinds of surgery, an X-ray outfit and good laboratory facilities are essentials. Diagnosis can only be made properly by the last two means in many cases. Life can only be saved or prolonged by the first in not a few conditions.

The number of beds in India's mission hospitals varies from ten to two hundred. Recently the Christian Medical Association appointed a committee to draw up a list of the essentials for a fifty-bed hospital. This unit was adopted, as it has been found desirable, by experience, to have at least two full-time doctors on the staff. A qualified medical assistant is also needed. There should be two compounders and about ten nurses, and a missionary nurse as superintendent. It has been found best to employ male nurses in men's hospitals in India. These

are usually trained in compounding also, and so receive
the title of " nurse-compounder ", though " ward-
master " and " brother " are sometimes used.

The training of nurses is a function of many of the
larger hospitals. Mission boarding-schools supply most
of the candidates, and they should have had at least
four years of education in English. Hospital records
are invariably kept in English. The nurse must be able
to read and understand them, and to enter her own
notes. In some hospitals she is permitted to enter her
notes in the vernacular. After finishing a probationary
period of from three to six months, a three years' course
of study is taken. After graduation the nurse may
remain on the staff of her hospital, but many are inclined
to seek more remunerative service in the large city
hospitals. They are in great demand there. Life as a
nurse in a large city hospital, or as a private nurse in
a city, is full of pitfalls, and there are few that can
escape grave temptation. This is a matter that gives
grave concern in Calcutta. In Bombay there are one
or two hospitals where a nurse can serve under matrons
who seem to succeed in shielding them from harm.
Fortunately a large number of nurses marry soon after
finishing training, and become mothers whose children
have certain distinct advantages.

The financing of hospitals is a problem that draws
forth much discussion. Much money is involved. For
the fifty-bed hospital that will treat about 1000 in-patients
a year, and perhaps 7000 out-patients, an annual budget
of no less than Rs. 20,000 is desirable. This excludes
missionaries' salaries. Each in-patient will cost about
Rs. 15 and each out-patient about 12 annas. The
Rs. 20,000 will not cover the cost of replacing all expensive apparatus nor of extensive repairs. It is really
too modest a figure, but most mission hospitals in India
manage, somehow, on less. This at once shows that

they are not equipped and staffed up to the desirable
standards. Towards meeting the annual budget local
receipts from fees and gifts will yield from one-fifth
to the entire amount. There are now about a dozen
" self - supporting " mission hospitals in India (missionary salaries again excluded). The majority meet
one-half or more of their expenses from local receipts.
" Is self-support desirable ? " This question has been
asked in No. 26 of the current Mission Hospital Survey
questionnaire with the purpose of determining whether
the stress put upon the necessary payment of fees is in
danger of overshadowing the Gospel message. Without going into the discussion here, it may suffice to say
that there are not a few medical missionaries who feel
that there is a real danger here : that, since " charitable"
hospitals are never self-supporting in the West, they
cannot be made so in India without jeopardizing an
important part of their purpose. Many are convinced
that an endowment, preferably, or an annual appro-
priation that will meet at least one-third of the budget is
very desirable. In some areas it should meet not less
than two-thirds. Government grants-in-aid are enjoyed
by very few mission hospitals. The number of such
grants and the amounts given are tending to diminish
throughout India.

There are now 212 mission hospitals in India,
distributed as follows :

Aden	1	Gwalior	2
Assam	9	Hyderabad	11
Baluchistan	1	Kashmir	3
Baroda	1	Madras	59
Bengal	10	Mysore	7
Bihar and Orissa	13	N.W.F. Provinces	4
Bombay Area	21	Punjab	27
C.I.	5	Rajputana	8
C.P. and Berar	12	U.P.	17
Delhi	1		

The Gospel message in a Christian hospital falls on
hearts that are softened by suffering. Such hearts are
often longing for a comforting assurance. The attending relatives and friends are in a state of sympathetic
anxiety. As improvement in a patient's condition becomes manifest there is added a sense of gratitude, felt
among all concerned. No more fitting soil for God's
message can be found. There still remain some days
before the journey homeward can be undertaken. The
average stay in hospital is about a fortnight. During
these days much can be learned. Many false conceptions and prejudices at least will be dispelled. The
doctors and nurses in most hospitals take a definite part
in giving the message. They are usually assisted by the
part-time service of one or more evangelists and Bible-
women. Evangelistic workers in the districts invariably
find that people who have been to a hospital give them a
cordial reception and listen attentively to their message.

(c) *Sanatoria.*—The proper treatment of pulmonary
tuberculosis is a specialty and demands for itself
special institutions. These are best situated in a
favourable climate and at a moderate altitude of 2500
to 5000 feet. Large open sites among hilly or rolling
country are desirable. The advantages of isolation are
thus also obtained, for this form of tuberculosis is
contagious. The disease is spreading rapidly and now
ranks as one of the most common causes of death in
India.

Missions have been called upon to enter this field
where fearless, self-sacrificing, attentive service is needed.
It is a field that has been neglected too much by other
public and private agencies. There now exist eight
mission sanatoria : three in the Bombay Presidency ;
two in Rajputana ; one each in the Central Provinces,
United Provinces and Madras Presidency. All of these
except one are comparatively small and inadequate.

The one at Arogyavaram, Madras Presidency, is, however, as has been said, the largest and best sanatorium in India. It has 150 beds. Eleven missions co-operate in its maintenance, and the Madras Government gives a goodly grant-in-aid. For the other Provinces of India a similar Union Mission Sanatorium is indicated. The missions of Bombay and of the Punjab are taking steps to develop such sanatoria, and they deserve every encouragement. Other Provinces should do likewise.

The smaller institutions which exist in various parts of the country are also needed. Particular interest attaches to one not yet mentioned. It is conducted by the Christian Church at Rajahmundry, independent of mission initiative. This Church has secured a pleasant site about two miles out from the city, on a low hill-top. Here several substantial foundations for wards were laid, the superstructure being, for lack of funds, of thatch. About a dozen patients can be cared for. A qualified Christian doctor is in charge, whose salary of Rs. 150 a month is met, with other current expenses, by the Church. This is a most praiseworthy enterprise.

(d) *The Care of Lepers.*—Of the 66 leper asylums in India conducted by missions, 37 belong to the Mission to Lepers and all but six of the others are aided by it. This mission thus assumes the entire care of 5228 lepers, and shares in the care of 1693 more. It also conducts about twenty homes for untainted children, and aids in the support of four other such homes in India. For these institutions and for twenty-two others in the Far East this mission expended last year £8286.

Leprosy is a chronic disease in which, often for long periods at first, there are but few symptoms. The onset is usually insidious and the first patch may be discovered accidentally. Later on, when the skin is affected by many bacilli, nodules are present; and such cases are decidedly contagious.   Gradually a resistance may be developed ; the bacilli are overcome but not before they have injured the nerves of the face, arms or legs. These affected nerves in turn, failing to function properly, allow contracting deformities to develop.   The areas supplied by injured nerves are poorly nourished ; bone absorption occurs ; and secondary infections easily occur.   Insensitive areas are also injured by burning, etc., and the resulting ulcers heal very slowly.   It is only in the very early stages that there is much hope of arresting the disease before much damage is done. Even this may take months to accomplish.   Those in the later stages, with infectious nodules, or, lastly, with trophic ulcers, may, for all practical purposes, be considered patients for life.

In properly conducted leprosaria the patients are grouped and housed according to the stage of their disease, and appropriate treatment is given.   This requires a trained medical staff and the proper facilities for their use.   Many patients are able to work at their trades in the institution, or can be taught simple farming that will interest them and return an income to the institution.

The finances of such institutions show a *per capita* cost of from Rs. 7 to Rs. 17 a month.   It is probable that where the latter figure obtains better results will be found.   Since there are at least 300,000 lepers in India (some authorities make the number larger) their care calls for a large philanthropy and it is creditable that missions have heard and are heeding this call.   But much more needs to be done.

(*e*) *Medical Schools*.—The three Mission Medical Schools include two for women, one each at Ludhiana and Vellore, and one for men at Miraj.   Formerly, two other small schools for men existed at Neyyoor and Jammalamadugu respectively, both stations of the

London Missionary Society. But both of these schools, after each training about fifty men, were closed more than a decade ago. The Edinburgh Medical Missionary Society also established at about the same time a Medical Training Institute for men at Agra, using a Christian Hostel for the purpose in connection with the Government Medical School. This Society still gives scholarships to Christian men from North India for medical training.

The importance of providing a body of Christian men and women to staff the large number of existing mission hospitals and dispensaries—about 400 institutions in all—not to speak of the unsupplied villages of India, is obvious. No greater need exists. No other department of medical service is of larger importance.

In this domain of medical education, co-operation between missions is working successfully at Vellore, and active steps are being taken to make the Miraj School a union one. This is most desirable, since otherwise it is difficult to provide the necessary staff, buildings, and equipment. Government requirements for the registration of medical practitioners call for high standards in these particulars that are not easily met by a single mission or by a small group of missions. Every mission in India that undertakes medical work for men should take this problem seriously to heart. At Ludhiana the school for women is interdenominational, but it is not a union school. It has been affiliated with the Lahore Medical School, and has received large grants for buildings and maintenance from the Punjab Government. Should this relationship ever cease, co-operative mission support would probably be necessary to keep up this important school.

(f) *Miscellaneous Agencies*.—Without unduly prolonging this chapter adequate mention cannot be made of the training of village midwives, of the help given in the conduct of Baby Welfare Weeks, of the district touring, of the physical examinations of school children, of preventive inoculations for epidemic diseases, of the medical care of missionaries, by medical missions. These are not passed over because they are unimportant, but because they are mere incidents in the busy routine service.

In the realms of preventive medicine and of medical research very little has been done, and much should be done, by missions. The inadequacy of the staffing of mission hospitals accounts for the deficiency. This is regrettable, and the necessary remedy ought to be applied. A wider vision and a longer arm are wanted. May He whose resources are unlimited inspire His servants to undertake the larger service.

(g) *Co-operation with other Mission Work.*—The medical department of missions has been regarded too long as almost an extraneous affair by many missions. In large international, interdenominational conferences, as at Edinburgh in 1910, the programme ignored it. At Jerusalem, 1928, it was given a place, but not so great a place as its importance warranted. The problems involved are not insignificant. Why are they not taken more seriously by the Church at large, and by every Christian in particular ? Surely the time has come for a more enlightened and truer evaluation of this form of work. It is indeed, " not merely a key to open the door into the non-Christian communities, but an integral part of the missionary enterprise ".

Among its rightful activities, the medical arm conserves the health of the oncoming generation of India's Christians, giving them better bodies than those of their neighbours ; it likewise attends to the ills of all mission workers ; it would educate many of them to undertake this work for themselves and for many others ; it reaches a helpful hand in true Christian spirit to many a sufferer, irrespective of his caste, age or creed ; it replaces, finally, opposition with a friendly gratitude. In such ways God is glorified, peace is initiated, goodwill among men is fostered ; and thus cometh the King into His Kingdom.

CHAPTER IX

THE PROBLEM OF POVERTY

By S. Higginbottom

" We who are strong ought to bear the burdens that the weak make for themselves and us."—Romans xv. i (Moffatt).

By poverty is meant such an insufficiency either of the right food, or of clothing and housing, that there is physical weakness and inability to do a fair day's work. That there is poverty in India is evident to all. Dr. H. H. Mann, formerly the well-known Director of Agriculture of Bombay, spoke of the distressing poverty in many of the villages of the Bombay Presidency. *The Times of India*, October 22, 1927, quotes him : " The empty stomach was the greatest obstacle to progress in India "; " Thirty-four per cent of the people are not in a sound economic condition even in the parts of India regarded as prosperous ". Professor D. S. Dube of the Allahabad University estimates that over 60 per cent of the population of India do not get more than three-quarters of the jail standard of food grains each year.[1]

This poverty is a problem, in its extent and complexity one of the most baffling in India. In this brief chapter I can only indicate a few of the causes, and in no case is there opportunity to exhaust the subject

[1] Cf. p. 127, note, above.

147

completely or to point out the far-reaching effects on the life of the people. We shall consider :

1. The economic consequences of social customs.
2. The economic consequences of disease and ill-health, and the consequent low expectation of life.
3. The economic consequences of the attitude of the people.
4. The economic consequences of the use made of the resources of the country.
5. The economic consequences of religious beliefs.

In this study there is no desire to show disrespect to the non-Christian religions of India, but a desire to learn the truth, without either racial or religious bias, in the belief that a sympathetic study and understanding of the causes of poverty will suggest ways of getting rid of some of it.

1. *The economic consequences of social customs.*

(*a*) Caste (in one aspect, social), by limiting and restricting occupation, restricts production, and therefore contributes to poverty.

(*b*) Caste fails to develop the best in each individual. If a person of a certain caste be born with certain natural gifts and abilities, which in a free and mobile society, by their exercise, would enrich greatly the whole community, he is frequently prevented *by caste* from exercising these gifts. The innate gifts frequently atrophy from lack of use, and the whole of Indian society is therefore the poorer.

(*c*) Caste also compels the poor to engage the services of others to do work (for which they can ill afford to pay) that in most other countries is done by the poor themselves, *e.g.* the work of washerman, water-carrier, sweeper, barber, hand-weaver. These are generally regarded as caste occupations. Those engaged in them seldom have full-time work all the year round. They therefore receive only part-time wages which are not enough for a decent standard of living.

(*d*). In many quarters there is failure to appreciate education. The failure to educate women is not only bad for them, but it involves their children. An ignorant mother seldom realizes the economic value of an education for her sons ; or, at best, regards it as a means of securing a job. She seldom looks upon education as an enrichment of life, in addition to being of economic value. Education that gives no money return would itself be a cause of poverty. The mother is the greatest factor in the education of the child in his most plastic years. She cannot hand on to her children more than she has. If she is ignorant and illiterate, her children have little chance of getting much from her. There is in India, among certain communities, little understanding of the fact that education is worth while for its own sake, that the child is worth an education because it is a child. Further, there is a direct money return for education. The higher the education, the greater the return. It is ignorance not education that is expensive. If it could be proved that education would secure larger financial returns, then it might be more generally welcomed. But that just because an education enlarges life's horizons it is justified, is hard to bring home to many. Yet this is precisely why education is the most profitable investment for society : it awakens and stimulates unsuspected powers and resources. This is surely one of the reasons for America's success—that almost all her children go to school. And it also explains Japan's speedy rise to become one of the world's great Powers.

(*e*) Again, there is the investment of available money in jewellery for the women. In India, because a non-Christian widow cannot inherit other property according to law, jewellery becomes the only protection to the widow. A change in the law is needed, so that a widow may inherit securities. This would release large sums of capital now tied up unproductively in jewellery. Frequently the jewellery is bought with money borrowed at high rates of interest. This jewellery produces no economic return, but, on the contrary, jewellery that is worn very much wears away and becomes lighter, and within a few years is of less weight and value. This is a reduction of working capital that is worse than hoarding, bad as that is. Hoarding says : " I was afraid and went and hid thy talent in the earth ; lo, there thou hast that is thine ". Hoarding is condemned, not because it loses the original capital, but because it makes no productive use of capital.

(f) The fragmentation of holdings of land grows out of the Indian social customs of inheritance, which, while avoiding certain objections in the system of primogeniture, do so at the expense of greater evils than they avoid. Fragmentation of holdings increases cost of production to such a high point that frequently the farmer has no margin of profit. He cannot compete with those who have consolidated holdings. The time lost in getting to and from his scattered fields, the added labour of watching several widely scattered plots, the difficulty of getting manure to the fields, and of carrying the harvest to the village threshing-floor, all add greatly to the cost of production. But the farmer on a fragmented holding gets no extra return for his extra labour. The market price is one, irrespective of the difference in cost of production. The farmer has to bear this higher cost of production that is suffered through scattered holdings. Mr. H. Calvert, C.I.E., I.C.S., has persuaded several villages in the Punjab to consolidate, to the great advantage of the village. Mr. Brayne, I.C.S., has consolidation of holdings as one of the planks in his programme for village uplift in Gurgaon. By co-operation consolidation has recently been effected in the Saharanpur and Benares districts.

(*g*) Weddings and funerals with their attendant ceremonies frequently involve a family in debt which can never be cleared off. Money can be borrowed for these things when it cannot be borrowed for economic improvement. Also many who will gladly hang a millstone of debt round their necks for a wedding do not dream of increasing their production to pay off the debt. The be-all and end-all of life to many is as it was in the days of Noah—" eating and drinking, marrying and giving in marriage ". Society demands these extravagant wedding feasts, and woe to the family that does not conform to society's demands.

2. *The economic consequences of preventible diseases and ill-health* fall heaviest on the poorest. Recently in a group of medical men I asked what was the greatest single cause of India's poverty. One prominent member of the group said " Malaria ". He knew districts where a large percentage of the population were disabled for three months each year through malaria, and often spent the other nine months in getting over the effects of it, and were never in first-class physical condition. Malaria so reduces the general resistance that many fall an easy prey to other diseases. A great deal of the ill-health of India is preventible, *e.g.* plague, cholera, typhoid, dysentery, but to prevent these diseases demands the active co-operation of the people. Ill-health is responsible for the high death-rate in India, which robs India of much of its most valuable product, *i.e.* human life. I quote freely in this section from *American Human Wealth*, by Woods and Metzger, published by Crofts, New York, 1927.

Woods and Metzger say :

In New Zealand the expectancy of life is	62 years.
In England and Wales (period 1910–1912)	53·43 ,,
In United States of America .	over 55 ,,
In India	less than 24 ,,

Recent studies by qualified men reveal the fact that the money value of the lives of the people of the United States is from five to eight times the value of all the material property of the United States. The life value is estimated to be

For the 1920 U.S. population .	$1,490,000,000,000
For the 1926 U.S. population .	1,600,000,000,000

M. Barriol, a French actuary, in 1910 estimated the average value of an individual in each of six countries as follows :

United States of America	£944
England	828
Germany	676
France	580
Austria-Hungary	544
Russia	404
India	?

A friend who has studied this problem says he does not think that it would be over £70 for India. Without venturing an estimate of the money value of the individual in India, we can make certain deductions. The figures for the six countries above are based on a working life of much longer duration than the duration of working life in India. It costs almost the same to bring a life to the productive stage, whether the productive life be long or short. If there be no productive life, or if it be very short, the net money result is an economic loss to society. If the productive life be long then the result is an economic gain. Now if the average length of life in India is, say, about twenty-four years, the average productive period begins at fourteen, and the average working life is ten years. Because the working life begins early, the average education and skill of the worker is low and the average money return is low. In the United States the expectation of life is over fifty-

five years. The working life begins at eighteen (which
implies higher education and more training than in
India for the average worker). Thus the average working life is over thirty-five years, and in general each
working life adds to society's accumulation of wealth.
Every addition to the length of the working life is
therefore a gain to society.

India has a large part of its population being supported until productive age is reached. This involves
a great drain on the producing population of India.
There is not enough of the productive part of the population producing for a sufficiently long period to offset
the loss involved in those who die before the working
life begins or who only produce for a comparatively
short working life. There can be no question that here
we are considering one of the root causes of India's
poverty. India is most prodigal and extravagant in
the use of what has the greatest money value—human
life. Her infant mortality and her high general death-
rate cause untold misery, suffering, mourning and de-
pression. The heart-ache of the mother whose arms
are empty is sad indeed. But beyond this mental and
physical distress lies the waste of human life which can
be expressed in terms of wealth. Dr. Bentley, Public
Health Officer of Bengal, was recently quoted as saying
that in Bengal in 1926 490,000 children died before
attaining the age of five years. 191,000 of these died
within the first month. Over 60,000 mothers died in
child-birth. Dr. Bentley calls attention to the great
loss of so much potential wealth-producing life. From
this standpoint must be mentioned the evil of child
marriage, which increases human wastage and prevents saving ; thus the accumulation of capital becomes
almost impossible.

India is not to-day over-populated if modern systems
of agriculture were in vogue. Nearly one-third of her

culturable area lies fallow.   India's population may need
redistributing, both geographically and according to
occupation, so as to take from the too congested areas
and from agriculture, and place the surplus in the
sparsely populated culturable districts, and into other
industries.

The first command given by God to man as recorded
in the first chapter of Genesis is, " Be fruitful and
multiply ; replenish the earth and subdue it ".   This
goes contrary to the teaching of " birth-control " exponents, according to whom more than a limited number
of children are regarded as an evil.   The facts are, that
as man has multiplied, and at the same time *subdued
the earth*, he has always been able to care for his increasing numbers.   New inventions, new nethods, new dis-
coveries have pushed back the dread day prophesied
by Malthus.   As man subdues his material world, he
gives it value and meaning.   Material things have no
value apart from man, but while he is giving value to
the material world, he is at the same time increasing his
own money value faster than he causes the material
things to increase in value.   Truly that which is spiritually, morally and socially right is also economically
right.   They are but opposite sides of the same coin,
inseparable for a complete life, individual or social.

3. *The economic consequences of the attitude of the
people.*—As one goes among the villages and talks with
the folk, he finds a lot of shrewd wisdom, much to
admire of courage and patient fortitude.   Yet as I
return from a village the outstanding impression left
on my mind is the attitude of hopelessness of the
ordinary villager.

A few months ago I sent out a questionnaire to a
number of people who have knowledge of rural India,
and asked for their opinions as to the causes of poverty.
I was surprised to find how many put down " laziness "

as one of the chief causes of poverty. I have been
thinking of the reason for this " laziness ", and recall
incidents that make me believe that much of the
" laziness " is induced by the feeling that effort put
forth brings no commensurate reward ; that although
one may toil, another will reap the harvest. Why
should one work harder if one gets no share in the extra
return? I hesitate to write of actual experiences of my
own, where sometimes the landlord, or the money-lender,
or the petty officials seemed unwilling for the ordinary
villager to rise in the social scale. Any extra burst of
energy on his part was met by a concerted pressure
to " keep him in his place ", which is often the place
of the serf. Very frequently the low caste man is not
allowed to improve his dwelling, or to carry an umbrella,
or wear decent, clean clothing. The attempt to improve his material condition is taken as a revolt against
his fixed place in society, which is considered to be at
the bottom, with no chance to rise. That this revolt
must be put down and the low caste man kept low is
too often the attitude of those above him. In talking
over their lives with these people, one finds that they
know what would improve their lot, they know how to
carry it out, but because of social oppression they fail
to make the effort, they remain dispirited, dejected and
hopeless. The economist regards hope on the part of the
worker as of the greatest importance to material progress. Tennyson says: "Work without hope is dead".
The Apostle uses the very suggestive phrase, " The
GOD of hope ".

" Laziness " is often one of the effects of malaria, dysentery, hookworm or intestinal parasitism, from one or
more of which a large percentage of the people of India
suffer. But when all such allowances have been made,
there yet remains an amazing amount of indifference to
material betterment which is easily within the reach of

the villager.   Show him better methods that yield better results, that call for no extra outlay, that are within his powers ; even then he will not respond.   He is not willing to pay the cost of extra effort.   A change of psychology is needed, a different outlook on life, a new and hopeful attitude to his world must be induced in the villager.   There are few districts where the village farmer is gainfully occupied for more that three-quarters of his time, even with his old uneconomic way of farming.   The fat part of the year eats up the lean part of the year.   The farmer is seldom willing to change his system so as to give him a longer working year.

4. *The economic consequences of the use made of the resources of the country.* — India has made comparatively little industrial progress.   We find so great a man as Mr. Gandhi arguing against the introduction of modern labour-saving machinery and urging India to stick to the old methods and the old hand-power. The cause of this attitude may be the fear of repeating some of the fearful social injustices of the industrial revolution of the West.   India needs to keep awake and protect herself against these evils.   But an industrial revolution can take place with continuous betterment of the workers.   It would be most unfortunate if the industrialization of India were gained at the cost of the exploitation of the poor.   This is a very real danger to-day in India.   Modern industrialism in India has often exploited the poor.

Present-day facts show that the more highly industrialized nations have the higher standards of living, while the industrially undeveloped have standards of living that are very low.   There is no nation to-day that is working with its bare hands, or with crude and inefficient machinery, that enjoys a decent standard of living.   When a man cranks a tractor or turns the wheel that starts a steam engine, he is controlling much more power than his own individual muscular effort. The use of machinery increases production. The more there is produced, the more there is to share with all those who produce. The only hope for a higher standard of living in India is in greater production, which can only come as the result of more and better machinery, and improved methods.

In the United States, where wealth is increasing at an unprecedented rate, the proportion of the population engaged in farming is rapidly decreasing, though agricultural production is rapidly increasing. A little more than a century ago 90 per cent of the population were engaged in farming. From the Civil War until the beginning of the present century about 60 per cent of the population were farmers. Since 1900 the proportion has dropped until to-day less than 30 per cent of the people of the United States are engaged in agriculture. This 30 per cent produces food for the 100 per cent with a large exportable surplus. This is only possible because of the widespread introduction of larger and better and more powerful machinery on the farms, better transportation from field to market and better marketing methods. The population released from the farms has very largely been absorbed by the industries that make the agricultural machinery and transport it and the crops, also by the luxury industries—the making of pianos, motor cars, etc. The production per man engaged in agriculture in the United States is many times the production of the Indian farmer.

One great need of India is to get other industries going to take surplus population from the land, which to-day in many parts of India is carrying too heavy a burden on such small, scattered holdings, with such primitive tools and methods as are common in most parts of India.

Another economic misuse of material wealth is the

failure to apply organic and other refuse as manure to
the soil.   Not only is much cowdung burned, but also
leaves, weeds, stubble that should be ploughed into the
soil to increase the humus.   During the cold weather,
in the villages near the Institute farm at Allahabad,
many of the women and children spend much of their
time gathering dried twigs, leaves, sorghum and millet
stubble, coarse grass and ripe weeds.   I have seen heaps
of this stuff, often several hundred pounds, made into
a fire and throughout the night the fire kept going,
the villager with only scanty cotton clothing, entirely
inadequate to keep him warm, no woollen blanket or
coat, and the night too cold for him to lie down and
sleep.   So for a good part of the night, sitting round the
fire, he toasts on one side and freezes on the other,
turning round and round.   He comes to work the next
day listless, haggard, physically incapable of doing a
fair day's work.   He seems to walk in a daze, con-
gealed, till the sun is well up and he can warm his
almost naked body in its genial warmth.

I have estimated that the organic matter that goes to
keep the fire going has a manurial value greatly in
excess of its fuel value.   If it had been mixed with the
soil, it would have increased the yield sufficiently to
provide money for better clothing and more abundant
food and thus the bodily heat could have been maintained.   The fertility of the soil could be progressively
increased in most villages by using as manure much
that now is either entirely wasted or improperly used.
India wastes in this way enough to make her well-to-do.

5. *The economic consequences of religious beliefs.*
—The veneration of the cow has led to such an increase
in the number of cows that they now have outstripped
the available food supplies.   This insufficiency of food
has led to deterioration in the quality of the cattle.   The
yield of milk of the ordinary village cows has decreased,

and is decreasing progressively, until only a small percentage of Indian cows pay for their keep. The oxen,
because underfed, are not as big as they would be were
they properly fed. The tractive power of bullocks varies
as the weight: the heavier, the stronger. Better cultivation would be possible with larger bullocks, and hence
larger yields. " Cultivation is manure." Further, the
veneration of every cow irrespective of her breed, age,
quality, or milk production prevents that selection of
breeding stock which is essential to cattle improvement.
The latter depends upon the eliminating of inferior
animals, upon breeding only from the best and feeding
them properly. Within the largest population group in
India everything of the cow family must live until it
dies of old age. I estimate that 90 per cent of the cattle
of India are a drain on the economic resources of the
country and are kept at a loss which reaches crores of
rupees annually.

The veneration of the monkey makes commercial
orcharding a very precarious business in many parts
of India, and impossible in others. An abundance of
cheap fruit would do much to improve the general
health of the people. Few countries can grow so many
varieties of good fruit as cheaply as India. Yet in many
parts, for most of the year, fruit is a luxury within the
reach of the well-to-do, and beyond the reach of the
poor.

Bombay Bulletin, No. 12 of 1927, puts the direct loss
due to the depredations of wild pig at seventy lakhs
of rupees per year. This is an estimate that anyone
familiar with the facts regards as conservative. But the
indirect loss is much greater than the direct. Were
there security in the field, better and more profitable
crops could be grown than are grown under the fear of
attacks by wild animals. Many of the most profitable
crops are not attempted by the farmer, where soil,

climate and market are favourable, because these crops are so attractive to the wild pig and other wild animals. The menace of the wild pig destroys hope and effort in many parts of India. For about two months the Institute has employed three men on about 200 acres using a calcium cyanide pump to kill rats, which are very destructive to ground-nuts, potatoes, sweet-potatoes, lucerne, wheat, barley, gram, maize, fruit. The work of these men will have to be continued for months more or we will suffer severe financial loss. In addition to the above, porcupines, jackals, flying-foxes, crows, green parrots and squirrels do an appreciable amount of damage, and have discouraged us from attempting to grow certain otherwise profitable crops for which our land is suitable. The cost of protection is so great that there would be a loss. All animal life, harmful and destructive, as well as domesticated and helpful, is regarded with a degree of veneration unknown outside of India. When I complain to the farm labourers and ask their help in fighting the animal pests, they say these animals are entitled to their share of the produce, and make little effort to co-operate in their destruction. The late Sir Ganga Ram in his interesting studies estimates the wastage of food grains in India at about 10 per cent. Also Professor D. S. Dube of the University of Allahabad estimates the wastage of food grains to be about 10 per cent of the total production in British India. Both these Hindu gentlemen consider the losses due to animals as a large part of the total wastage of food grains.

This veneration may grow partly out of the belief in transmigration which is held so solidly by large numbers of the people of India. There is a common and deep-rooted prejudice against killing any animals, although cruelty to animals is practised largely and seems to arouse little resentment among those who worship animals. The ordinary Hindu farmer does not usually

assent to the idea that man is to have " dominion over
the fish of the sea and over the fowl of the air and over
every living thing that moveth upon the earth ". He
does not believe that God made him to have " dominion
over the works of His hands ; all sheep and oxen, yea,
and the beasts of the fields ; the fowl of the air and
the fish of the sea". His disbelief that he is to have
dominion over the animal creation, and control it, can
be shown to cost him much more each year than the
total cost of the Government of India. This enormous
loss can be removed only by the active co-operation of
the people of India. On the part of many this would
involve a change of attitude in regard to the place of
veneration of animal life. Animal worship would have
to cease. This direct and indirect loss due to animals
falls very heavily on the countryside and contributes in
large measure to the poverty and hopelessness of the
rural population.

As one studies the problem of India's poverty it
becomes increasingly evident that there is no one sure,
quick remedy. Before education can become effective
(and one of the remedies is the right kind of education)
there must be created and awakened a desire for better
things. There must be a change of attitude of heart
and mind. I have studied many suggested remedies,
co-operation of various kinds, rural betterment and
uplift, all of which have an important place in the programme. But these remedies are all secondary. There
must be found a " prime-mover " that can touch the
springs of life and bring union and progress where now
there is chaos and stagnation. " The level of a people's
life can never be higher than the level of its thinking."
Therefore the unceasing effort must be to elevate the
thinking of the village folk of India. The longer I live
in India the more I believe that in the application of
the Gospel of Jesus Christ, fully, persistently, as He

M

lived it and commanded His disciples to practise it, is India's only hope.   And there is no other adequate.

There is much prejudice against such a proffered solution.   Some say it begs the question and fails to take into account all the factors.   I have thought much on this, and am driven back by the logical method of exclusion to reassert that a thoroughgoing acceptance of Jesus Christ as Saviour and Lord, and just as thoroughgoing an application of His Gospel to all the affairs of life, will bring India to her rightful place among the nations and solve her poverty problems. Her spiritual, moral and social poverty is the cause of her economic and political poverty.

How is it that one stratum of Indian life under one system makes such a poor showing in progressive living and cumulative achievement?   Part of this stratum is either entirely stationary or going backwards.   Part of it takes Jesus Christ as its Lord and Master, as well as its example and model, and immediately the old things pass away; and the part that follows Jesus Christ enters literally here and now a new heaven and a new earth. Children, both boys and girls, are educated.   Medical care is given.   Sanitation finds a place in daily life. Disease is prevented.   Economic conditions are greatly improved.   Higher education is enjoyed by many, who take their place in the public life of the people of India. Moral conditions improve.   Wherever the Bible goes and its precepts are followed, there the standard of all human relationships is raised.

It is the social and religious system, not the individual, that makes the difference.   Christ is the Life and the Power in the system, religious, social, economic, political and moral.   The way to develop a full belief in India would be to study the history of the Indian Protestant Christian community.   This history would show that India is not hopeless and incapable of improvement. While it is true that many Indian Christians came from the best blood and social traditions of non-Christian India, yet a large majority of the Indian Protestant Christian community have come from the outcaste and untouchable classes. Jesus Christ has exalted them.

Indian society is not peculiar in this. The West can match in unfavourable conditions almost anything in the East. Mankind is the same at heart, no matter what the colour of the skin. There is a curious monotony in the category of sin, nothing ever new in sin. Natural and unaided mankind at heart, whether in East or West, is incapable of sustained goodness. Jesus Christ in the heart of mankind provides this sustaining power.

Now, in India, Christian missions have been pioneers in much that has stood for the betterment of the people. The direct preaching of the gospel of love and sal-vation, the educational work of missions, the medical work of missions, the literary work of missions, the social work of missions, the industrial work of missions, the agricultural work of missions are all done by men and women who recognize that God is using their differing gifts to express one great, controlling motive and purpose: that God so loved the Indian world that He gave His only begotten Son, that whosoever believeth in Him should not perish, but have everlasting life.

There has been sometimes in the Christian mission enterprise a failure to appreciate the wideness, and scope, and many-sidedness of the Gospel. Preaching is of superlative importance. Yet it is not a complete gospel. To heal the sick, cleanse the lepers, feed the lambs, feed the sheep, to heal the broken-hearted, to preach deliverance to the captives and recovering of sight to the blind, to set at liberty them that are bruised are all co-ordinate with the oral presentation

of the Gospel. The Gospel of Jesus Christ is as wide
as the needs of man, spiritually, socially, politically,
industrially, economically. Economic truth is God's
truth, even as spiritual truth. Failure to obey it ensures
loss, just as surely as failure to follow spiritual truth
entails loss. He asked for which of His works, not
for which of His sermons, they sought to stone Him.

There are encouraging signs that missions are
strengthening the weak places in their programme.
Industrial and agricultural missions are now recognized
by many as an integral part of the propagation of the
Gospel—good news for body, mind and spirit. The
danger is that they try to manage without properly
trained men, who are indispensable if these enterprises
are to make their proper contribution to the spread of
the Gospel. To serve tables the Apostles chose men
of honest report, full of the Holy Ghost and wisdom.
This was in order to leave the Apostles to do the work
of prayer and ministry of the Word. There may be
something in this for us to-day.

CHAPTER X

PUBLIC QUESTIONS

By J. F. EDWARDS

THIS is not a chapter on Indian politics, but an attempt to show how the Christian movement in India can best help in establishing the reign of Jesus Christ as King in every part of Indian society. Nor is it our purpose to adjudicate on India's greatest " public question ", the problem of her future constitution. What Mahadev Govind Ranade wrote over forty years ago applies to-day : " The sole *rationale* of British rule in India is its capacity and its providential purpose of fostering the political education of the country ". Our faith in the overruling Providence of God and in the political wisdom of both countries assures us that a solution will be found of this problem affecting one-fifth of the human race. On the question of India's constitutional development, the conviction of the present writer is that a larger measure of self-government will mean a greater opportunity for churches and missions, since the Indian mind will be less disposed to associate these with what is called the bureaucracy. Above all else, India's dominating desire is to see in her rulers, Indian and British alike, more of such personal character as conforms to the standard set up in the New Testament, and where this is not forthcoming, India loses faith in her rulers, whoever they be. Therefore, in declaring unfalteringly that the character needed in her public leaders, and that the unity required to dispose of India's factions, can only come from the Spirit of Christ, the Christian movement is making its own distinctive contribution, though indirectly, to the making of an Indian nation.

Whatever direct contribution the Christian Church is to make towards solving India's " public questions " can best be made by seeking to mould Indian public opinion, thereby helping to overcome what Government spokesmen insist is the one serious obstacle to the drastic social reform India needs. There is probably no more acute " public question " in the minds of Indian social reformers at the present time than that arising from their profound dissatisfaction regarding the comparative sterility in measures of social reform since Lord Bentinck in 1829 abolished *satī* or widow-burning, though the Reformed Councils are agreed to have somewhat quickened the pace. Reformers blame the Government, and Government say they cannot go too far ahead of public opinion. Mr. C. F. Andrews, who probably knows the Indian mind better than any other living non-Indian, in a recent issue of *Foreign Affairs*, is driven to conclude " against the natural bent " of his own mind that the remedying of India's " acknowledged social evils ", including even the wrongs suffered by the depressed classes, is " being retarded rather than accelerated under the present system of Government ". Many will wonder whether in reaching this conclusion Mr. Andrews may not have underrated the stout opposition to social reform still being put up by Hindu and Moslem orthodoxy, both in the legislature and out of it, and whether he may not also have underestimated the deep appreciation of the Reformed Councils by the depressed (or " suppressed ") classes themselves. But the editor of *The Indian Social Reformer* (Feb. 25,

1928) agrees with Mr. Andrews ; and it is worthy of note that even under the Reformed Councils there have been critical occasions when India's clearly expressed desire for social reform has been overruled either by the action or the inaction of officials.

Two glaring instances in the Legislative Assembly of 1925 will suffice ; the first being the Age of Consent Bill in March, and the second when the Assembly on September 2 voted by 69 to 39 " that the ultimate policy of Government should be prohibition of production, manufacture, sale and import of intoxicating liquors, save for medicinal and scientific purposes " with local option as " the first step ". Every non-official Indian member present voted for this resolution, but up to the time of writing nothing has been done to give effect to the wishes of the people's representatives. The object of the Age of Consent Bill on March 24, 1925, was to " protect girls below the age of 13 ; to protect them against strangers up to the age of 15 ; and to protect girl-wives up to the age of 14 from the injurious approaches of their husbands ". Speaking on this subject a few months later, Dr. S. K. Datta, the Indian Christian representative in the Legislative Assembly, stated : " I speak as a Christian ; to me the most terrible thing was that the downfall of the Bill was brought about by the combination of European Christian members of the Government with orthodoxy against the reform," the official whips having been put on to defeat the third reading. It is impossible not to sympathize deeply with Indian impatience regarding official timidity, but an impartial verdict will not overlook the fact that it was a similar Age of Consent Bill in 1890 that led Mr. B. G. Tilak to invoke the wrath of the Hindu gods on Government for venturing to impinge on the domain of religious custom. Though the reform aimed at was meant to save India from the curse of premature motherhood, every Hindu who supported the measure was denounced as " a renegade and a traitor to the cause of Hinduism ". Orthodox India is now sending similar protests to the Viceroy against the Sarda Hindu Child Marriage Bill (which proposes to raise the marriage-age for girls to 14, and that for boys to 18) reminding His Excellency of Government's promise of " religious neutrality ". On the other hand, that noble woman, Dr. Mathulakshmi Reddy, Deputy President of the Madras Legislative Council, affirms that " without the help of legislation we will have to wait till Doomsday for getting rid of these social evils " These and many other facts point to three conclusions, viz : (1) that nothing but a vast body of healthy Indian opinion can release India's present Government from its promise of " neutrality " ; (2) an equally strong and healthy public opinion will be needed for drastic social reform in India under any form of complete self-government ; and, therefore, (3) it must be regarded as a sacred part of the Christian task in India to help in creating such public opinion.

Seeing then that the Kingdom of Christ cannot be established in India without very drastic social reform, how far shall the Christian movement give itself to this delicate duty of shaping Indian public opinion ? In this connection missions are sometimes accused of remaining too aloof from India's public events and the churches are charged with being denationalized. There is truth in both contentions, and there is perhaps an even more subtle danger to which Mr. Arthur Mayhew refers in his notable book, *The Education of India*. Though Mr. Mayhew believes India's Government to have been " the most conscientious Government that the world has ever seen " he avers that " in its failure to reach the heart or affect the springs of constructive activity " the Government system needs supplementing by much more

of definite Christian enterprise, and he insists that
missions have suffered a loss of influence with India's
educated classes owing to association with a Government " neutral " in religion.   We believe this expresses
the mind of not a few progressive Indian leaders, who
feel that missions and churches themselves are sometimes almost " neutral ", because so often silent, on
urgent matters of social reform.   Not that missionaries
are expected to meddle with party politics, for it is
because they have kept outside and above these that
India's ear has been kept open for the Christian message.
The charge of aloofness and denationalization we are
not concerned to rebut, for happily there are many facts
on the other side, nor is India ungrateful for these facts.
It is matter for justifiable pride, for example, that the
masses of every district in India are indebted to the
" strong mission influence " of Alexander Duff in the
drawing up of that *magna charta* of Indian education,
Sir Charles Wood's Despatch of 1854.   The whole of
South India thanks God for men like William Miller of
Madras who " left an indelible mark on the standards of
life, and on probity both personal and public ".   Since
the organization, and especially since the Indianization,
of the Christian Councils, Provincial and National,
throughout India, much encouraging work has been done
by united effort for the removal of India's social evils.
One of the most dramatic moments in the communal
strife that has torn present-day India was when the
President and Vice-President of the National Christian
Council for India, Burma and Ceylon (the Metropolitan
and Dr. Datta) attended the Unity Conference in Delhi
during Mr. Gandhi's fast of September 1924, and Dr.
Westcott laid down the Golden Rule of Jesus Christ as
the sovereign remedy for India's communal ills.   And
who could write any adequate account of the economic
and racial strife during recent years in India and over-

seas without narrating the amazing labours of Mr.
Andrews, who many years ago left the Cambridge
Brotherhood to found throughout India the wider
Brotherhood of Christ, and who to-day is the intimate
friend of Mr. Gandhi and Dr. Tagore, as well as the
accepted mediator of India's labouring classes ?   Our
plea is that a great deal more remains to be done and
that India expects every one of us to fulfil our God-
given " ministry of reconciliation ".

In facing this difficult part of the Christian task in
India, the task of creating a state of public opinion more
in conformity with the mind of Christ, churches and
missions may build on the encouraging and wellnigh
universally admitted fact of India's " tacit recognition
of the values that are in the mind of Christ as the
supreme criterion for all human conduct, public and
private ", and on this matter " Mr. Gandhi's appeal to
the Sermon on the Mount as the supreme criterion of
private and public conduct " is rightly considered " one
of the unerring signs of the times ".[1]   That " the
penetrating Christian ethic is already powerfully influencing India " is the verdict of that careful observer
of everything Indian, Sir Stanley Reed, delivered from
the platform of Bombay's largest public hall in January 1928.   How inadequately the ethic of Jesus is
being applied to India's public situations is indicated
by the fact that the missionary weekly journals, Protestant and Romanist included, circulating among
India's 320 millions can be counted on one's fingers with
a few fingers left.   Mr. Gilbert Chesterton has warned
us that there is enough dynamite in the social teachings
of Jesus to blow all modern society to rags.   Certainly
there is evidence of this in India, for wherever Jesus is
taken in earnest, masses of the population are raised from
servitude and degradation to useful and happy citizen-

[1] K. T. Paul, *British Connection with India*, pp. 40, 51.

ship ; while its disintegrating influence on moral and
social evils has been so deep that Dr. H. D. Griswold
could say in *The Indian Standard* for February 1928,
that " there are in Hinduism to-day large numbers of
people whose thinking is more dominated by Christian
than by orthodox Hindu ideals," and that " to this
extent Christianity in India has affected Hinduism as a
society " ; hence " the measure of social reform which
is slowly taking place in Hinduism ".

But the enormous amount of nation-building yet to
be done, and the fact that " Christ the Constructive
Revolutionary " is waiting to accomplish it, constitute
a clarion-call to all His servants.   We are engaged in a
holy war in which we need to " fuse personal piety with
social passion", a war against evil entrenched in the name
of religion from which there is no release till the work is
done.   " While there is a lower class I am in it ; while
there is a criminal element I am of it ; while there is a
soul in prison I am not free."   The need of such Christ-
like identification with our fellowmen is the reason why
every one of us should detect an echo of the voice of his
Lord in the complaint about the loss suffered by India
whenever there is aloofness or denationalization on the
part of Christian people, a complaint for which there has
been much less ground since men like Narayan Vaman
Tilak demonstrated their patriotism equally by devotion
to India's culture and by denunciation of India's wrongs.

Other important considerations call us to a more
vocal attitude in relation to India's social evils—assuming always that our social applications of Christian
principle must be based on sound information as well as
sympathy.   There is our responsibility for doing all in
our power to purify the environment surrounding our
four and three-quarter million fellow-Christians, and the
building up of a pure Church cannot fail of itself to be
one of the greatest factors in the building up of a pure

India. We have an equally important duty to that large section of Indian reformers who, while attracted to Jesus Christ, feel repelled by His defective Church in India and elsewhere. The profound conviction that Jesus Christ alone could save his country was one potent reason leading Narayan Vaman Tilak, " the Rabindranath Tagore of Western India ", to dedicate his great powers to Christ, and there are many others who will be drawn to Christ through the channel of patriotic social service. By working side by side with such men in social service ourselves, both missionaries and Indian Christian leaders, we can give them a direct lesson in Christian dynamics and help to fortify their convictions as they daily confront a dead weight of conservatism in their own homes. Resolved as many of these men are that social injustices must be ended even at the cost of social disruption, they are paying a price inside their own circle of which Westerners cannot dream. They are in deed and truth " carrying a cross ", and to such heroic souls we have a most solemn duty. What we covet for the Indian Church is that more Indian Christian leaders shall co-operate with these men in facing India's problems, and that the two groups together shall carry on the traditions of bodies like the Servants of India Society, bringing about " an Indian evolution of the Spirit of Christ ", " a Christ-inspired Indian mind and soul ". This we believe to be the surest method of creating that Christian public opinion which alone can solve India's " public questions ". Were it not for that most widespread of heresies, the " heresy of labels ", we should probably realize that this process is already well advanced, for there is much truly Christian work being done all over India, by those who as yet have not proclaimed themselves under Christ's banner : " He that is not against us is for us ".

Restricting our attention to certain particular

" questions ", on account of limitations of space, let us take first the *Problem of Race and Colour*. There have been moments during the past decade when a missionary was ashamed to meet thoughtful Indians, such moments being those during the bitterest stages of the Kenya and South African questions, and the first announcement of the exclusion of Asiatics from the United States. This last has led American missionaries in India to send to the United States authorities a protest against " the discriminatory clauses " as being " a violation of Christian principles which we hold to be the surest guide in international relations ". Recent history makes clear that racial antagonisms are so deep as to make the prospects of the human race ominous if Christ is ruled out, and India itself is saying that " the progress of Christianity in the world is being retarded by the incurable race-prejudice of its white votaries, who lamentably fail to rise to the height of Christ's religion of love ".[1] In what spirit India's ambassador to South Africa, the Right Hon. V. S. Srinivasa Sastri, has performed his selfless service was shown in an article he contributed to *The Natal Mercury* of Christmas Eve, 1927, in which he said : " Christ's commands know no limit of race or colour, no mere geographical or political boundary ; they would discipline us into one brotherhood ". One of the chief subjects discussed at the Jerusalem meeting of the International Missionary Council was " in what ways the Christian forces can make the largest possible contribution to the furtherance of racial understanding and goodwill ". The pronouncement made by the Council is worthy of the closest study.

Caste, Untouchability, Communalism are all a plain denial of Christ's principle of brotherhood. In India every aspect of life has a religious basis, and caste and all the evils linked with it have their origin in *karma*,

---

[1] *The Indian Messenger* of the Brahmo Samaj, Calcutta.

the Hindu theory which holds that one's present status is the inevitable fruit of past lives. Accordingly, India's out-castes were born such as punishment for ill deeds done in a former existence. This view is at the very core of Hinduism, which for two thousand years past has been the negation of nationality, split up as it has come to be into 2300 separate castes, as shown in Sir Herbert Risley's authoritative enumeration. Hence it is that the uplift of the out-castes and even non-Christian work on their behalf are the direct outcome of Christian teaching ; hence also, India has been coming to realize that the uprooting of caste is an essential condition of India's national regeneration. In the moving picture of social progress in India during the past four decades, unfolded by the President of the Fortieth National Social Conference held in Madras in the closing days of 1927, one feature was that India's " hereditary cast-iron caste system is rapidly disintegrating ; we can hear almost every day some part of this mediæval system crashing to the ground as if struck down by unseen hands ". One of the most striking spectacles in modern India has been Mr. Gandhi's campaign against untouchability, while the orthodox pundits have been fulminating against him ; part of his message being that, if India attained full self-government before untouchability was removed, it would be a curse and not a blessing. It is all the more tragic, therefore, that " Mr. Gandhi's intervention in this reform, while it gave it more extension, actually reduced its value and importance ", for social reformers " do not regard his efforts as going far enough ", as he has " seemed to show excessive consideration for the irrational prejudices of caste Hindus ".[1] That " the caste system is inherent in human nature "[2] is Mr. Gandhi's position. Against such a view the sublime

---

[1] *The Indian Social Reformer.*
[2] *Young India*, Dec. 8, 1920, and Oct. 6, 1921.

figure of Jesus is an impressive protest, and how that figure is influencing India in this matter is shown by the fact that when the late Maharajah of Kolhapur, one of the greatest champions of the untouchables, was asked why he was eliminating caste regulations from his State, he replied that he " got the idea in Miraj Mission Hospital ".

We have already referred to the Golden Rule of Jesus as the antidote for communalism, and it is worthy of note that Professor L. F. Rushbrook Williams observes: " It seems difficult to deny that the solution of this vexed question must ultimately lie along the lines laid down at the Delhi Conference ".[1] If, therefore, churches and missions are to help India to triumph over caste and communal strife, we must ensure that we ourselves are " free from the spirit which breeds such strife ", as the resolution passed on this subject by the National Christian Council of India reminded us. And there is need of the reminder, for Sadhu Sundar Singh has never ceased to point out that the spirit of caste in some parts of the Indian Church is like elephantiasis in the Church's feet; and the Christian Church in India can never afford to forget the pronouncement of that converted Konkanasth Chitpavan Brahman, the Rev. Nilkanth Nehemiah Goreh, concerning whom Pandita Ramabai wrote: " I think no one would have had the power of turning my heart from the Brahman religion but Father Goreh " On our subject Father Goreh laid down the principle that " Christianity with caste would be no Christianity at all ".[2]

Wrongs against Women provide a black list among India's " public questions ", viz. *Child Marriage*, *Premature Motherhood*, *Infanticide*, *Prohibition of Widow Remarriage*, *Prostitution*, " *Devadāsīs* ", the

[1] *India in 1924–1925*, p. 322.
[2] C. E. Gardner, *Life of Father Goreh*, pp. 6, 275.

Purdah System, the *Low Age of Consent*, the "*Nautch*", and the *Sale of Brides*. Probably the degradation of India's womanhood has done more than anything else to lower India's prestige in the eyes of the world, but there is no subject on which there is greater need of accurate information on the part of those who would effect reform, a condition unfortunately not fulfilled in Miss Mayo's *Mother India*, which deals with some of these subjects. The official census returns are bad enough, revealing, as they do, that the birth of a girl is still viewed as a misfortune in many parts of India, and the persistence of infanticide.[1] The 1921 Census figures for child-wives and child-widows in India were as follows : 218,463 wives under five years of age, 2,016,687 between five and ten years old, and 6,330,207 between ten and fifteen, making a total of 8,565,357 child-wives under fifteen. The child widows under five years of age numbered 15,139 (of whom 759 were under twelve months old), those between five and ten years of age numbered 102,293, while those between ten and fifteen numbered 279,124, making a total of 396,556 child-widows under fifteen years of age.[2] Here, again, India's evil customs are directly due to the Hindu theory of *karma*, that the wife is to blame for her husband's death, even though she may never have seen him, her loss of her husband being the due penalty for her wrong-doing in a former existence. Social reform in India, therefore, drives one back on the need for religious reform, and on the need for the Christian message.

It is very clear that Indian apathy concerning girls' education and other reforms affecting women will not be removed until the attitude to women is changed. But it will be futile to attempt such reforms by means of education alone. " All the education that we have

[1] *Census of India, 1921*, vol. i. Appendix VI.
[2] *Ibid.* vol. i. Part II. p. 46.

been receiving for the past hundred years seems to have produced but little impression upon us, for I note that the *purdah* is being retained even in educated households ", says Mr. Gandhi.[1] Can we imagine what it means for some forty million women in India to be living " more or less " behind the *purdah* ? And can the Christian Movement help in this matter more effectively than by directing India's attention to the greatest Champion of the rights of woman ?   Jesus is her greatest Champion, because what counts most with Him is woman's soul, and this law of Jesus is receiving practical application in India by the influence of earnest Christian women behind the scenes of the All-India Women's Educational Conference and twenty-two Provincial Conferences, which are insisting that " consent " and motherhood below the age of sixteen violate both natural law and divine law, since the meanest woman has a right to some voice in choosing the father of her child, which is impossible at present in India.   This same law of Christ condemns all " toleration ", " segregation ", or " regulation " in relation to vice-areas in our Indian cities, where children of tender years are being trained in " the profession of prostitution ".   It is a law that will also abolish the calling of the *devadāsī*, which on the best authority means nothing less than dedication to a life of vice in the name of religion. One of the most hopeful movements in some of the most wicked centres in India is that for self-reform among these women, who are organizing to save their children from the hell through which they themselves have passed.

" From the moral standpoint there is no defence of the *Indian Opium Policy* ", said Mr. Gandhi in a letter to the office of the National Christian Council of India in 1924, and the recent history of this question shows

[1] *Young India*, Feb. 3, 1927.

N

how much can be done by the co-ordinated efforts of
Indian Christian leaders and missionaries. One of the
most notable speeches ever given in the Legislative Assembly at Delhi was made during the important opium
debate of March 12-13, 1925, by Dr. Datta, the Indian
Christian representative, who urged a new inquiry into
opium conditions in India. The ground had been
thoroughly prepared for Dr. Datta's appeal by an eighty-
page pamphlet entitled *Opium in India*, making out a
prima facie case for such an inquiry, and written by
the Rev. W. Paton, secretary of the National Christian
Council, at the request of the International Missionary
Council, from evidence gathered by Provincial Councils
throughout India. That constructive criticism is welcomed by the Indian Government is shown in the striking tribute from the Director of Public Information,
who describes Mr. Paton as " one of the leading critics
of the Government of India's opium policy—and one of
the fairest ".[1] How much can be accomplished by constitutional and thoroughly Christian agitation is demonstrated by the fact that Indian revenue from opium
export fell from 801 lakhs of rupees in 1910 to 183 lakhs
in 1923, the reduction being attributed by India's public
men to " the British Nonconformist conscience ".[2] On
the other hand, missions have not hesitated to give credit
where credit is due. At Geneva, in November 1924,
Mr. Kenneth Maclennan, secretary of the Conference
of British Missionary Societies, agreed that on opium
export the Government of India had given an example
to the world, and a little later Lord Reading as Viceroy
intimated that India's limiting of opium export to
strictly medical and scientific purposes involved India
" in loss of net revenue of approximately £1,200,000
sterling a year ", while Lord Irwin, in May 1927, forcibly

---

[1] *India in 1925–26*, p. 250.
[2] *Assembly Debates*, March 13, 1925

reminded the Indian States of " international under-
takings ". At the same time missionaries and Indian
Christian leaders deplore the fact that India is the
world's greatest exporter of opium and its second largest
producer ; that although the League of Nations Committee allows six seers or twelve pounds avoirdupois
per ten thousand of the population per annum as legitimate consumption of opium, the average figure for
India is twelve seers or twenty-four pounds ; and they
press for a new inquiry in every Indian province, because
facts are against the verdict of the Royal Commission
of 1893, which made out that opium is required medicin-
ally to compensate for the scarcity of doctors, the truth
being that opium consumption is higher in Bombay
and Calcutta where there are more doctors. An official
report on Bombay housing conditions states that " 98
per cent of the infants born to women industrial workers
have opium administered to them " ;[1] while Calcutta
consumes as much as 143 seers per 10,000 of the population per annum. Happily the Bengal Government has
appointed a special committee for inquiry and report,
with a distinguished missionary as one of its four
members. On the whole of this question sterling work
has been done by Mr. C. F. Andrews, whose *Assam
Congress Opium Enquiry Report* (September 1925) is
a classic example of opium investigation, being "indispensable, careful and accurate ". The verdict of this
Christian humanitarian is that " if opium, as a poison,
is regarded as a dangerous drug in the West, it should
equally be regarded as a dangerous drug in the East ",
and sold only under " a Dangerous Drugs Act ". A
very special " appeal to the missionaries to help us "
comes from all the seven Congress Nationalists who
formed the Assam Committee, and a similar appeal
came to India's churches and missions from opium's

[1] *Bombay Labour Gazette* for Sept. 1922.

chief victim, China, in a letter dated September 24, 1924, signed by the Chinese National Christian Council's officers, appealing for India's help to deliver China from the opium curse. Such appeals deserve a worthy response. And in view of much Indian apathy and ignorance on this subject and " the winking of Indian public opinion at the habitual eating of opium ", there is need of *The Servant of India's* appeal to a certain class of critics that they would " be better employed in rousing popular feeling, not against the Government, but against the opium evil itself ".

India's *Drink Evil* has never been more correctly described than by Lord Morley as " India's new, deadly and additional plague". Hinduism and Islam, comprising some seven-eighths of the population, demand complete abolition as the one remedy, and successive annual sessions of the All-India Conference of Indian Christians express emphatic agreement. " The whole country is crying itself hoarse for prohibition ", said *The Servant of India* on January 26, 1928, while " the Government is still thinking in terms of maximum revenue from minimum consumption " ; and Mr. Gandhi urges his English friends " no longer to obstruct our national passion for prohibition ". That " passion " was expressed unanimously once for all in the memorable debate of September 2, 1925, to which we have referred, when Mr. N. C. Kelkar hurled forth his jibe about the " trinity of the Bible, the Bottle and the Bayonet ".[1] Unquestionably the most emphatic way to help India in her drink struggle is for the Christian Church in India and in every other land to set an example of personal total abstinence, for India cannot understand any middle course on this question ; Sir William Wanless has expressed doubt whether it is morally possible for the average Indian to be a " moderate " drinker.

[1] *Legislative Assembly Debates*, vol. vi. No. 9.

The measure of responsibility of the " Christian " West for India's drink traffic is shown by an authoritative estimate that more than one-half the foreign liquor imported into India is consumed by Indians. Mr. W. P. Livingstone not long ago, in *The Record* of the United Free Church of Scotland, had an article on the drink question as " The Most Important Matter before the Church ", and for ourselves we are growingly convinced that there is no other single factor so alienating India both from the British Commonwealth of Nations and from the Christian Church as is the drink evil. Moreover, it is a menace to the Indian Church itself, as " one of the blatant social evils in our own community ", says the Conference of Indian Christians. " If your brother is being injured because you eat a certain food, then you are no longer living by the rule of love. Do not let that food of yours ruin the man for whom Christ died. Your ' rights ' must not get a bad name. . . . The right course is to abstain from flesh or wine or indeed anything that your brother feels to be a stumbling-block " (Moffatt's translation in Romans xiv.). The Indian case for total prohibition has never been more lucidly stated than by the late Honourable Lord Guthrie, Senator of the College of Justice in Scotland, who in his article on " Prisons " in Dr. Hastings' *Encyclopaedia of Religion and Ethics* says that " if crime is to be prevented, it must be done by the State securing ", among other things, " that the existing temptations to use alcohol, either in moderation or excess—such temptations being often found at the maximum where the power of resistance is at the minimum—shall be ended ".

Gambling in India, especially in industrial centres, is regarded by many as a greater menace even than alcohol, and since it causes many " to stumble ", it calls for stern condemnation. Churches and missions may help much by definite instruction on the social and

economic dangers of sordid speculation and by setting
forth the Christian antidote in heroic and adventurous
service, such as " the spirit of Toc H " inspires. Only
by this spirit showing itself in the lives of the 156,000
Europeans in British India (including the British garri-
son) and the 113,000 Anglo-Indians can the gambling
spirit be exorcised. In regard to both drink and the
race-course, Christian people who are in India from
Western countries may help India immeasurably by
willingly foregoing these luxuries for India's sake and
for the Indian Church's sake.

No survey of India's public moral problems will
discover their solutions in orthodox Hinduism with its
spurts of outward revival and its " steadily increasing
inner decay ". Nor is reformed Hinduism much better,
for "no miracles may be expected and it may take ages",
says Mr. Gandhi of his own spiritual pilgrimage. But
Christ's people know " He has done all things well "
whenever He has been given full sway as King, and
that "miracles" happen daily wherever He reigns. He
stands in the midst of Indian society and, in the words
of the little papyrus sheet discovered a few years ago,
cries : " My soul is pained for the sons of men ; for they
are blind in heart and see not ; poor and know not their
poverty". If Jesus is to be *heard* in Indian society, we
need to strengthen existing agencies in certain directions.

(1) We need a far more effective Christian journalism
all over India, for, as His Holiness Pius XI has said,
" if such a large number of newspapers and publications
of all kinds constantly contradict Christian principles
and produce scandalous news and even pornographic
material, then it is a real apostolate to multiply the
means and activity of that press which alone is able to
steer clear of such mischief, which awakens noble and
pure thoughts in the hearts of the readers and enlightens
them with the animating light of the Gospel ".

(2) In our boarding-schools, high schools and colleges we have the future India in our hands, and by simple courses of study on India's moral questions we may create a growing army of social workers.

(3) The sense of civic responsibility must be quickened in the Indian Church in relation to its own immediate environment everywhere, leading every member to take his part in finding " the constructive equivalent of caste jealousy " and to offer mediation if necessary.

(4) National and Provincial Christian Councils, and all organized Missions and Churches, while keeping above party strife, might well publish more frequently judicious and constructive statements of Christian principles, showing their bearing on particular social problems, and thus helping to Christianize public opinion.

(5) The Christian Church's greatest contribution to despairing India on *all* her problems is to put Christ so vividly at the very centre of India's whole life that her people " may be overflowing with hope by the power of the Holy Spirit " (Romans xv. 13, Moffatt). For we have nothing else to give India's people if we do not give them the transfiguring Spirit of Christ. Let every social worker in India therefore pray :

> Bread of Thy Body give me for my fighting,
> Give me to drink of Thy sacred Blood for wine,
> While there are wrongs that need me for the righting,
> While there is warfare, splendid and divine.

CHAPTER XI

AN ENGLISH LAYMAN'S CONTRIBUTION

By J. Arthur Davies

THE title of this chapter suggests at least two possible lines of treatment. I might discuss from my layman's standpoint what I conceive the Christian Task in India to be—contribute, in fact, the views of an interested sympathetic outsider upon the work of what may be called the " professional missionary ", especially in relation to its goal. Or I might, assuming agreement on that goal, point out in what ways the English layman in India can contribute to its achievement. The two subjects are, of course, closely related, and I shall attempt to tackle both.

It is no doubt peculiarly appropriate to the writer of Chapter I to expound the nature of the task, but a layman, irresponsible to any Church or institution, has perhaps a greater freedom of exposition, and a presentation of things therefore as he sees them may be of value on the assumption—which I admit is not always or unqualifiedly true—that the onlooker sees most of the game. On the other hand, I recognize that my irresponsibility is in itself a handicap, for if I cannot speak for any missionary body, neither can I pretend to do so in the name of laymen in general. There is no such person as a typical layman, nor perhaps even a generally representative one, and any attempt to express the average opinion of the laity must in practice—however judicial and fair-minded the writer—resolve itself into a personal statement of attitude and impression. The best that one can expect is a sincere and frank setting out of the writer's own position, and if, in fact, a very large number of laymen would consent thereto in general terms, that best is so much bettered.

I would start with what seem to me two incontrovertible propositions : first, that the aims and methods and the driving inspiration of all missionary effort abroad must depend in the last resort upon the religious atmosphere in the homeland ; and, secondly, that that atmosphere has been profoundly changed during the last few decades. The first of these propositions requires no elaboration, and the second demands a capacity for exposition to which I can lay no claim. Indeed, I wish I could add that it too needs no elaboration here, for if it is not proved by the reader's own experience of the life around him, of modern literature, of discussions in the drawing-room and the club, of the character of sermons, of the things that interest and hold the man in the street and the man in the pew, nothing that I could say would convince him. And yet I feel that the proposition requires emphatic statement on account of its vital, fundamental importance, and also because it seems to me that in the ranks of the clergy and elsewhere there are still too many who, from either timidity or an incapacity to read the signs of the time or a mistaken loyalty to the traditions of the fathers, do not sufficiently recognize that this very profound change has taken place. Science has revolutionized men's preliminary, elementary ideas, so that the background on which we build our philosophy of life, our religion, is almost unrecognizably unlike that of our fathers. The earth is, or should be, no longer for any of us the centre of the universe. Man is no longer a

" special " creation.   These new conceptions and many
others like them are in themselves of stupendous import,
but something even more profound than the most far-
reaching changes in particular conceptions has taken
place.   The " scientific attitude " has become a dominating factor in all our thought.   In our pursuit of
religious truth as well as in our study of Botany and
Physics we are no longer content to accept without
question.   We ask for fact and experimental proof in
this sphere of interest as insistently and as sceptically
as we ask for it in that of Geology or Astronomy.   As
a consequence, many of the " facts " upon which our
ancestors thought their faith was built have been questioned and, for most of us, swept away.   In particular,
historical criticism and the study of comparative religion,
the work of unprejudiced scholarship upon text and
source, the wide publication and popularization of the
results of research, have united with other causes to
create an atmosphere for our familiar breathing that
would have choked and stifled our great-grandparents.
Working hypothesis has taken the place of infallible
certainty.   Authoritative dogmatism condemns itself to
our thinking as surely in the realm of religious statement
as it does in that of Medicine or Psychology.   We
respect and allow for error, believe in change and
growth, no less in the utterances of the inspired prophet
than in the theories of the scientist.

What is the effect of all this upon the character of
our twentieth-century Christianity ?   Of that there may
be many estimates, from the more conservative view
that the orthodox positions have been unmoved, and
all that has happened or is needed is a resetting, a re-
statement, of ultimate truths that remain the same
yesterday, to-day and for ever, to the more revolutionary
ones that the whole foundations of the Faith have been
shaken and require thorough renovation and repair.   I

omit still more extreme views on either side. There is, for instance, the Obscurantist who would set back the hands of time, and bitterly deplores the loss of " simple faith " and the " irreligion " of these modern days, or the uneducated Fundamentalist who gets rid of facts by ignoring them. And, on the other hand, there is the positive Materialist, who seems to have acquired nothing from the modern extension of his vision of the wonders —material and spiritual—of God's Universe beyond the amazing conclusion that there is no God. By a large and growing number of intelligent persons, sympathetic to the Christian Message, the claim would be made that the fundamental appeal of that Message has remained the same in spirit as it was for their fore-fathers, but that the expression of that spirit has been considerably altered—that the Holy Spirit, leading ever to fuller realization of truth, has given to this age revelations that previous ages were not ripe for, that the new thought has in fact modified and amplified the old, even rendered parts of it obsolete or unimportant, that there have been of late accretions to Christian Truth comparable in importance to those which added to the " simplicity " of Gospel teaching the wealth of Greek Philosophy and the Roman sense of discipline and social duty.

Again and again in the history of Christianity there has been such change and growth. New truths have been absorbed, and the Christian Faith, after a period of strain and stress, has arisen again, the same and yet not the same, for, being alive and dynamic and not a dead, static thing, it has adapted itself by God's grace to the new light it has received. Men and women are still striving for that realization of their highest and best self, which our fathers called " conversion ", that reconciliation with God known of old times as " Atone-ment ", that sense of the ineffably Holy One and that

communion of saints which were given alike by the
Sacraments of the Catholic and the Silence of the
Quaker.   And at the same time they are reaching out to
new truths (or are they but old truths newly expressed?)
shadowed forth by such words as adventure and service.
But in the new light much that once seemed essential is
assuming a secondary importance.   A theology there
must be, an intellectual explanation and theory of God
and His working in the world; but expressed in words,
and being the outcome of human thought, it must be
full of error, of symbol and reaching-out, rather than
of reality and attainment.   Creeds therefore no longer
stand where they did.   Christianity is primarily a life
or attitude towards life rather than a creed.   Churches
too, organizations for united worship based upon
common dogmatic statements of theological belief, sit
very lightly.   Some regard them as useful, others as
necessary evils rather more apt to obstruct than to help.
A very large number would repudiate any special claim
they may put forward to " divine institution ", however
much respect or even affection and loyalty may be due
to them as time-honoured organizations of human origin.

If my diagnosis of the present position at home
bears even an approximate relation to the truth, its
bearing on the Christian Task in India is obvious.   We
may approve, or we may fear or even detest, the
modern attitude, but we cannot ignore its influence
upon missionary effort.   The modern Christian layman
who has won through for himself to at least a modified
freedom from ecclesiastical shackles can have no desire
to impose them upon others.

What, then, is the present position in India?   I
cannot, I think, do better than cite the evidence of Dr.
Timothy Lew of the Yenching University, Peking.
In 1927 he was in England speaking of the Christian
Movement in China.   India is not China, but there are

many striking similarities between them, especially in
the character of the great upheavals, political, social
and religious, that have resulted from their contact with
Western life and thought. Moreover, the same missionary bodies are at work in both countries. I need therefore make no further apology for my witness. Dr. Lew
declares the Christian Movement in China to be characterized by six distinct features. I shall deal with them
seriatim, asking how far they may be applied to the work
in India, and using them as pegs on which to hang my
own observations upon the conditions of the missionary
field there. The first three characteristics may be taken
together, and, put shortly, they are: (1) *an infallible
Bible*; (2) *infallible dogmas*; (3) *deep-seated denominational divisions*.

Do these deserve the same prominence in a description of Christian India? As an observer from the outside, I should be slow to give a confident answer; but
there are signs that some of them are not altogether
absent as by-products at least of Christian work in
India. In practice, however, I believe that the teaching
given by missionaries is of just as varied a character as
that given by the clergy in England itself. On the whole,
indeed, I should say that the missionary tends to be
rather more broad-minded than the priest or minister
who stays at home, partly because it is to the more
adventurous and imaginative that the call comes, partly
because in the midst of a heathen world the necessity
of co-operation between Christian workers compels them
in pure self-defence to a wide mutual tolerance, but
most of all for a reason that I shall elaborate later, viz.
that contact with alien cultures and faiths forces any
man who is at the same time sincere and sensitive
to new and wider outlooks upon life. Among Indian
Christians indeed, and still more among the religious
members of the domiciled Anglo-Indian community,

there is a very much larger proportion of believers in literal inspiration and in the infallibility of their own little Bethels than one would find in any home congregation. This is due to the teaching their grandfathers received, combined with the absence of any systematic provision for education for these classes in those results of modern scholarship which are nowadays generally accepted even by the most conservative. Indian pastors are for the most part very poor, and consequently cannot afford an expensive library. I would suggest to missions an extended recognition by them of the need these pastors have for guidance and training.

A far more serious danger of the situation, however, lies in the spirit of partisan denominationalism that Christianity has, I will not say introduced or even consciously fostered, but been unable at any rate to check efficiently. Must religion ever be a divisive force? That seems to be the belief of many. On this very ground, for instance, the Servants of India Society, whose members are sworn to poverty and devoted, with what one can only call religious intensity, to the political and social service of their country, have deliberately excluded religion from their programme either as a purpose or as a motive. But what of the Christian household in India, the family of Him Who prayed that His followers might all be one in Him and in the Father? Long before any Westerner set foot on Indian soil, the Syrian Church was established in Travancore and Malabar. Its history is largely lost in obscurity, but by to-day, without much blame ascribable to the foreigner, it has split into half-a-dozen sects whose mutual quarrels and litigation are still a continual byword of reproach and scandal. It cannot then be said that the Westerner introduced sectarianism into India. It is part of the original sin of the Indian — indeed of every human being—till in the ideal fullness of the Christ we overcome this enemy too. Our peculiar fault is that we have added our denominations to the welter—our denominations that are so often more largely the outcome of the political and social conditions of Europe than based upon any vital, fundamental religious distinctions of world-wide significance. The fault of the Indian convert is that he has greedily swallowed our sects, and added to them his own territorial, linguistic and caste distinctions. Not content with being a follower of the Master, in Whom was neither Greek nor Jew nor barbarian, neither bond nor free, he prides himself on being a "Tinnevelly Tamil Brahman C.M.S. Church of England Christian".

Here again the wiser missionaries are out for something bigger and better than that, and there is to-day a growing tendency to co-operation and united work. In educational work this is very marked, and great Christian colleges like that of Madras, which used at one time to be Free Church only, or that of Masulipatam, which was once Church of England exclusively, have now the support in men and money of many missionary boards at home, and may be said to have lost all taint of narrow denominationalism. In evangelistic work, too, the existence of such a body as the South India United Church is itself a triumph, or perhaps, to make a more just claim—for its path is set with many snags and difficulties—an indication that the evil of division is being realized and attempts made towards a greater unity. But the problem remains. A few years ago I heard a very clear exposition by an able South Indian Christian of the evil and absurdity of the denominationalism that was being thrust upon them. In the chair was a Baptist missionary. " I thoroughly agree ", he said, " with the speaker. What we want is the simple Gospel message. Therein lies our only hope for unity—but of course ", he added with a smile, " part of that message is adult baptism." That is the trouble. As long as adult baptism, or indeed baptism in any form, or the need for Episcopal ordination or special sacramental grace, is regarded by sincere Christians as of the essence of the Christian Faith, the Christian host will remain divided. And the impatient, irreverent layman cries out, " A plague upon all your shibboleths ".

In passing to Dr. Lew's fourth feature—*that the indigenous cultural background is being ignored by Christian workers*—we come to the consideration of a very important matter of principle and policy. Jesus Himself was a Jew, and so were Peter and Paul, and it would seem impossible, therefore, to present Christianity except on the background of the Jewish history out of which it arose. Moreover, the formation of the Bible as a combination of the Jewish Scriptures with the Christian writings of the New Testament has stereotyped the position for good and ill. And perhaps there is no cause for regret in this, for the Bible is so Oriental in its thought and setting that it is by itself largely in harmony with the culture of India. Indeed it is possible that it may be more truly appreciated there than it ever has been in our Northern and Western climes. But among the more conservative Indian Christians there are movements—as, for example, that of the Christo Samaj of Madras—of protest even against so much of connection with the history of an alien people as acceptance of the Bible demands. " We want an Indian Christ ", they say, " not a Jewish." One may justly show the fanciful impracticability of such a demand, and even its origin in political rather than strictly religious aspiration, without diminishing its significance. But modern Western Christendom is not the child of the Bible alone. In addition to what it has acquired from Palestine, it has, for good and evil, absorbed into its system and life large elements from the civilizations of Greece and Rome ; and our " Protestant Christianity " has added thereto further ingredients from Teutonic and Scandinavian sources.

Two questions arise at once. First, is it our duty in presenting Christianity to India to disentangle these accretions to the Faith and give a " Bible Gospel " alone ? Secondly, is it possible for us to do so ? I think I have sufficiently indicated already that some kind of affirmative answer should, in my opinion, be given to the first question. It may be very difficult for us to agree on what is essential and what is not so in the Christian Message, but we may well agree that the Christ is something bigger and more important than the interpretation of Him that we have given in our sects, limited and exaggerated as they have been by historical, and often very doubtfully religious, considerations. But we must guard ourselves against the idea that there is some peculiar purity and value in " Primitive " Christianity. Indeed, such a view seems to me to smack of an unworthy pessimism and paganism—as if the golden age were in a dead, unrecoverable past. Surely the Christian Faith is in a Kingdom to come, a belief that in spite of, or even indeed through, our errors and failures we are by God's grace attaining. The early Christians were as capable of error as we. I need only refer, for instance, to the common belief among them—shared possibly even by Paul himself—that the end of the world was at hand, or, at a rather later time, to the exaggerated asceticism that sent so many of them to seek the Christ as hermits in the desert, rather than in the market-place, as citizens and fathers, amongst the things of their brother men. When Christ left His disciples He promised them the Holy Spirit to lead them on into fuller truth. The experience of the saints counts for much, and it is not by looking back alone that we shall learn this fuller truth. Slavery does not seem to have shocked the early Christian conscience. To-day

O

it has become intolerable.   Have we not thereby grown
in the knowledge of the Christ ?   I think, too, that we
should boldly and thankfully accept the fact that our
Western Christianity has been enriched by its absorption of beauties and truths from other sources than
the Bible.   Plato and Aristotle have been our schoolmasters as well as Peter and Paul in our struggle upward
to the Christ that is to be.   Our Faith is richer for
Roman ideals of citizenship, for Norseman courage and
sturdy independence.   We must not look then for
essential Christianity chronologically, nor in a limited
school of teachers alone.   Whatsoever things are pure
and just and right are ours.   Treasures new as well as
old are in the storehouse, and it would be the height of
folly to disown the jewels which later Christian generations have added.   Besides, it would be impossible—
which answers my second question—even if it were
desirable to attempt the task.   For better, for worse, we
are what we are, and we can only give to India all the
highest and best that we ourselves have gathered.

But if this freedom is ours, we cannot but grant a like
freedom to India.   She has her own history, her own
culture.   God has been revealing Himself to her through
the eye of prophet and saint and sage.   It is on the
foundation of her own past that her future must be
built.   This is surely the message that Dr. Stanley
Jones has given in *The Christ of the Indian Road*.   We
must preach the Christ we ourselves have apprehended,
but then we must leave Him fearlessly on the Indian
Road to find His own way into Indian hearts, and—
what is far more difficult to tolerate—allow Him to be
interpreted by strange tongues and in strange manners.
Will the Mission Movement in India be big-minded
enough to see this vision, courageous and imaginative
enough to fulfil it ?   I believe it will.   There was a time
when the missionary believed that Hinduism was entirely

of the Devil, and his function was simply to destroy and supplant it. That time has passed, and it is largely recognized to-day that as Christ was the fulfilment of the Jewish Law, so may He be of those aspirations and strivings which have hitherto found their expression in Hinduism. Such a book as Dr. Farquhar's *Crown of Hinduism* embodies this typical present-day attitude. Unfortunately we are human, and still too easily visualize Christ, if not as of the particular form of Christianity we ourselves adorn, at any rate as of some common denominator or highest factor of Western Christianity. In practice we expect the convert to renounce his own traditions and follow ours, be baptized, call himself John or Moses, join a Western Church, and adopt the customs and the costumes of the West. The result is that Indian Christianity is imitative rather than original, not an expression of the highest and deepest experience of the Indian's own life so much as a reflection or shadow of the experience of others. At its worst his model is not the Christ at all, but the Englishman. With many notable exceptions, the Indian Christian, therefore, is far too often a camp-follower rather than a soldier in the Christian host.

But I believe the Missionary Movement to-day is advancing to a third stage. It is beginning to understand that it goes to India not merely to give but to receive, to learn as well as to teach. Christianity may be the crown of Hinduism, but it is also not too ridiculous a statement to make that Hinduism is the crown of Christianity. To elaborate this point one would need a whole book. I can merely throw out a hint or two of its significance. In the first place, it means at least this, that there are elements in Indian culture—in the vast background of her indigenous religious experience —which must find a place in any living expression of Indian Christianity. It means further—unless we

believe that the Thirty-nine Articles or the Shorter
Catechism is the last word of God's Spirit—that in the
building up of the Christ Universal that is to be, Indian
thought and tradition, freed from the incubus of a slave
mentality, has a contribution to make of unique and
vital value.   The psychological effect of this recognition
will be incalculable   No longer a slavish copyist, but
an independent self-respecting co-worker in the establishment of the Kingdom, the Indian will bring his own
treasures—not merely those he has borrowed from the
Englishman's storehouse—to the feet of the Master.
Mr. Gandhi, with his deep reverence for Christ and his
consistent application of His ethical teaching to his own
life, has refused to give up his Hindu tradition or be
baptized.   Many Christian people will understand and
sympathize with him in this, while some of us may even
welcome the challenge his life offers to " our " Christianity, for it compels us to a heart-searching inquiry as
to what is the essential core of the Christian Message.

The fifth feature under Dr. Lew's analysis is *the
special Government protection that surrounds Christianity*.   This is without doubt a very important matter
for consideration, but, as it is related more to political
than to religious issues I shall only make very few
remarks upon it.   I think there can be no doubt that
Christianity, the religion of service rather than of
mastery, has suffered grievously in India from the strange
irony of being the religion of the ruling caste.   For
thus, unfortunately, it has become identified by association throughout the East with Imperialism, a term of
opprobrium applied by the Oriental struggling for free
self-expression to that spirit of domination and repres-
sion in the spheres of politics and economics that he
regards as his deadliest enemy.   It is this misunderstand-
ing which has created the bitter hostility to Christianity
which marks some of the political movements in China.

If India has on the whole been more fortunate in this respect, the danger still exists and needs constant wary walking.

The sixth and last feature that Dr. Lew draws attention to he rather curiously describes as *Involuntary Humanism*, meaning thereby the human service for social betterment rendered by the Christian missionary. The titles of the various chapters of this book are significant of the important place such " humanism " occupies in India and in the minds and hearts of Christian workers there. Dr. Lew seems to have used the epithet " involuntary " because he had some doubt whether missionaries intended—originally at least—this application of the Gospel of Love to human redemption in this world. We need not debate the point. To the modern Christian at any rate service lies at the very heart of the Gospel Message. A clear-cut theology may or may not be a necessity. But we have New Testament authority and the experience of the Christian centuries to assure us that love of one's fellowmen is not an accidental concomitant, but an inevitable inference from, and consequence of, the Christian Faith. One can never indeed disentangle body from spirit, life from one's theory of life, but more and more clearly one realizes that spirit is so much more important than body, life than creed, that many would accept the proposition that, if you look after the Christian life of service, you may leave theology to look after itself. Not he who says "Lord, Lord", but he who does the will of the Father, shall convince himself and the world of that Father's Love. If so, will it not become more and more the business of the missionary not to make " converts ", but to extend the Kingdom of Christ, to exalt the life of service and love, to inspire men by precept and example with the sure and certain faith that God is Love, " visiting the widows and the fatherless ",

" going about doing good " ?   It is a hard saying, but perhaps our missionaries would be twice as valuable, twice as effective, as heralds of the Christ that is to be, if they could completely forget they were " Christians ", with all the political and sectarian associations of that word, and become in name just the brothers that in fact so many of them in practice are to Hindu, Moslem and Christian alike.

So far I have attempted two things: first, to describe the attitude of the modern Christian, and, second, to give some indication of the reactions such an attitude must have upon the problems of the Mission Field.   The reader may repudiate my diagnosis entirely.   He may think I have grossly exaggerated the character and tendency of the revolt against definite, systematic Christianity with its creeds, its Churches, its forms and orders.   Or, admitting the substantial accuracy of my picture, he may deplore as degeneracy changes which I regard as triumphant fruits of the working of the Spirit of God.   On one thing, at any rate, we may agree—that in so far as Christianity is an inspiration for conduct, the responsibility of the layman is no less than that of the cleric.   It seems to me, indeed, that from my point of view a clearer vision of the layman's contribution to the Christian task in India becomes possible. In the past his function was the vague and negative one of not discrediting by his life and conduct the religion to which he was presumed to belong.   As long as the task was regarded as primarily one of theological propaganda, he was not expected to take any active part in it.   It was not indeed his job; he had no training for it; and rules, express if he was a Government servant, implied if he was in business, prohibited any such attempt. But if Christianity is a positive life to be lived, the Christian layman is called upon to live it in his occupation, whatever it may be, as surely as the missionary with his specialized work in the school or the hospital or on schemes of social, economic or intellectual development and reconstruction.

But there is a further and more urgent call. Hitherto in general the layman in India has fought shy of missionary circles or of any close association with missionary work. If my review of the position is true, not only has he no excuse for aloofness, but it is his bounden duty to take a part in the common endeavour, not necessarily or indeed as a rule by identifying himself with any missionary body or policy, but by giving of himself, his leisure and his mind and heart to a deep personal understanding of the peoples among whom he lives. That differences of manners, of customs and of tradition, trivial to a broad outlook, but strengthened by very real psychological distinctions of an emotional and mental character, do create barriers between East and West is a fact almost too patent to need mention. The political, social and economic problems of the day, with their clash of conflicting interests, the passions they raise, the dust and heat of controversy, serve to estrange still further from each other men of differing types of civilization and cultural background. The whole conditions of the European's life in India tend to place him in a rigorously exclusive caste. Till recently he was the " ruler " ; the Indian was the " ruled ". And though —formally and outwardly at least—that is all being rapidly changed, the spirit of domination remains, and with it the fact that out of all numerical proportion the positions of vantage and responsibility in Government service and business alike are in his keeping. What I may, for want of a better expression, call the club-habit accentuates the evil tendency to separateness. It is natural that birds of a feather should flock together, and that the Englishman should spend his leisure hours entirely at his club in the company of his own kind; natural

too, perhaps, and understandable that it should be a
primary rule of his club that no Indian should become a
member. But the results seem to me deplorable. It may
be an unjust estimate of the position, but I believe it to
be true, that many of the men who spend forty years of
their lives in India never for a moment come into contact
with the soul of its peoples, or learn by personal sympathetic insight anything of its eager, passionate life.

I do not think there is any substantial justification
for complaint against the personal, individual morality
of the average British layman in India. There is indeed
a freedom from many of the restraints of life at home
that leads some, no doubt, to excesses from which they
might have escaped had they stayed in England. But
on the whole the sense of *noblesse oblige* that arises from
a position of responsibility in the midst of an alien people
tends to inspire a peculiarly keen recognition of personal
honour and social duty. The Briton has, in fact, a well-
deserved reputation not merely for efficiency in his work,
but also for cleanness of living and straightforward
honesty of word and purpose and action. Moreover, he
takes a notable part in all those movements that may be
included in the generic term of " social work ". But
" good works " are not Christianity. Though I bestow
all my goods to feed the poor, and have not that
virtue whose characteristics even Paul could do no more
than hint at, it profiteth nothing. Heaven preserve us
from sickly sentimentality, and from that indiscriminate
—I would almost say dishonest—incapacity for facing
facts, that says one man is as good as another. There is
a tremendous variety of gifts and of the lack of them.
Many are the qualities, characters, manners, capacities,
cultures of mankind, and it is not required of the
" Christian " that he should lump all men together as
physical, intellectual or moral equals, or even abjure
all personal affinities, attractions, predilections. But, if

there is any meaning in the Christ in Whom there is neither Greek nor Barbarian, bond nor free, Jew nor Gentile, we must as Christians, without ignoring, transcend our distinctions by a humble recognition of our own limitations and imperfections, and a faith in the infinite possibilities of the Divine sonship not only for ourselves and our friends, but for all men. The Briton in India—God forgive me for anything harsh and pharisaical in my judgement—seems to me a Briton first and foremost, and only a long way after a man and a brother.

Throughout this chapter I have been critical and fault-finding. I would end it by a prayer that my reader may have the grace to see the constructive purpose behind my carpings. Christ is bigger than any or all of our systems and creeds and respectable conventions and manners. " The Christian Task in India " is the bringing of the people of India—the British sojourner no less than the native Indian—into the Fellowship of the Kingdom of God. The first business of each one— missionary and layman alike—is to make clear his own vision as to the nature of that Kingdom—and then by God's grace to fulfil it.

CHAPTER XII

INDIGENOUS CHRISTIAN EFFORTS

By P. Oomman Philip

ORGANIZED Christian missions have been carrying on their operations in India for only a little over one hundred and fifty years. It is, therefore, vain to expect to find in this land any indigenous Christian efforts in the sense of movements that have sprung up originally on Indian soil. There are, however, Christian activities noticeable in different parts of the country, some of them local, some country-wide, which, though they may have at first come into existence under the stimulus and inspiration of the Western missionary movement, have been made, in more senses than one, their own by Christian Indians, and which depend for their existence and growth on the care and support they are prepared to extend to them. The oldest of these ventures does not perhaps go back beyond forty years, and the youngest may be only a few years old. Their significance, however, is far beyond what may be indicated by the years they have been in existence. First of all these efforts are an expression of the spirit of Christian service which is taking hold of the Church in India. Secondly, they stand for a legitimate desire to render this Christian service untrammelled by the limitations involved in taking financial help from Western churches. Thirdly, they represent a venture, much needed in India at the present day, for discovering ideals and methods of Christian work that would be suitable to the peculiar conditions of the land.

As indicated already, these efforts have been stimulated to a large extent by Western missions. Individual Western missionaries had often a great deal to do in initiating even the most outstanding of these. This is only in accordance with the declared object of Western missions of establishing the Christian Church in the lands to which they are sent, and then laying upon this Church the responsibility of completing the work missions began. The fact that Westerners had a share in initiating such efforts need not discount their indigenous character. The important point to be considered is how far the Indian Christians associated with these efforts have been making them really their own. In this connection it is useful to recall how the great political institution of India, the National Congress, owed its origin to ideas first put forward by one or two British friends of India, and followed up by faithful, steady help to the Indians who took up these ideas. The subsequent history of the Congress shows that this help received from foreign friends at the time of its initiation has not stood in the way of its development as an organization of great national importance, through which the political aspirations of the people of India find effective expression. It has been more or less so in the case of indigenous Christian efforts in India. The inspiration for such efforts, and in some cases the very initiative for them, might have proceeded from Christian men of vision who came to India from the West. Whether most of these ventures have been later made their own, and developed by Indian Christians in an atmosphere of freedom, is the important question we have to ask.

Understanding indigenous Christian efforts in the

sense indicated above, we may proceed to consider the nature and extent of their operations. They fall into three main divisions : (1) missionary efforts for evangelizing some of the regions of India not touched by foreign missions ; (2) educational ventures ; and (3) movements which seek to influence students in colleges, and to mould the thought of Indian Christians as a whole.

(1) The most noteworthy missionary effort under the first head is what is known as the National Missionary Society of India. This society was organized twenty-three years ago with the object of " evangelizing the unoccupied parts of India and adjacent countries ", and of " laying upon Indian Christians the burden of the responsibility of evangelizing India ". A study of the Census Report of India for 1901, undertaken by a group of Indian Christian young men soon after its publication, revealed the fact that in spite of the work carried on by scores of missionary societies from the West for the past one hundred and fifty years, more than one-third of the people of India had, humanly speaking, no chance of hearing the message of the Gospel in their lifetime. It was realized that for this work of making the Gospel known in these regions, entirely unreached or unreachable by foreign missions, the Christian Church already in existence in India should be turned to for help. At the same time the fact that Indian Christians were divided into several denominations was considered as an obstacle in the way of their joining forces to undertake the work. However, after some preliminary conferences, in which some prominent missionaries took an important part, and after wide consultation with foreign missionaries at work in India, the society was formally organized on Christmas Day, 1905, at Serampore, a place hallowed by the labours of pioneer missionaries like William Carey and Henry Martyn. Though Indian Christians generally do not

attach much value to the denominational differences
that have come to them from the West, it was significant
that when the National Missionary Society was organized, it was done not on an undenominational basis but
recognizing the denominations that existed in India.
This was perhaps due to the fact that attempts made in
the past by certain ardent Indian Christians, notably
Kali Charan Banurji in Bengal and Dr. Palney Andy
in Madras, in the direction of doing away with denominations, far from achieving their purpose, only tended
to add to the number of the existing denominations. In
view of such experience, the organizers of the National
Missionary Society were wise in making it an interdenominational effort, in which Indian Christians of
different communions could actively participate without
compromising in any way their denominational loyalties.

The Society came into existence at a time when
a great awakening of the national consciousness was
taking place in India. The Indian Christians, by their
associations and training generally indifferent to movements which had a political complexion, were at first
inclined to stand aloof from the rest of the country when
the national movement swept over it. But a movement
like the National Missionary Society aiming at the
evangelization of India " with Indian men, Indian
money and under Indian direction " helped the Indian
Christian community to discern the spiritual elements
in the national movement, and to realize the contribution
they as Indian disciples of Christ could make towards
its enrichment. The highest service that Indian Christians could render to their country was conceived, and
rightly conceived, as sharing with their countrymen
the unique knowledge and experience of God derived
from Jesus Christ. The National Missionary Society
was also fortunate in its first organizers. Mr. V. S.
Azariah (now Bishop Azariah) and Mr. K. T. Paul were

among those who first carried the appeal of the Society throughout the length and breadth of the country, and from a thousand platforms and pulpits they made Indian Christians of all churches and Provinces realize the importance and privilege of the task to which they were summoned.   The enthusiasm aroused and the idealism stirred up were promptly organized and directed along channels of definite Christian work in some of the neglected parts of India.   In this way the Society was led within a few years' time to start work in " un-occupied " districts situated in the Provinces of the Punjab, the United Provinces and Madras.   In later years work was started in other places as well, and the Society has now eight centres of work in different parts of the country.

It has already been mentioned that the Society is an interdenominational effort.   Paradoxical as it may seem, this interdenominational co-operation has been possible only by maintaining strict denominationalism in the different fields of the Society.   That is to say, while the income of the Society comes from Indian Christians of all churches into a common treasury and is administered by committees drawn from members of all churches, these committees also settling questions of general policy, members belonging only to one denomi-nation are sent to a particular field as workers.   The ordination of workers and other ecclesiastical matters are regulated by the ecclesiastical authority of the denomination concerned nearest to the field.   In this manner the work of the Society in the different fields is related ecclesiastically to the following communions : the Anglican Church, the United Church of Northern India, the Lutheran Church, the Mar Thoma Syrian Church and the South India United Church.   Under this arrangement the Bishops or the Church Councils, as the case may be, of these bodies co-operate with the interdenominational committees of the Society. But in the matter of the appointment of workers, the supplying of the funds needed for the work and the general direction of the work, the National Missionary Society as such is solely responsible.

From its very beginning the Society attracted to its service some of the best of educated Indian Christians. It required a great deal of faith and courage on the part of these men to throw in their lot with the Society at a time when there was nothing stable about it. Though the Society has somehow not been able to retain all the men who heard the call and enlisted themselves as its workers, it should be admitted that it has done invaluable service in holding aloft among Indian Christian youths the high ideals of Christian service.

One of the principles of the National Missionary Society, from which it has not swerved, has been that no financial help be solicited from foreign countries. There was considerable misgiving in the early years as to whether Indian Christians would be able or willing to contribute the money needed for its work. In the year 1906, the first year of the work of the Society, the income from voluntary contributions was only a little over Rs. 2000. There has, however, been a steady rise in the income from year to year and now the average annual income of the Society from voluntary contributions is about Rs. 60,000. This is a small amount when compared with the incomes of some of the Western missionary societies. But when we consider that Indian Christians are generally on a lower economic level than their non-Christian countrymen [1] and that various and insistent demands are made on their generosity by their own churches and missions, this is very encouraging.

---

[1] The average income per head of the Indian population even on the most generous estimate of Anglo-Indian economists is only Rs.116 or about £9 per year. For another estimate, see p. 127, note.

A significant feature of these contributions is that the bulk of these is made up of small subscriptions offered with faithful regularity by the middle class and the poor. Behind these gifts of money there is a great deal of genuine prayerful interest. In comparison with the vast activities of foreign missions in India, the work done by the National Missionary Society in all its eight districts taken together is insignificant. In the number of workers, in the range of activities, in the institutions established and maintained, and also in the number of those admitted into the Christian Church, even some of the smaller and more recently established foreign missions may have far greater results to show than this Society. But the uniqueness of its work consists in the fact that it is being carried on as a purely Indian effort. Indian Christians increasingly support the work not because it is extensive and shows striking results, but because they feel that it is something which in spite of all its limitations they can really consider their own. A sure indication that Indian Christians are really making this effort their own is that it has been slowly evolving methods of Christian work suited to the conditions of this land. The results achieved in this respect may appear as negligible to those who expect indigenous Christian efforts to revolutionize missionary methods in a day. For one thing, Indian methods are not something that can be produced to order. If they are to be worth anything in the economy of God's Kingdom they are to grow out of the experience of those Christ-possessed men, who, being familiar with all that is best in Indian life and thought, bring to bear on it the values and standards of Jesus Christ. This is necessarily a slow process. Secondly, the atmosphere favourable for the development of such methods is lamentably lacking among Indian Christians, the large majority of whom have derived their training and outlook on these matters from Western missionaries, and as such, look with anything but favour on any departure from methods with which they have been made familiar. In spite of these disadvantages the National Missionary Society has been tackling this problem, and the Ashram method of Christian life and service which has been adopted with such remarkable success in Tirupattur, its South Indian field, may be cited as an illustration of the discovery and application of methods best suited to Indian conditions.

Organized on strictly denominational lines and depending for their support on groups of people belonging to a particular communion, there are several indigenous missionary societies which are called " Home Missions ". They seek to carry out in a restricted sphere the aims of the National Missionary Society. A number of the organized Church bodies in India prefer to give expression to their missionary spirit through these Home Missions of their own to co-operating with an all-India organization like the National Missionary Society. It should, however, be mentioned that there are at least three Church bodies in South India, which, while maintaining their Home Missions take also an active share through the National Missionary Society in the evangelization of some part of India far away from their own region. A few of these Home Missions have been in existence since before the National Missionary Society was started, but a good number of them were organized after it, perhaps stimulated by its example. All of them claim to be indigenous efforts depending for support on the contributions of Indian Christians belonging to the denominations concerned, and with the management and direction of policy entirely in the hands of Indians. How far these conditions are actually realized depends upon the extent to which the denominations at the back of these Home Missions are free from the tutelage of foreign missionaries Some of these

P

efforts merely consist in a Presbytery or Church Council maintaining an evangelist to preach the Gospel in some place within its area.   On the other hand, some of them carry on well-planned work among non-Christians, involving the employment of high-grade workers and a considerable annual budget.   The Ludhiana Church Council, for instance, has been carrying on steady work in the Karnal District of the Punjab for the last thirty years, and its present annual budget is over Rs. 3000, raised entirely from the congregations connected with the Church Council.   In the South, where there are larger numbers of Christians than in any other part of India, we find a number of such efforts.   The two most noteworthy of these are the Indian Missionary Society of Tinnevelly, connected with the Anglican Church, and the Mar Thoma Syrian Christian Evangelistic Association.   The Tinnevelly Society was started twenty-four years ago with the main object of evangelizing some parts of the Hyderabad State where no Christian agencies were at work.   Out of the work of this Society has grown the well-known Dornakal Mission of which the Bishop of Dornakal is the head.   He first went to Dornakal as a missionary to the Telugus of that area, sent by the Tamil Anglican Church of Tinnevelly.   The Indian Missionary Society of Tinnevelly has an annual income of over Rs. 20,000 contributed by the Indian Christians of Tinnevelly and other Tamil Dioceses of the Church of England, and it is the " home base " of the Dornakal Mission.   The Mar Thoma Syrian Christian Evangelistic Association is the missionary society of the Mar Thoma Syrian Church, one of the branches of the old Syrian Church on the west coast of South India.   This Association represents the first missionary effort organized on modern lines in the long and chequered history of this ancient community of Indian Christians.   Started forty years ago on a very small scale for the purpose of evangelizing their non-Christian neighbours, it has now grown into an efficient Christian agency carrying on extensive work among the depressed classes, and maintaining a large number of educational and other institutions both for Christians and non-Christians.   It also co-operates with the National Missionary Society of India by undertaking to send the men and money needed for its work in the North Kanara District of the Bombay Presidency.   The average annual income of this Association from voluntary contributions is about Rs. 25,000.   The Church which is behind this missionary organization, it should be remembered, is itself an indigenous one, with its own Indian bishops and depending entirely on its own resources for the support of its bishops, clergy, churches and institutions.

Before proceeding to consider the other types of indigenous Christian efforts, it may be helpful to try to appraise the value of the various Indian missionary ventures briefly described above, and indicate the lines along which they may be strengthened.

All these missionary efforts of the Indian Church have come into existence as the result of a realization of the immensity of the task of making Christ known to the people of India, of the utter inadequacy of the work so far done by missions from the West, great though that work has been, and also of the responsibility that is upon Indian Christians for evangelizing their own country.   Men of faith and vision in the Indian Church saw the work waiting to be done and they sounded forth the call to service.   The response of the Church is what we find in some measure in these indigenous missionary societies.   They have served as channels for giving expression to the missionary spirit of the young and growing churches.   Through them a large number of Indian Christians are led to think of others and of their needs and give out of their best for them.   In the process they have gained inward spiritual strength and been helped to measure up to the ideals of Jesus Christ. We have to make thankful acknowledgment of all these. And yet it is impossible to ignore the fact that the movement represented by their activities is still feeble and needs considerable reinforcement. What, then, may be the elements of weakness that prevent these efforts from fulfilling their highest purpose ?

When the missionary interest of any body of people is organized along certain definite channels of service they are bound to share the limitations and weaknesses of that body. If the spiritual life of the community behind a missionary movement is at a low level, it is naturally reflected in the movement itself. So also the dominant ideas and ideals of the community influence the movement for good or evil as the case may be. The Indian Christian community has inherited from the non-Christian communities to which they originally belonged, has learned from Western missionaries and has also acquired by imitation and assimilation several characteristics, good, bad and indifferent. One should not be surprised if these characteristics give colour in one form or other to movements which have their origin among Indian Christians.

The apprehension of the missionary task is in need of adjustment and expansion, so that it may appeal to the highest among Indian Christians. Evangelization has been understood more in terms of the preaching of the Gospel, with the definite object of enlisting as many baptized adherents as possible in the Christian Church, than in terms of permeating the life of the country with the spirit of Christ. The emphasis has been on individual conversions to the great neglect of the equally important task of bringing to bear on social, communal and national life the principles of Christ. The Indian Christian community as a whole still clings to the belief in which it has been nurtured by the foreign missionaries of an earlier generation, that matters like the social reform, the economic improvement and the civic and political education of our neighbours have to be left severely alone by Christian workers.   The result is that what happened to the churches in the West is happening to the churches in India also.   While they compass sea and land for a proselyte, the open sores of social, economic and other evils are left unattended by the churches, as matters which are of no concern to them. In India also the Churches through their missionary organizations go in search of " unoccupied " fields for evangelization, ignoring the fact that there are large areas in their own social, communal and economic life which are not yet " occupied " and Christianized.   No serious attempts are made to grapple in the spirit of Christ with evils like caste, class and race prejudice, worldliness, the exploitation of the weak by the strong, and other evils existing within the Christian community itself.   There is an element of unreality in all this, which wideawake sincere disciples of Christ cannot help taking note of.   The younger generation of educated Indian Christians with vision and insight are already beginning to react to the situation.   The future of Indian missionary efforts looks gloomy if, along with the preaching of the religion of Christ to non-Christians, earnest efforts are not also made to relate that religion in a vital manner to all conditions of life, whether within the Christian community or without it.   This alone will make high acts of heroism for the Christian cause supremely worth while for the best Indian Christian men and women.

Indian Christians have imbibed from the religious atmosphere with which they are surrounded a great deal of the belief that matter is essentially evil, and, as a result of that, the most spiritually minded among them have a tendency to despise all material aids in the carrying on of religious work. Their ideal of a Christian worker is a wandering *sannyasin* who is a celibate, who owns nothing in this world, and who throws himself on the charity of others. They cannot quite reconcile themselves to the idea that a Christian worker should be given an allowance to keep him above need and to enable him to carry on the work without any anxiety about the support of his family. Though the exigencies of church life and religious work under modern conditions are making Indian Christians accustomed to the salary system for Christian workers, and other business-like arrangements for carrying on religious work, there is, deep down in the minds of many good Indian Christians, a lurking fear that all this is something un-Christian and unspiritual. There is a similar attitude towards organizations also. It is to be remembered that the National Missionary Society and other Indian missionary societies have to find support and make progress among people who have such a mental and spiritual background. Perhaps this may be a reaction against the over-organization which so often characterizes Christianity in India. The point to be noted is that very little attention is being given to the study of this attitude, which is fairly widespread among Indian Christians, with a view to reconciling it with the highest teachings of Jesus Christ, and of applying the results of such study to the work of evangelization which the Church in India is facing.

(2) Under the second class of indigenous Christian efforts come some striking ventures in Christian education, initiated and carried on by Indian Christians. Within the last few years the conviction has been growing among thinking Indian Christians that for the building up of the Church in India there is nothing which is more important than institutions where

education can be imparted to Indian youths in an atmosphere of Christian fellowship, conserving and cultivating at the same time all that is of value in Indian culture and life. Residential institutions where the teachers and the taught can live together and share experience and knowledge were needed for realizing this ideal, and it was felt that these institutions could really fulfil their purpose only if they were staffed and managed by Indians. It was remarkable that almost in the same year two groups of educated Indian Christians set themselves independently to work out this ideal in two different centres in South India. The aim of the one group was to establish a Christian Residential High School for the Tamil country, and that of the other, a Christian Residential College for the Malayalam country, where the large community of Syrian Christians live. The Residential High School venture had unfortunately to be abandoned after the group of men behind it had, against tremendous financial odds, bravely kept it up for some years. The lack of adequate financial response from the Indian Christians of the Tamil Districts was the chief reason for the failure of this noble venture. But the faith and heroic self-sacrifice of the young men who were associated with this effort will not soon be forgotten in South India.

Happily, the venture of the other group, the Union Christian College at Alwaye, Travancore, has been a great success. This group consists of a few distinguished graduates of the Madras University, most of them former students of the Madras Christian College. They are members of the different sections of the Syrian Church, and the great hope that they have is that the young men of the Syrian Churches passing through the College in the formative periods of their lives may be helped to catch something of the spirit of Jesus Christ, and to go out into the world with a character fashioned after His. Started in the year 1921 with 64 students as an Intermediate College, it was soon raised to a First Grade College, preparing students up to the B.A. degree examination of the Madras University. It has now an average total enrolment of over 200 students, a large majority of whom are Christians. The residential character of the College is maintained, the students and the professors living in the College, as is rarely done in India. The College is under the management of a Council on which representation is given to the different sections of the Syrian Church. About Rs. 200,000 has been raised by the Council for buildings and equipment, among the contributors being several well-known non-Christian Indians. The recurring expenses are met from fees and grants from the Government of Travancore. While the College maintains an Indian atmosphere, and the direction of the whole enterprise is in the hands of Indians, and the Principal is an Indian Christian, there is provision on the staff for any European or American educationalist who feels he can throw in his lot with the group which forms the staff of the College. There have been Europeans working as professors of the College on this basis and in the most cordial spirit of brotherhood and equality.

Inspired by the example of the Union Christian College, a Residential High School for Girls under the name Christava Mahilalaya embodying most of the ideals of the College, was started last year at Alwaye. A group of Syrian Christian men and women are behind this enterprise also, and there is every prospect of its becoming a success and fulfilling a great need in that part of the country.

To meet the educational and economic needs of a group of villages around Hadapsar, a village near Poona, and to present Christianity to the inhabitants

of this rural area, an Indian Christian, who is the
Government Advocate of Poona, has been on his own
initiative carrying on a notable piece of work since
1913. The work, which is among middle-class Hindus,
who are agriculturists, centres round a well-equipped
middle school with auxiliary institutions like a dispensary and a library. There is also a place of worship.
Improved methods of agriculture, the co-operative
credit movement, adult education and temperance are
promoted among the villagers. And through all this
service there is the presentation of the message of
Christianity, which is beginning to make a deep impression on the people. With a view to increase the
accommodation now available in the school, and to
improve the possibilities of the whole work, buildings
are now being erected at a total estimated cost of
Rs. 1,60,000. A good proportion of this amount has
already been raised, and a remarkable fact in this connection is that the bulk of it has been contributed by
non-Christians. This shows that non-Christians are
not unwilling to help forward Christian work when they
know that such work is to result in real good to their
countrymen.

(3) We have now to consider the third class of
indigenous efforts, which seek to influence Christian
students in universities and shape the thought of Indian
Christians. The Student Christian Association of India,
though working on the lines of the Christian Student
Movements of other countries and in affiliation with the
World Student Christian Federation, is indigenous in
the sense that it has Indian personnel, and that the
funds needed for its work are raised in India. Through
Student Camps, through the promotion of Bible Study,
through literature and through the visits of the secretaries of the movement, Christian students in the
colleges scattered in all parts of the country are linked

together and helped in various ways. The annual budget of this Association is about Rs. 12,000, the whole of which is raised in India.

There has been in existence in Madras for some years a body known as the Christo Samaj, which is somewhat nebulous in its organization and intermittent in its activities, but which exercises a great deal of influence on the thought of the younger generation of Christians. It consists of a group of educated Indian Christians, some of them converts from Hinduism, who think boldly and independently on questions affecting the faith and practice of the Christian Church. They are nationalist in their outlook, and seek to interpret in terms of Indian thought the varieties of Christian experience. They have also been subjecting missionary methods and policies to careful examination from the Indian point of view and publishing the results of their study in booklets. The Christo Samaj group made its influence felt most when, as a group, it conducted the *Christian Patriot* of Madras. This paper has now changed hands, and consequently the fresh and thought-provoking discussions of this group on questions affecting Christian thought and Christian movement in India do not get the publicity they deserve. Whatever may be the present condition of the Christo Samaj, those who have been in any way associated with it will admit that it has done a great deal for promoting independent thinking among Indian Christians, and helped them in some measure to understand in their Indian setting the eternal verities of Christ and His religion.

The Christian efforts briefly described above, because of the fact that they are of India and have grown out of the felt needs of the country, have an important place in the work of the Christian Movement. In the volume and extent of the work, they will not be able for years to come to approach anywhere near the highly organized missionary efforts which the Western Churches are carrying on in India.   Nor is it desirable that they should aim at approximating to the standards of efficiency and organization developed in the West.   The economic resources of Indian Christians, not to speak of cultural and other considerations, will make it impossible for them to travel along the same road as the foreign missions. But these Indian efforts, it should not be forgotten, are the growth of only the last forty years among a community of Christians of a little over two millions, divided into several denominations and scattered in various provinces, the large majority of whom are economically on or below the poverty line and still struggling to find their feet amidst the conflicts of culture and opposing loyalties which they have to face, both in their Church and civic life.   As such, they demand careful and sympathetic study by all those who are interested in the progress of the Christian Movement in India.

CHAPTER XIII

CO-OPERATION

By William Paton

ANOTHER essay in this book deals with the subject of the unity of the Christian Church in India. The present writer must preface his treatment of the subject of Christian co-operation in India by the confession of his faith that, even more than the co-operation of separated Christian bodies, India wants the unity of the Church of Christ. Some have been found to argue against organized co-operation on the ground that it tends to weaken men's sense of the pain and evil of disunion. This attitude seems to be somewhat wrong-headed, but it is nevertheless true that practical co-operation up to the limited extent which disunion allows is only a poor substitute for the power and glory of the united Church.

The case for missionary and Christian co-operation in India, or indeed anywhere else, is therefore to be based on the fact that Christian unity in life and practice is necessary to the worthy presentation of the Gospel, and that, the Church of Christ being divided, co-operation between the separated parts in some measure averts the evils of disunion, and in some measure brings the blessings of union. One of the most important though least noticed aspects of the recent Conference on Faith and Order, held at Lausanne, was the prominence which some at least of the delegates saw to be lent to

movements for practical co-operation by the undoubted
failure of the Churches represented at Lausanne to make
any appreciable progress on the road towards organic
union.   The Stockholm Conference of the Churches on
Life and Work has probably benefited by the comparative failure of Lausanne.   Serious men and women who
realize the desperate need of the world for the Christian
way are bound more and more to turn to practical
methods of achieving something in common, if, as
appears to be the case, the goal of full unity is regarded
as remote. Similarly the International Missionary
Council, which is probably the most continuously effective piece of international Christian co-operation at
present existing in the world, must to thoughtful men
acquire an enlarged importance for the same reason.
What is true on the most general view is equally true
of India or any other country.   India has given rise to
what is probably the most important, far-reaching and
carefully considered proposal for organic unity that any
part of the world has seen, with the possible exception
of Canada and China.   But even in India the goal of
organic unity is remote, and the task of achieving
common prayer, thought and action among separated
bodies over as large an area of life as possible is therefore
the more insistent.

We may here refer to the impatience manifested by
many good men regarding the multiplication of conferences, which is alleged to be the chief symptom of the
co-operative missionary movement. These complaints
are not always serious, nor do they always come from
those who have from experience the best right to speak.
Let it be acknowledged, however, that there is a certain
inevitable cumbrousness in the process of achieving co-
operation—it cannot be avoided.   If there are separated
Christian bodies preserving their own sovereign independence, but desiring, nevertheless, to mitigate the

evils of disunion by co-operating as far as possible, it
cannot be denied that from time to time, in one kind of
gathering or another, their representatives must meet.
Christian work of every kind depends upon the contact
of personalities, and there can be no profounder mistake
than to imagine that co-operation can ever be effective
through the issuing of memoranda, through correspondence, or through anything short of personal meeting
between the individuals concerned with the common
tasks in question.   One may, therefore, justly admit that
there is much cumbrousness and much occupation of
time involved in making co-operation real, but the inference to be drawn from this is not that co-operation is a
waste of time.   The true inference is that this cumbrousness should be regarded as part of the price we pay for
disunion, and the acceptance of it a warrant of our
sincerity in trying, in spite of everything, to achieve
unity of prayer and work.   People who sneer at " the
conference trick " ought to be told plainly that they are
sneering at one of the major manifestations in our time
of the real passion for unity.

Co-operation in India has in one form or another
been found ever since the development of the modern
missionary movement.   The Calcutta Missionary Conference was founded under the influence of Alexander
Duff, and in all the larger missionary centres of India
there have been established missionary conferences,
some of them of respectable antiquity.   They have in
all cases been confined in the main to periodical meetings,
at which opportunities for prayer and for social intercourse were provided, and papers read on subjects of
general interest.   In some cases the oversight of definite
pieces of co-operation, usually of a local, and often of a
temporary character, has been undertaken by these
conferences, but in the main their function has been to
promote in an informal way friendly contact between

those engaged in the work of Christian missions. Of a
wider range, and perhaps of more significance, was the
South India Missionary Association, wound up not long
ago, which for a number of years maintained in Southern
India a considerable degree of fellowship among missionaries of all denominations, and was undoubtedly the
progenitor of that spirit of co-operation for which South
Indian missions have been so honourably distinguished.

The development of organized co-operation dates
from the winter of 1912-1913, when Dr. John R. Mott,
as chairman of the Continuation Committee of the
World Missionary Conference, held in Edinburgh, 1910,
visited India. He held conferences in each of the major
provincial areas of India, concluding with an All-India
Conference held at Calcutta. Out of this gathering
emerged a complete organization for the promotion of
missionary co-operation throughout India, Burma and
Ceylon. In each province of India (and in Burma and
Ceylon) there was organized a representative Council of
Missions. Each Council was representative of all, or
nearly all, the missions working within its area, representation being roughly in proportion to the size of the
work carried on by each body. For India, Burma and
Ceylon as a whole there was organized the National
Missionary Council, composed of three delegates from
each provincial council, together with a number of co-
opted members.

These councils in the judgement of all who know anything of their work, have contributed very greatly to the
development of the true spirit of co-operation among
Christian missionaries in all parts of India. If they had
done nothing more than to secure the bringing together
of those engaged in common work they would have
justified themselves, and this, by their annual meetings
and the smaller committees through which they carried
on their work, they undoubtedly achieved. They did,

however, much more. Such institutions as language schools, the provision of common standards of examination in language study, the better organization of Christian literature, the facing of common problems in education and many other subjects were fruitfully essayed by these councils. The National Missionary Council during the ten years of its existence, until it became the National Christian Council, had two outstanding achievements to its credit. It was able to frame and to obtain widespread acceptance of a scheme of rules for the observance of comity between different Christian missions. Those who only know the widespread acceptance of these rules of comity sometimes forget the labour and care which was spent on elaborating their principles. It will be sufficient here to say that the rules envisage both those missions which are prepared cordially to accept the principle of territorial demarcation, and those which by reason of some doctrinal or ecclesiastical principle cannot accept such demarcation absolutely, but are willing to do their best to avoid friction of every kind. Provision is made for arbitration by the Provincial Council or the National Council, by the consent of both parties to a difference, but such arbitration has been very rare, simply because the spirit of the rules has proved so potent.

The other main achievement was the safeguarding of the work of the German missions during the war and the period immediately after its close. Probably it is in dealing with government and in kindred matters that the need for co-operation and for the existence of a representative body is most universally acknowledged. The Roman Catholic Church was not less deeply concerned in the preservation of the work of missions of " enemy " nationality than were Protestants, and it had its own institutions and methods which it used in dealing with the situation *vis-à-vis* Government.

Protestant Missions used the Provincial Councils of Missions and the National Missionary Council. The Government of India recognized the National Missionary Council in the same way as the India, Foreign and Colonial Offices in London recognized the Conference of British Missionary Societies and the Conference of Foreign Missions in North America, as the bodies with which they would deal on questions affecting the admission of non-British missionaries to India. When it is realized that a Christian community in different parts of India totalling several hundreds of thousands of souls, and large educational, medical, evangelistic and other work were concerned, it will be understood that the services of this co-operative organization in ensuring the maintenance of the work were of no little value. The work itself was maintained by the efforts of American, Continental and British societies, and of the National Missionary Society of India. Mission Trusts were formed, representative of Government and of the National Missionary Council, and the work of the leaders of the whole movement not only in India, but in London, ensured the maintenance of the principle of missionary freedom at a time when many old customs were being shaken, and in the new world created by war and post-war conditions Governments were beginning to assume new powers. Now that the German missions have returned to India and the work so hardly maintained is returning to their care, it is pleasant to reflect on the reality of the succour which missionary co-operation was able to bring to their work in the time of its need.

The period of the war was, as everyone knows, a period of great change and development in India. The political movement associated with this period is so well known that it needs only to be mentioned here. It may, however, be said that on all hands there was an increased realization of the fact that any useful all-India

Q

or provincial organ of co-operation must be not only missionary, but also Indian.   The Provincial National Councils at all times contained a number of Indian members, but so far as these bodies were representative, they were representative of missions, and not of the Indian Church in its various branches.   In 1921–1922, under the leadership of Mr. J. H. Oldham, the National and Provincial Councils considered the reorganization of their work, and it was decided to make two important changes.   In the first place the National Missionary Council was reorganized so as to be composed to the extent of not less than half its members of Indians, Burmese or Ceylonese.   The Provincial Councils followed suit, changing their names to Christian Councils (the Bengal and Assam Christian Council, the Madras Representative Christian Council, etc.), and became representative not only of the missionary bodies, but of the Indian Churches, in such a way as to become composed in roughly equal numbers of Indians and of missionaries.

The other change was the provision of a whole-time secretariat.   The National Missionary Council from its foundation had the great benefit of the half-time services of the Rev. Herbert Anderson, the secretary of the Baptist Missionary Society, and one of the best known missionaries in India.   The development of the work of the Council made it plain that more help than this was necessary, and it was decided to appoint, to begin with, one full-time secretary, and to move as soon as possible towards a staff of three.   In 1922–1923 the National Christian Council had a full-time European secretary ; in 1924 an Indian secretary was appointed also ;   and in that year the United Free Church of Scotland lent one of its most able women missionaries to assist the Council, particularly in relation to educational problems.   She was succeeded in 1927 by a missionary similarly lent by the American Arcot Mission. The Council has, therefore, for four years enjoyed the services of three full-time workers, and whatever the value of its work may be judged to be, it is certainly due not only to the reforming of its constitution, but to the securing of a staff adequate to see that resolutions are carried out, information collected, evidence sifted, and the work necessary to the achievement of practical co-operation carried on.

So much for the machinery of co-operation in India. We turn now to consider some of the departments of work, and the way in which the development of co-operation has been manifested in them.

Probably there is no department of Christian work in India where the spirit of co-operation has been so manifest and has brought forth so many fruits as in the sphere of education. Institutions such as the Madras Christian College, supported now by seven missions, or even more notably, the Women's Christian College, Madras, supported by fourteen missions, are a demonstration of the degree to which the growing needs of education in India have made co-operation necessary, and of how wonderfully that co-operation has been forthcoming when needed. It is natural that union institutions should be more easily found in the college field than among high schools, simply because the college draws from a larger area, and its work concerns a larger number of separate bodies. Increasingly, however, in the sphere of high schools the need for co-operation is becoming manifest, and one may quote examples such as the union school at Delhi and the union school at Bishnupur, Bengal, as recent examples of the missionary determination to seek increased efficiency in co-operation.

Why is co-operation found increasingly necessary in the sphere of education? The answer is two-fold. In the first place, as is shown elsewhere in this book, standards of education are rising in India. Institutions which adequately served their day and generation are finding the demands made by modern standards increasingly hard to meet. At the level of university teaching the provision of scientific equipment is a heavy and almost intolerable burden on missionary finance. While Christian schools and colleges have their distinctive type to maintain, and stand pre-eminently for education in character and for life, they can never maintain their place in India if they become academically second-rate. This general rise in standards and pressure of competition, both from Government and from private agencies, is one main reason why co-operation has been found more and more necessary as the years pass.

Not less important is the sense which is strong in Christian educators all over India, both Indian and missionary, of the distinctive type which Christian education should seek to achieve and maintain. The zeal of Indians for education, and their willingness to flock in large numbers even to poorly equipped institutions, has always brought with it a certain temptation to the principal of the school or college. It is not difficult to yield to the pressure of numbers, which means fees, and to allow an institution to develop which, by reason of its size and the comparatively slight contact of the Christian staff with the students, ceases to have any distinctively Christian value. When we speak of " Christian value ", we do not think only of the specific work of evangelization, but also and equally of the maintenance of a spirit and tone in the school, an ideal of service, an intimacy of personal contact, which are all part of that real if somewhat indefinable thing known as Christian education. We do not think that anyone who knows intimately Christian schools and colleges in India would deny the remarkable growth among educators of the sense that this distinctive type is in peril, and that it is in peril not from any attacks made on it from without, but from the failure of those who ought to maintain it. When, however, the staff or council of a Christian college or school sits down to consider how it can strengthen the spirit and deepen the life of the institution, it finds itself faced by great practical difficulties. Whereas in Christian schools for girls, Indian conditions still bring it about that the majority of the girls are Christians, this is not the case in schools for boys. Accordingly, there has grown up a movement in favour of the formation of at least some schools in India where the majority of the boys will be Christians. Again, the staff of a school which is to be Christian in spirit as well as in name ought, if possible, to be composed of Christians, and not only of those who may technically be called Christians, but of those to whom the function of the Christian teacher is in the nature of a vocation. Such men are not found easily in England or America, and it is natural that they are not found easily in India. Here, again, is a stimulus to co-operation, and it may confidently be affirmed that the most powerful motive to co-operation in Christian education to-day in India is the desire for the improvement of the spirit, atmosphere and life of the Christian schools and colleges. Many missionary educators would be willing to face the maintenance of a smaller number of schools, with the consequent shrinking in the numbers of pupils who pass through their hands, if by so doing they could ensure a more fully Christian atmosphere in the schools, and a consequently profounder effect upon the pupils, both Christian and non-Christian.

No less than that of higher education, the sphere of village education has been notable for the growth in co-operation. Here, as is necessary, co-operation takes a different form. A great Christian college may rightly be a union institution controlled by a governing board representing many different Churches. Nobody would suggest that a union primary school should be established in a jungle village, and it is important to remember that co-operation can take many forms besides the formation of union institutions. In 1919 the British and American missionary societies sent to India a Commission on Village Education, of which the chairman was the Rev. A. G. Fraser, of Trinity College, Kandy, Ceylon. This Commission, whose report was published under the title *Village Education in India*, surveyed the whole sphere of primary education conducted by the missions in the villages, and its report was widely studied all over India. The result was that many individuals in charge of village schools began to experiment with new methods, and a sense of the inadequacy of village education and of the glaring defects of the existing regime became widely disseminated. No one can doubt that the greatest single factor in the improvement in village education, as conducted by missions, has been the example of certain notable schools, particularly that conducted by the American Presbyterian Mission at Moga, in the Punjab. One may sum up the matter of co-operation in village education by saying that it has meant the sharing by Christian bodies in all parts of India of experience, both of success and of failure, gathered by one and another in remote regions. It fell to the National Christian Council to make this possible, in large measure by the publication of literature, and, most of all, by the holding of conferences in different parts of India, where those concerned with village education came together to hear, discuss and criticize descriptions of the work done at Moga and in other institutions. Visits were paid to these *foci* of experiment, and there are now in other provinces in India centres where valuable experiments are being carried on. Government recognizes these, as any student of annual and quin-

quennial reports will see, and a recent book on primary
education, written by a Hindu inspector, derived nearly
all its examples of fruitful advance in this field from the
work of missionary schools.

Another department of education in India in which
co-operation has been highly developed is that of the
training of the ministry. There is no name better
known in the history of Indian missions than that of
William Carey, and no place better known, perhaps,
than Serampore. The college he founded there has
gone through many vicissitudes, but the old charter
given by the Danish king has been in recent years re-
affirmed, and Serampore College is able, as no other
Christian college in India is, to give its own degree in
divinity. The council of the college in London and the
senate in India are fully interdenominational, representing all the great non-Roman communions, and the
students are drawn from all parts of India. Unfortunately the burden of finance has fallen almost entirely
upon a single body, the Baptist Mission. The Serampore degree is available to students of other colleges of
the same grade, and Bishop's College, Calcutta, the
premier Anglican theological college in India, and the
United Theological College, Bangalore, supported by a
number of missions in South India, enter their students
for the B.D. degree as internal students of Serampore.
The Bangalore College is a notable piece of co-operation,
and one may mention also the theological seminaries
at Ahmednagar, Pasumalai, Saharanpur and Tumkur
as among the more notable centres where two or more
bodies are collaborating in providing training for the
ministry. It may seem ungenerous in the face of this to
say that much greater co-operation is still needed, but it
is so. There is hardly anything more important for the
future of the Church in India than the training of the
ministry. Moreover, it is merely futile to discuss the

transference of authority from missions and missionaries to Indian Churches and Indian Christians, unless steps are taken to provide for the men who are to assume new responsibilities a training not less adequate than that accessible to the missionaries whose work they assume.   Missions are nearly all under-staffed in India, and, even with the measure of co-operation already achieved, much still remains to be done if we are to escape from a situation where men labour to teach a range of theological subjects with which they cannot be fully conversant.   Some have dreamt of a centre of Christian learning in India where there would be not only training for the organized ministry, but opportunity for those who wished to go deeper in the study of Christianity, to sit at the feet of those who had made themselves expert in the different departments of that study.   It may perhaps be said in explanation of the slowness with which some feel that the needed co-operation is brought about, that there is no department of Christian work in which not only in India, but in all countries, denominational feeling and tradition are so manifest as in theological training, and where, consequently, even with all goodwill fully present, the drawing together of forces is slow.

Mention may also be made of co-operation in the sphere of medical missions. Mission hospitals are practically always conducted by a single missionary body, and it is not the function of missions to maintain large and centralized hospitals, which would illegitimately compete with the proper functions of Government. Compared with China, India has singularly little to show in the way of medical training conducted under the auspices of the Church, and the reason is of course the existence of an organized system of medical training maintained by authority.   There are, however, three medical training colleges organized and maintained by missions ; two for women at Ludhiana and Vellore and one for men at Miraj in the Southern Maratha country. Ludhiana and Vellore are co-operative institutions, the latter particularly having in recent years called forth large support, especially in America. Miraj has been maintained through many years by the energy of Dr. (now Sir William) Wanless, the famous American Presbyterian surgeon, whose name is a name to conjure with all through Western India. Plans are now on foot to make this institution, the only one in the whole of India where doctors of the sub-assistant-surgeon grade are training under the auspices of a Christian body, into a union institution. On its present basis it has provided Indian Christian doctors for hospitals over a large part of India. Medical work, by reason perhaps of its distinctive nature, has, in the view of many, shared less in the general spirit of co-operation than any other part of mission work in India. Among themselves the missionary doctors have maintained communications through the Medical Missionary Association with its admirable Journal. This Association was in 1925, in conformity with the spirit of the time, made into the Christian Medical Association of India, and is open to Indian and other Christian doctors who are not in the limited and technical sense missionaries. This Association in collaboration with the National Christian Council is now completing a survey of medical missionary work in India, which it is hoped will form the basis of action and lead to development of policy in years to come.

Much the same may be said of the share of missions in industrial and agricultural work. It is rare for an industrial school to be conducted under the joint auspices of two or more bodies, while all over India there are small industrial or agricultural schools maintained by single missions. There have been, however, for many years, associations of industrial and agricultural missionaries, and more lately the Provincial Councils and the National Christian Council have given attention to this work; and through bringing workers together, making regional surveys and making widely known advance and experiment, where such has proved significant, they have done something towards the improvement of this type of work.

Christian literature is an entirely different department of missionary work from education and yet closely akin to it. If, as has been suggested above, changing conditions should make it necessary to limit the number of missionary schools and colleges in the interests of efficiency, it may still be within the power of the Christian forces, through the use of literature, to ensure that the number of people reached by the Christian message is not less but greater than before. The great obstacle to extended co-operation in the production of Christian literature is the most fundamental of all, namely, the existence of the different vernaculars. Much can be and is being done to circulate literature in English all over India, and the Association Press in Calcutta and the Christian Literature Society of Madras have taken a notable share in this. The vernacular is a different matter, and while in each language area there is a co-operative publishing concern, some of these are very weak, and live, financially speaking, from hand to mouth.

One of the more important departments of the National Christian Council's work is that styled the Indian Literature Fund Committee. This fund was begun as the outcome of a survey of Christian literature in India, made principally by the Rev. A. C. Clayton of the Christian Literature Society. This survey, with the revelation it contained of the great need for Christian literature and the still very inadequate response made to that need, led to the formation of the scheme for gaining larger funds for literature and distributing them to the different areas in accordance with their need. The Indian Literature Fund is controlled by a committee representing the contributing bodies and the provincial organizations. It is not a publishing society. Its functions are to receive statements from the different language areas of need either for the subsidizing of workers or of books, and to distribute to the different areas such funds as it has annually at its disposal, in accordance with a just view of the relative importance and needs of the different areas. There is no part of Christian work in India where a greater advance could immediately be made by the provision of even relatively small funds than in this department of Christian literature. It may, perhaps, be added here that, unlike some other countries, India has been relatively free from that violence of theological dispute, and the more horrible manifestations of the *odium theologicum*, which in some countries have made the co-operative production of Christian literature largely impossible.

In what has gone before, the spheres of co-operation discussed have fallen under two heads — co-operation in the joint maintenance of different pieces of work, and co-operation in the sharing of thought and experience in regard to work carried on by different bodies in their separate capacities. There is one other type of co-operation which may be mentioned here, namely, co-operation in regard to public questions.

We do not propose to enter here upon any discussion of the vexed question of the degree to which missionaries or other Christians should enter into politics. It is common ground to all that there are at least certain great moral issues in regard to which the Christian conscience ought to be able to express itself. Further, Christian opinion in the last fifty years has markedly developed in appreciation of the bearing of the Christian

ethic and spirit upon the whole order of society. The
movement represented in England by " Copec " may
be cited as a notable instance of this tendency in
Christian life in the West. In India, not less than in
the West, Christians have the duty of expressing and
making effective the Christian judgement on such public
issues as claim attention. In India, not less than in the
West, such judgement to be of any value whatever must
be informed by knowledge. Too often Christian assemblies have been prone to rush into public view with
resolutions on matters of general importance without
either the knowledge which will give the resolutions
meaning or the forethought and power to follow them
out in action.

It may be claimed as one of the necessary functions
of a body such as the National Christian Council of
India, that, on such matters as are felt by the general
Christian body to claim the attention and judgement of
Christians, it should be able to focus thought and make
the Christian judgement a reality. An instance may be
taken in the opium question in India, where the officers
of the Council were able to amass a great deal of information throwing light upon the use and abuse of opium
in India, material which it is widely conceded was of
value in helping to create public opinion, and thus to
lead to the great improvement in public policy in this
matter in recent years. At the present time, the Council,
with the assistance of an experienced British woman
investigator and student of social problems, is making
a study of the development of industrialism in India,
with the specific purpose of supplying a foundation of
ascertained facts, on the basis of which the different
Christian bodies, singly or together, may be able to find
ways of service. It is well known that in certain areas
in India the development of factory life has been so
great as to create most menacing problems. All Indians

are concerned with these questions, Hindus and Moslems, as well as Christians. Hindus and Moslems, however, are not slow to say that just because the industrial problem has come to India from the West, and religious bodies in the West have had to face it and think about it in the past, probably Christians can render peculiar service in India while the industrial development is still in its infancy. There is a growing conviction that this is so, and that with adequate knowledge and vision it may be possible in India, where industrial development is inevitable, still to avoid some of the evils which have followed in the train of industrialism in the West. Clearly, however, such service cannot be rendered adequately by separated denominations ; some kind of common study and consultation is necessary, and here again we find the pressure of actual need emphasizing the importance of Christian co-operation.

In bringing this brief survey of co-operation to a close, we may note as worthy of record the fundamental principle on which it is based, and which can only be neglected at the risk of the entire structure falling to the ground. It is the principle that the co-operative organization, Christian council or whatever it may be, has no legislative or mandatory power unless such is given to it by the bodies which compose it, and that it exists in virtue of another kind of authority altogether, namely, the authority of persuasion and reasonableness. Those who sigh for short cuts to quick results will always be impatient of the processes of co-operation among separated Christian bodies, each of which claims, and rightly claims, control of its own policy. It may, nevertheless, be held that a body whose authority resides solely in the value and quality of the work which it does, whose views may be disregarded by anyone who disagrees with them, and which cannot compel the acceptance of any of its opinions, exerts authority in a very

Christian sense ; it exists as the servant of the whole, and its authority resides in the thoroughness of its work, and in the degree to which as an organ of the common mind it truly expresses and adequately informs those for whom it speaks.   There are not a few who, without in any way disparaging the importance of the approach to Christian unity through a consideration of questions of faith and order, feel also that the kind of impalpable unity which grows up amongst those who have become habituated to working together along the various lines described above is a not less significant harbinger of a coming day.

One thing remains to be said, and it is perhaps the most important of all. Education, Christian literature, public questions and other sections of the missionary undertaking have been shown as demanding and receiving some measure of the spirit of co-operation. The fundamental work of missions is evangelism, not as a separate activity from all these, but as the one which inspires them all. In India it has never seemed well, unless in certain very special cases, to undertake very great campaigns of united evangelism. Men like Dr. Stanley Jones, in work which, while among a special class, has the support of all the Churches, have utilized the organization of co-operation in India in carrying on their work. The main effect, however, of the spirit of co-operation upon evangelism in India has been precisely in its least obvious and organized form. It has made it easier for men and women, Indians and foreigners of many races, drawn together in a common task for the love of India and the love of Christ, to exchange experience in the deeper things of the Spirit, to learn from one another and together to learn from their Master. It is probably more difficult to estimate the value of co-operation in the great work of evangelism than in any other single thing. In religious work the most real is the most impalpable. Those who are most deeply engaged in co-operative work would probably feel that no measure of success in the more obvious forms of co-operation would compensate for failure in this deeper realm. In the long run the modern development of missionary co-operation will be judged, and ought to be judged, by the degree to which it has been used for the deepening of devotion, the extension of the passion for souls, the focussing of attention on spiritual reality, the opening of the channels by which the Spirit flows. We make no estimate here of success or failure, but it is plain that the whole movement of co-operation, now so powerful throughout the world, would not have gained, and would not hold the attention of men, and would not claim the selfless labour it does, were it not that in it men are finding God, and in the fellowship of common search and labour are becoming more certain of His Will.

CHAPTER XIV

THE CHURCH OF CHRIST IN INDIA

By Nicol Macnicol and P. Oomman Philip

If Christ is indeed, as the old mystic said, " the root in every man "—and this is assuredly one of the bed-rock convictions of our faith—then, when from that root the first green shoots thrust their way above the earth, the Church of Christ is born. Until life has asserted its presence by growth, until, to change the metaphor, the sleeping Christ within the soul of a race or people stirs and wakes to life and to activity, the Church is only a potency, a prophet's vision for days that are yet to come. It is a great hour in a nation's history when the watcher is able, lifting up his eyes upon the fields, to perceive not by faith alone, but sight, that they have begun to clothe themselves in greenness "The Great Church awakes," the Bishop of Bombay told us recently, looking out upon the world. We can claim that in some of the missionary lands at the present time this awakening of the Christ that has so long slept in men's drugged souls is taking place, this coming into real being and consciousness of the Church of Christ. And one of the lands where this can be seen, unless desire deceives us, is surely India. It is so easy for our longings to mislead us, and yet the signs seem unmistakable that indicate a real quiver of life, a real stir and movement both among those in that land whom the Church acknowledges and among not a few who are unacknowledged and outside. The time therefore seems not inopportune for us to examine the situation more closely and to consider whether these things are indeed the tokens of growth they appear to be, and if so to inquire further whereto they will grow. If not Brahma but Christ is awaking in India, then we may hope that a new Yuga, a new Age of power, is about to dawn.

There has been a Church in India for at least fifteen hundred years. Whether or not St. Thomas sold himself into slavery that he might carry to that land the message of Christ, some messenger—if not he then another—brought it across the Arabian Sea from Syria and established that Syrian Church that remains in Travancore to this day. It has remained a small Church and divided ; it has shown little power of growth ; and yet that it springs from the Root which is Christ and draws its life from Him is proved by the fact that, through the barren and troubled centuries, it has lived on. Thus it comes about that of the 4,754,000 Christians of all kinds in India and Burma nearly one-fourth are to be found in the States of Travancore and Cochin. That total makes the Christian religion the fourth largest in India and Burma in the number of those who profess it—though far, of course, behind the two dominant religions—and the third largest in India alone.

Next in seniority to the Syrian Church comes the Roman Church. Roman Catholicism began its history in India with the coming of the Portuguese in 1478, and first among its apostles in the passion of his devotion to Christ—a Christ whom we to-day may perceive more truly but certainly not more lovingly—was St. Francis Xavier. A third era in the growth of the Church was marked, on the one hand, by the publication in 1820 by Raja Ram Mohun Roy of *The Precepts of Jesus the Guide to Peace and Happiness* and, on the other, by

R

the coming to India at the end of the eighteenth century and the beginning of the nineteenth of the first Protestant missionaries, heralds of an increasing multitude—among them Carey, the Bible translator, and Duff, the Christian educator. Through the nineteenth century two Christian streams have flowed by these two channels throughout the land, one underground and unnoted, the other manifest to the eyes of all, but both of them elements that have gone to the making of the Church of Christ that India is coming now to know and that is coming now to know herself. Only the 4,754,000 of whom mention has already been made can be numbered as within the Christian Church. How many there are besides into whose hearts " by secret sluice " the Spirit of Christ has flowed and who, perhaps largely unconsciously, are governed by Him and are members of His Body, we cannot tell. Probably those truly controlled by Him and effectively united to Him are few. In India, as elsewhere, there are many who call themselves Christians but " whose life breaks through and spits at their creed ". There are many also, as elsewhere, who pay to Him a fitful allegiance, knowing Him a little, reverencing Him more, but following Him only at a distance, and often unawares. Such " half-believers of a casual creed ", and indeed all who refuse to be called by His name, we must leave out of our account in this brief study   There are 4,754,000 in India and Burma who, in one sort or another, reckon themselves Christians, and by what these are we must judge the present, and conjecture the future, of the Church of Christ in India. But it is specially to those who are non-Roman that we shall direct attention, and it must be mainly by what we know of them that our conclusions shall be governed. Our survey must accordingly be incomplete, but, thus limited, the Church we are considering numbers a membership of 2,730,000.

The first question we must ask in regard to this Church is as to the witness of her life. Can she be said to be in India fulfilling the Church's calling and so to be " continuing the incarnation " ? To answer this question aright one must realize the elements that have gone to the making of the Indian Church. We must note the fact that Christianity, being a message of redemption from every enslaving evil, has in all history drawn to it first the most oppressed and most despairing. There is no country where there are more to be so drawn than there are in India. As soon therefore as the message of Christ came to be in any measure realized and its hope to shine, however dimly, eager multitudes turned towards it. The first, indeed, to enter the Church were not of that sort ; they came as single spies, finding truth, falling in love with the divine beauty. They were usually men of high caste, and of outstanding ability and strength of character. They were few, but they lighted a torch here and there ; and here and there the flame of these torches spread to a conflagration. It was among the " depressed " and " untouchable " classes, who are usually reckoned in India as numbering sixty millions, that these forest fires broke forth. There is no need to describe the condition of contempt to which these people are, for the most part, condemned. It is enough to say that they dare not drink from the same wells as their fellow-Hindus and that they dare not worship in the same temples. A story which Mr. Gandhi tells and which, he says, reveals " our shame and their shame " gives a hint of the demoralizing consequences that have followed from such treatment. He tells how in Orissa a man " with a half-bent back, wearing only a dirty loin-cloth ", came crouching before him. " He picked up a straw and put it in his mouth and then lay flat on his face with arms outstretched." It is these unhappy despised people who have within the last forty years

thronged into the Christian Church. It has opened the
gate of hope for them. The result is that the Census of
1921 reports that there were in that year two and a half
times as many Indian Christians as there had been in
1881.

No doubt the tidal wave that swept during these
years into the Church has begun now to slow down and
to recede. Other emancipators are on the field besides
the messengers of Christ, and other, less worthy, motives
than those of compassion are turning men's eyes towards these oppressed people and moving them at
least to talk of helping them. The Church has leisure
now to look at herself and consider how far she is truly
to be described as Christian. When she does so she
cannot see herself (what Church can ?) as " without
spot or wrinkle or any such thing ". The wrongs
inflicted through the centuries upon these fugitives
from oppression still work out their evil consequences.
When ignorance, superstition, fear have been so
deeply wrought into the soul, they cannot be exorcised
in a moment by a word, even by the great re-creative
word of Christ. Not at least unless that word has really
reached the understanding and the heart. But thousands of these people were drawn into the Church by
nothing more than a sense of bondage and a dream of
deliverance. In their case the Root that is Christ has
no more than begun as yet to send forth tendrils. The
fact that so many of these serfs have found freedom
within the Christian Church is at once her glory and a
heavy burden crushing her to the earth.

It is of the crushing burden that those who realize
the high calling of the Church are at the present time
most fully conscious. This fact creates most of the
problems for which her leaders are seeking a solution
almost despairingly. Mr. T. R. Glover has told us how
in the early centuries the Christian " out-thought "

the pagan, " outlived " him and " out-died " him. The
fleeting glimpse that these outcastes have gained of the
love of Christ may indeed in not a few cases enable them
to suffer for Him and even to die for Him, for suffering
is their lot. They may be able to say truly what a " poor
Amboinese " said in the days of St. Francis Xavier,
" I don't know what it is to be a Christian, and I don't
know what God is, but I know one thing which Father
Francis taught me, that it is good to die for Jesus
Christ ". But how to " out-think " the Hindus who kept
them in ignorance for centuries is a far-off attainment
for them yet, and how to " outlive " them is a lesson
that such depressed classes cannot but be slow to learn.
This is all the more the case since in India among the
higher classes there have been not a few who have
journeyed along the highway of the Spirit. How hard
then it must be for those who have come up from slavery
and ignorance to make good their claim to have found
the Way and the Goal. " Hindu India refuses to accept
the claim when from among its own sons have arisen
men and women who have attained nearer the Christ
ideal than the Christians around them. Daily, hourly,
the Church in India is confronted with this challenge." [1]

The problems that present themselves in these circumstances to every loyal and eager Indian disciple
of Christ are such as the following : How can such a
Church bear that witness to her Lord, which the Church
lives to bear ? How can such a Church bear rule,
under Christ, within her own household ? And yet
if she does not, how can she be or become what the
Church of Christ should be ? How can such a Church
prove herself to be, in this land of India, the instrument
of the coming of the Kingdom of God ? These are
questions to which answers are being anxiously sought
at the present time and to which answers must be given.

[1] K. K. Kuruvilla in *An Indian Approach to India*, p. 141.

When we are perplexed as to what answer to give to
the question of the witness of a Church that is far off as
yet, in the case of very many of its members, from
Christ, the Source of its life, we remember with reassur-
ance individual Christians whose lives are lived in Him
and have been enriched and transfigured by Him. What
they are the whole Church may be and, we believe,
shall be. It may be sufficient to cite two such from a
single Province in India and to suggest that they have
their parallels in every Province of the land. These
are Pandita Ramabai and Narayan Vaman Tilak.
They both belonged to the Maratha country and were
born, lived and died within a few years of each other,
differing in the remarkable gifts with which they were
endowed, but alike in the surrender of these gifts to
the service of Christ Jesus.

Narayan Vaman Tilak, as is not seldom the case
at a flowering time of the Christian faith, found in
poetry a means whereby to express his gratitude and
exultation. He takes up and carries forward the tradition of desire for the divine fellowship that has come
to him from a great line of poet-saints of the past.
When he sings of Christ, he echoes notes of spiritual
longing that have come down through many centuries,
but he does so in a new tone of rapture and attainment :

The more I win Thee, Lord, the more for Thee I pine ;
Ah, such a heart is mine !

Thou dwellest within my heart.   Forthwith anew the fire
Burns of my soul's desire.

My arms have clasped Thee and should set Thee free ; but no,
I cannot let Thee go !

There is here the inhalation and the exhalation of one
who draws breath in the atmosphere of God, one who
has attained a Nirvana that is not death but life. And

certainly no less unmistakably do we see in Pandita
Ramabai a Christian whose service of the poor and the
despised was uplifted and borne onward by a tide of
power that could only flow from God Himself. She
was of the kin of St. Catherine of Siena, uniting a
passionate devotion to her Lord with an intense and
wholly self-regardless activity of service. Happy are
the people who possess among the sources of their
inspiration an example such as hers.[1]

Through these and such as these, we know that the
Church of Christ in India is indeed the Church of the
living God, and that the light that they kindled will
shine on with increasing brightness. We cannot doubt
that in spite of so much that fills us with dismay we have
here Christ Himself, and we have here therefore the
one, holy, Catholic and Apostolic Church.

If its growth is slow and its life stagnant, how can
these faults in it be remedied and the Church attain to
its full stature in Christ Jesus ? Growth—the growth
that comes from the possession of life and health—that
is, past all dispute, the chief need of the Church in
India. It is not in any wise as necessary that it shall
expand its borders as it is that it shall be strengthened
at the centre, that its faith in Christ shall be deep-
rooted—sincere and intelligent and passionate. The
Church needs first the Spirit of God, apart from which
it is nothing but dead wood. This central necessity
we take for granted ; our aim here is to learn how we
may discover and dig clear the channels by which the
Spirit shall flow abundantly, and to note what dams
these channels up and clogs them.

One of the first of the facts that we are aware of as
affecting these problems (but whether it is a help to

[1] Lives of both Narayan Vaman Tilak and Pandita Ramabai have
been issued in the Series of *Builders of Modern India*, published by the
Association Press, Calcutta.

the life of the Church or a hindrance it is not easy at once to say) is nationalism. This spirit, so vivid and sometimes so fierce in India at the present time, has invaded the Church of Christ, as it has every department of the life of the people. Its effect is to make the Christian in whom it is present turn back again to his own people and his people's heritage and hopes with a far stronger desire than before to be one with them. But his desire is to magnify India, not yet to magnify Christ. He is a nationalist, not yet a supernationalist, —not yet, that is to say, a full-grown Christian. And which of us—" imperialists " as we so largely are, even when we do not suspect it—can cast a stone at him ?

The great gain from this nationalist quickening is just that it is a quickening, and that it makes the Church less of an exotic. It sends roots into the soil, even if the soil is less rich than it might be. It is better that the Indian Church should turn away in petulance from her foreign helpers than that she should lean upon them so as to be unable to stand up upon her own feet.

Thus the Church is withdrawing herself, often with a certain resentment, from foreign dominance. A certain number of the people have begun to say, " This is our Church ". They do not perhaps say as yet, " This is Christ's Church "—but they may have taken a real step in that direction. The duty of the foreign missionary is to welcome this advance. He should rejoice to stand aside and give room to the growing child to live its life. He should say with St. Paul, " Not that we lord it over your faith—no, we co-operate for your joy : you have a standing of your own in the faith ".[1] A full recognition of this " standing of her own in the faith " must be willingly rendered by the foreign missions to the Indian Church. They must eagerly thrust upon her the central place that is hers as both right and duty

[1] 2 Cor. i. 24 (Moffatt's translation).

" under Christ " and accept it as their part to " co-operate for the Church's joy ". What is called the problem of the devolution of authority to the Church, which is occupying so much of the attention of foreign missions at the present time in India, is vitally related to the Church's growth. Co-operation and not domination—" co-operation for her joy ",—that is the channel of help by which the wisdom and experience of foreign Churches may flow into the life of the Indian Church, enriching it and strengthening it and causing it to grow.

This co-operation of foreign missions with the Indian Church which in different areas is at different stages of life and growth and which has a cultural and economic background so unlike that of the Western Churches is not as natural and simple as it may appear at first sight. The outcaste and the suppressed of India's population who in their hundreds find refuge every year in the Christian Church bring with them baffling problems. With a religious past in which animism and not any higher phases of Hinduism play the prominent part there is the ever-present danger of their transferring to their new faith the unworthy elements of fear of spirits and superstitious practices in which they have been brought up. The oppression to which they have been subjected for generations by the higher classes no less than the constant fear in which they have been living of unknown and unknowable evil powers conspiring at every turn to do harm to them has tended to crush out of them qualities like self-confidence, independence and love of truth, so very necessary for the development of a living indigenous Church. More than all these, there is the great handicap created by their social and economic condition. Reduced to the position of landless serfs and perpetually living below the poverty line, they have come into the Christian Church in search of a salvation which in their minds is inseparable from social and economic emancipation. Through education and through patient work extending over more than one generation the character of the community which enters the Christian Church has to be transformed before a mission in any given area can hope to find a body of people who will be in a position to take over from it some of its responsibilities. Only with growth in Christian character and with improvement in economic condition can they hope in due time to co-operate with foreign missions in some measure of equality. It is, however, a remarkable tribute to the transforming power of Christianity that as the result of the work of foreign missions for the past one hundred and fifty years we have in different parts of India to-day Christian communities that are already able to carry on the work of the Christian movement in their areas with very little help from foreign sources or that are rapidly working towards that consummation. There is reason to believe that the older Churches of the West behind foreign missions are eager that the younger Churches of India should take their full share in the responsibility for the propagation of Christianity and that they should also take over the management and control of their own affairs. The missions have on the whole been generous in turning over to Indian Church bodies, either in entirety or in sections, work which they initiated, built up and carried on in the past.

The adjustments in relationship that have been going on for the last two decades between missions and those Churches which have come into existence as the result of their labours have been governed by some important considerations. On the part of the missions there is the increasing conviction that wherever indigenous Churches are established missions should adopt a policy of retiring entirely or standing behind and rendering such help to the Churches as they feel that the Churches require to enable them after a definite period to go on without the outside help coming from missions. Thoughtful leaders in the Indian Church are equally anxious that in this period of transition their Churches should not be hustled into taking over wholesale work which, though done in their midst and for their benefit for years, has grown mainly outside of them, and for that reason may not easily become their own, in the sense that they can re-create them and adapt them to suit the genius and racial heritage of India. For another equally important reason they desire that the withdrawal of missions as missions, though necessary and important for the free development of the indigenous Church, should be a gradual and carefully thought-out process. It is apprehended that any sudden withdrawal of missions may result in cutting off the young Indian Churches from that fellowship and co-operation with the older and more experienced Churches of the West, which is so very necessary for the former at this critical period of their growth. The problem, briefly stated, is how to make available to the adolescent, growing Indian Churches the collective and historic experience of the Church Universal, how to make them enter into the heritage of the Church in all lands and all ages without in any way doing violence to their natural and free development. Both the leaders of missionary societies and of Indian Churches are keenly alive to the problems indicated above; and they are adopting policies and evolving methods which it is hoped will meet the situation.

As a first step, the Churches are assuming responsibility for activities which naturally belong to them and are fundamental to their life, such as caring for the congregations, fostering and developing their spiritual life so that they may become evangelizing agencies in their localities and looking after the education and Christian training of the boys and girls belonging to the

Church. Where the Churches are at a higher stage of development in regard to membership and economic status, they assume further responsibilities like maintaining elementary and middle schools, and in some cases secondary schools, as evangelizing agencies. There are also instances of Church bodies which are responsible for the conduct of institutions where higher and technical education are given. In all such cases the main responsibility is placed on the Churches, the missions standing behind and giving them financial grants mutually agreed upon or help in personnel as desired by the Churches themselves. That the Church is the body to which all Christian activities have ultimately to be related is an ideal towards which most missions are working. The steps adopted for giving effect to this ideal vary according to the denominational policy and the development of the Churches concerned. For instance, within the Anglican communion, the Churches are now organized with Diocesan Councils and Synods that are independent and autonomous. The various Anglican missions working in India co-operate in the work of the Church by practically merging themselves in these Diocesan Councils and by placing at the disposal of these Councils, which have a predominantly Indian membership, their contribution in men and money. In the case of the Presbyterian and Congregational societies, the Presbytery or Church Council concerned has set up Joint Boards of Indians and missionaries for administering the work taken over from foreign societies. The societies give to the Joint Boards grants which, supplemented with what they are able to raise from Indian sources, maintain the work transferred. In other cases committees for evangelistic work, educational work, etc., are set up, on which both the mission and the Church appoint representatives, and the mission gives grants for such work to these committees. These arrangements that have come into existence between Churches and missions are in the nature of experiments. Therefore, defects in their working are carefully noted by both the parties concerned and steps taken from time to time to remedy them. The relationship that is thus being established and developed between the foreign missions and the Churches in India is along the right path of advance, the path, namely, of partnership and co-operation.

The way of the wise foster-parent, of the wise educator, with the growing adolescent is full of pitfalls. In China the new lesson is being learned, it would seem, through the discipline of tragic experience. In India, also, we are having dark hours, estrangements, recriminations, suspicions. At such a time in a Church's growth "offences", it may be, "must come". The way by which they may be escaped, or healed, is the way—on both sides—of a fuller possession of Christ-likeness, of forbearance and respect and love. It is hard, very hard, to be independent, when one is poor —and the Indian Church is poor. It is sadly easy to be overbearing and dominant when one is rich—or at least richer than one's poor neighbour. How can the Indian Church in her poverty refuse to receive ? How can the foreign Church learn to give with a love that has in it no patronage ? Christianly to receive may be as blessed as lovingly to give.

The sum of the whole matter is that the Church of Christ in India needs "more life and fuller"—for she must grow. There are signs of this increasing life, sometimes in a rebelliousness that may appear petulant, sometimes in experiments that may appear dangerous. "We shall call ourselves Hindu Christians," say some. "We shall put away from ourselves", say others, "the sacrament of Baptism, lest it separate us from our brethren." To take risks, to seek spiritual adventures, to blaze new paths—these things which we see in the Indian Church of to-day may sometimes be due to recklessness and insincerity, but sometimes also to a courageous and resolute faith. When these new roads of adventure lead down among the despised and ignorant, who are within the Church but who are so far off as yet from Christ, and when in the spirit of Christ men hasten down these roads to help their brethren to realize their heritage in the Church, then the Church will begin to draw men's eyes. Love of India must blossom into a love that shall desire that all her ancient wisdom should be crowned by Christ. Then the Church in India shall bear a witness that shall give her in the land an unchallengeable authority. A Church that is nationalist, because it is rooted in the people's life and the people's dreams, and yet at the same time supernationalist, because it is above time—a Church that is self-reliant, strong, because her strength and her very self are in Christ—that is the true Catholic Church whether in India or in any land. She will not be ashamed to take the help of a foreign Church and foreign Christians, for those are her brethren for whom as for herself Christ died. "The egoistic satisfaction of giving things"—and the equally egoistic dislike of receiving them—"will be replaced" in the Church "by the joy of owning things together." The Churches of the older Christian lands and the Church of India will be helpers of each other's joy.

CHAPTER XV

TOWARDS UNITY

By the BISHOP OF BOMBAY

WE in India are the pioneers of unity to-day.

At the World Conference on Faith and Order in Lausanne (1927) the only insistent note of urgency came from the mission fields, and especially from the countries where Christianity is making its way in the midst of an ancient civilization—India, Japan, China. Others regarded unity as a matter of academic interest; others again wished to satisfy their consciences by schemes of federation; we represented unity as a matter of life or death for the Church.

It is not by any merits of ours that we are the pioneers of unity at the present day. It is the call of God. We are called to be the pioneers of unity, and this call makes itself clear in circumstances which are beyond our control and beyond our choice.

THE PRESSURE FROM THE INDIANS

The first of these circumstances compelling us towards unity is the pressure from the Indian Christians. They often put it into words, but it is always there.

Every one of them has left a great religious system which embraces all the relations of family and national

life.   He wants a Christendom which will give him a
similar support, social, economic and moral.

Indian Christians are impressed by their distance
from what they have left rather than their differences
from one another.   " The difference ", said Father
Nehemiah Goreh, " between a Hindu who worships a
cow and an Indian Christian who has ceased to do so,
is so great that any theological differences there may be
between Indian Christians make no impression upon
us."   Indian Christians are united by marriage ; they
gather together in associations, or in conventions ;
they experience an ever-deepening social and spiritual
unity.

They are indignant when they reflect that the
divisions in which they find themselves imprisoned had
their origin in the controversies of foreigners in distant
lands, in which they had no part and have no interest.

The more thoughtful know that division has for
centuries been the ruin of their own country ; and the
cruellest divisions are the result of caste.   They dread
the possibility of different Christian Churches becoming
caste-churches.

The more earnest have the conversion of India
at heart.   They find that patriotic young Indians will
join any society that promises to unite Indians, but
none that will divide them.   On the other hand, if
Christendom in India was one society uniting men in
peace and concord, that would be a very miracle.
Nothing could better commend the claims of its
Founder.

The more instructed know that every nation which
has been converted has made its contribution to the
Christian society.   They long that India should do the
same.

These great reasons outweigh and overcome the
tendency of Indians to faction.   The result is a constant

pressure towards unity from the Indians. We, English and Americans, are conscious of it and know that it is fundamentally right. The Indians are only demanding the thing which our Lord Himself desires, that those who believe in Him should be one.

THE PRESSURE OF PRACTICAL DIFFICULTIES ON MISSIONS

At the same time there has been for fifty years and more a pressure of external difficulties urging the missions towards unity.

As missions expand and close in upon each other, the scandals of competition become obvious. In some small villages three missions are at work; there are more in most large towns. Even where missions have agreed on a division of territory, those territories in many areas now touch one another. There is the difficulty of enforcing discipline. A man disciplined in one church goes to another and is not always repelled. There is the difficulty of varying standards of instruction before baptism. Some Christians had been so little instructed or tested when they were baptized that their life is a disgrace to the Christian name. There is the difficulty of the moral standard. Churches teach differently about marriage and divorce, and again about abstaining from alcohol or other things. The misery of seeing all this confusion from day to day forces missionaries to thoughts of union.

Again, in these days of straitened means the missionary societies feel more and more that overlapping is expensive, and they tend for that reason to combine for the more expensive kinds of educational work, such as colleges and high schools.

Besides these difficulties, all missionaries feel in their hearts that they ought to be able to invite non-

S

Christians to join the Church of Christ and to show them where it is in India.   The difficulty arises every now and then in an acute form, when an educated man who has been attracted towards the Person of Christ and His moral ideal wishes to take the great step of sacrifice and adherence and be baptized.   To whom shall he go to be baptized ?   In the days of the Apostles, and for nearly a thousand years afterwards, there was no practical difficulty about this at all.   He went to *the* church to be baptized.   When he was baptized, he was a member of the Church of Christ.   But now he must go to *a* church to be baptized, and he must choose which church he shall join.   There are educated men in India who have refused to make that choice. " I do not want to join any of the churches ; I might, if I could, join the Church of Christ."   The difficulty does not arise where village people have never seen any other Christians except the mission which happens to be working amongst them.   Their difficulties about the churches arise later.   Missionaries ought to be able to say to Indians of all sorts : " Here is the Church of Christ in India.   Join it and in it you shall find all the promises of the Gospel fulfilled.   The Light that lighteth every man shall lighten you.   The family of the One Father shall embrace you.   You shall find that in Christ there is no longer Greek nor Jew, Barbarian, Scythian, bond nor free, but you shall find a society, which is one man in Christ Jesus, which, after all the centuries of division, offers to India at last the peace of unity."

THE PRESSURE FROM THE SPIRIT

There is one more source of pressure which is quite beyond our control.   Those of us who have been engaged in the most difficult negotiations about unity have felt it again and again.   Certainly twice in the

recent negotiations in South India between the South
India United Church and the Anglican Church it
seemed, when we met, that we were sure to separate
and give up our task, but there was a power behind
us which we all felt, and that power was pressing us
together. It was as if we were young and wayward
children, and He was very quietly saying : " Children,
children, you must agree ". The sense of this pressure
does not obliterate the sense of difference in our views
and in our systems of life and government, nor that of
our responsibility for what has been entrusted to us.
We do not think that these things will not matter, but
that they must be so combined as to please Him. We
recognize that the primary motive of all our efforts is
not anything that arises in our own hearts or brains ;
it is not a calculation of advantage nor is it a consideration of the needs of the Indian field. The motive is
the Spirit, and that is the one force which keeps our
faces towards unity.

Tendencies towards Unity

In these three ways Christians in India have been
subject to circumstantial or external pressure towards
unity. They have manifested at the same time certain
tendencies towards it which must next be noticed.

(1) *Undenominationalism*

Undenominationalism is the tendency to emphasize
those great and precious things which all Christians
have in common, and to ignore things in which they
differ. Its spiritual centre in England was for many
years the Keswick Convention. Undenominationalism
was represented in India in very early days by the
London Missionary Society, later by the Zenana Bible
and Medical Mission, the Y.M.C.A. and the Y.W.C.A.

Some circumstances of Indian Christianity favour its influence. The gospel of conversion is very simple, and is preached in much the same way by all missionaries, and received in much the same way by all converts. These circumstances give a certain support to the greatest common measure theory of the essence of Christianity, which is the distinctive mark of Undenominationalism. Under its influence some successful union institutions sprang up in various places, of which the most notable is the Christian College at Madras. Under its influence again, an attempt was made in 1911 by twelve Churches scattered all over India to form " the Federation of Christian Churches in India " on a basis which said nothing of sacraments or ministers, and nothing decisive about our Lord Himself.[1] This Federation was to have councils in seven areas and a central council, and all the federating Churches were to have intercommunion and to recognize each other's ministries. This scheme fell into abeyance when it was found that the Anglicans, the Lutherans and most of the Baptists would not join it, and when, in the following year, a system of councils was adopted which was founded on a different tendency—the next which must be considered.

(2) *Interdenominationalism*

About the year 1900 the Student Movement in England took a strong turn in a new direction. This direction was symbolized by the invention of the word " Interdenominationalism ". From that date, students and their leaders sought to co-operate, not on the basis of saying nothing about their differences but on that of

---

[1] I have been assured that among those who drafted this basis " there was no thought whatever of in any way lowering the doctrine of the Person of Christ ". However true this may be, the basis as actually drafted could be accepted by any Unitarian.

frankly acknowledging them and seeking to learn from
them.   This change affected the conception of Christian
unity in that and the succeeding generations.   The
unity of Christendom, it was seen, would not be
brought about by ignoring but by combining differences.

The spirit of Interdenominationalism came to India
by degrees, and influenced the originally undenominational societies.   The Student Movement itself arrived in
India.   The National Missionary Society of India (1905)
and the Indian Christian Associations were founded
on interdenominational principles.   These principles
were the basis of the series of Provincial Missionary
Councils and the National Council, which were founded
as a result of Dr. J. R. Mott's visit at the end of 1912
The National Missionary Council met first in 1914.
These councils underwent a great change when Mr.
J. H. Oldham visited India in 1922, and made certain recommendations which were generally approved.
Henceforward it became a rule that half the members
of these councils must be Indians, and they were called
Christian Councils instead of Missionary Councils, and
aimed at representing churches as well as missions.

These councils are a good example of the spirit of
Interdenominationalism.   Their object is to get done
what the members feel can be only done or best done
in co-operation.   They are purely consultative and ad-
visory; their decisions are never legislative or mandatory.   They respect the different views of the churches
and missions represented on them ; they do not attempt
to force any church or mission into such co-operation
as it feels would compromise its principles.   They increase the effective unity of the Christian forces, even
while they are divided.   They give an unrivalled opportunity to the working of the next tendency which must
be noticed.

(3) *Friendly Intercourse and Conference*

Mention has already been made of the drawing together of Indian Christians in social intercourse and in conventions, etc.   The missionaries were at the same time being drawn together in similar ways.   In most of the large cities there have long been Missionary Conferences meeting once a month for prayer and discussion.   The custom of spending the hot weather holidays at hill-stations has furnished an opportunity for missionaries, whose daily life was lived far apart, to meet in social intercourse, in conference and in common worship.   Such gatherings, especially at Kodaikanal and Mussoorie, have produced notable results, both on missionary comity and missionary policy.   In the language schools which were instituted more recently, the missionaries using the same vernacular have become friends from their earliest years in India.   All these opportunities are proving of incalculable advantage to the cause of unity.

The National and Provincial Councils, already mentioned, in which the Church of Rome and the Salvation Army alone are unrepresented, have given further opportunities of a similar kind.   Men and women have met in these who were previously unknown to each other.   The unknown who belongs to another church is usually an object of suspicion and of mis-understanding.   In the councils many a misunderstood and suspected unknown has become a well-understood and respected friend.   Since the reconstitution of the councils in 1922, they have furnished a favourable opportunity for the interchange of ideas between Indian and foreign Christian thinkers.

It is one of the greatest achievements of the councils that, both for the Provinces and for all India, they have enabled *central thinking* of the greatest value to be done.

The statements on comity and on the conscience clause
drawn up by the Missionary Councils, and the Reports
on rural education, opium and medical missions presented to the Christian Councils, have advanced the
thought of the Christian community. Such central
thinking is a very definite preparation towards unity.
It tends to counteract one of the most disastrous effects
of separation, which is that, once two bodies of Christians have become separate, they add every year to the
original differences on which they separated new and
irrelevant differences, and thus develop different corporate characters. After fifty years the friends of unity
will not only have the old controversy to settle, they will
have to reconcile two groups of people who have acquired
different group-opinions. Central thinking, such as the
Christian Councils in India have done, checks the formation of new group-opinions. It may even substitute
common opinion for some existing group-opinions.

(4) *The Urge towards Corporate Union*

Far back in the last half of the nineteenth century
Christian men in India were beginning to turn their
attention to the problem of actual corporate Church
union. As early as 1871 a Conference between representatives of four Presbyterian Churches met in Allahabad to consider a union of all Presbyterians in India.
But that project was despaired of, and the Conference
had to be content with founding the Presbyterian
Alliance, the fourth of whose objects was : " (4) To prepare the way for an organic union among the native
Presbyterian Churches in India ". However, the Spirit
gave to this alliance a greater success than it had dared
to hope for. The Presbyterian Church in India emerged
from it as a single body in 1904. If anyone is doubtful
of the evil of separate Church organizations, let him

remember that it took forty-three years to unite the Presbyterians in India into one Church, and even then that Church did not contain quite all of them.

In October 1901 the American Arcot Mission and the United Free Church of Scotland Mission in South India had united together, and this united Church took part in the amalgamation called " The Presbyterian Church in India ", but in so doing reserved to itself the right of entering into a wider union. In 1905 the Churches of the London Missionary Society and those of the American Board of Commissioners for Foreign Missions in South India effected a union. Though both those missionary societies had started as undenomi-national, they had passed, in the course of time, almost entirely into the hands of Congregationalists. The Churches which they founded in India were for all practical purposes Congregational. In 1908 this Congre-gational union and the Presbyterian union in South India, united in what is now " The South India United Church ".

The step which in the order of time immediately followed this union was of an entirely different character. It was the attempt to form " The Federation of Christian Churches in India ", which has been already described in the section on Undenominationalism. However, as was there explained, this proved abortive, and thus the tendency to union in India was not diverted into the lines of federal union. The great endeavour for cor-porate union was resumed in 1917. The Presbyterian Churches again took the lead, and a long series of negotiations resulted in the formation of " The United Church of India (North) " in December 1924. (After-wards the name was happily emended to " The United Church of Northern India ".)

It is quite natural from the point of view of the Indians and of Indian history that organic union should be aimed at in India rather than federal union. Most Indian Christians would like to have general inter-communion at once. But this does not mean that they are interested in federal union. They want one Church, not a federation of Churches. Every Indian Christian is alive to the immense and insidious power of caste, and recognizes that it is quite as easy for federated Churches to be caste Churches as for unfederated Churches. If the terrible tendency to caste division is ever to be overcome in Christian India it must be by thorough-going organic union.

The tendency to corporate union has in it the capacity for producing so much greater effects than any other of the tendencies described, that I think the actual unions already consummated in South and North India, and the plans at present under consideration for a further union in South India, deserve a more particular and separate treatment.

Lest I should be thought to lack knowledge or sympathy in describing the two unions, I have obtained accounts of them from men who themselves took important parts in making them, to whom my best thanks are due for their contributions.

THE GENESIS OF THE SOUTH INDIA UNITED CHURCH

The Rev. J. H. Maclean of the United Free Church of Scotland Mission, Conjeeveram, has favoured me with the following account of the union of Churches in the south which resulted in the South India United Church :

The first definite steps for the unification of Churches in South India were taken in the year 1900, and were the direct result of the South Indian Missionary Conference held in Madras in the beginning of that year. The way had been prepared by a suggestion to one of the Presbyterian Missions from its home board that it consider the example set many years earlier by the union effected in South China between the mission churches of the Reformed (Dutch) Church in America and those of the Presbyterian Church of England. A few weeks after the Conference certain representatives of the missions in South India most nearly corresponding with these two—the American Arcot Mission, the Free Church of Scotland Mission (soon to add the word " United " to its name), and the Church of Scotland Mission—met and prepared a scheme for the co-operation of the three missions in several matters, more especially in the maintenance of a teachers' training school and a theological seminary. In so doing they were simply acting on the advice of the Conference. But, encouraged by the information about the union in China, they resolved to take steps for the union of these three branches of the Presbyterian Church, and in the following year the first Synod of the South India United Church was constituted.

At first only two of the three Churches participated in the movement, for the home board of the Church of Scotland Mission, while sanctioning the proposals for co-operation, hesitated about the ecclesiastical union. It was soon clear, however, that the movement was not going to stop with this small beginning. Certain proposals made by the Indian Presbyterian Alliance for the unification of all the Presbyterian Churches in India, and dropped owing to the difficulty of giving effect to them, were now renewed. In 1904 the Presbyterian Church in India came into being, and into it passed the Synod of the South India United Church. In entering this union, however, the Synod made it clear that if the way for a wider union in the south were opened up it would be free to sever its connection with the Presbyterian Church.

This stipulation was made in view of the fact that in the south also the idea of union was taking deeper root. In 1901 proposals were made for the uniting of the churches in South India and Ceylon founded by the London Missionary Society and the American Board of Commissioners for Foreign Missions. In the course of its inquiry the committee appointed by these two missions considered the question of uniting with the Presbyterian Synod, but it was thought best that the Churches which they represented should draw

together first. Accordingly, the first General Assembly of
the " General Union of the United Churches of South India "
connected with these two missions was held in 1905. The
negotiations with the Synod, however, were continued, and
at the second General Assembly, held in 1907, the Basis of
Union drawn up by a Joint Committee was heartily agreed
upon. Later in the same year the General Assembly of the
Presbyterian Church in India handed over its South India
Synod to be part of the South India United Church, and
the first General Assembly was held in Madras in July 1908.

The Church thus constituted was a much larger body
than its predecessor of the same name, for it included not
only the Churches of the two comparatively small Presbyterian
Missions, but the much larger Christian communities of the
London Mission in the Madras Presidency and Travancore,
and that of the American Madura Mission. It even went
beyond India and included the Jaffna Mission of the American
Board. Soon afterwards the churches of the Church of
Scotland Mission were added, and in 1919 a notable step
was taken by the admission of the churches of the Basel
Mission in the Malabar District, which accepted the Basis
of Union without alteration. The United Church thus
stretches from Calicut to Jaffna, and from Vizagapatam to
Cape Comorin. Its churches, organized under eight Church
Councils, are found in fourteen Districts of the Madras
Presidency, in the States of Travancore and Mysore, and in
North Ceylon.

The union effected in 1906 is also notable for the com-
prehensiveness of its basis. The statement often made that
the union was one of Presbyterians and Congregationalists
needs modification. The original South India United Church
was indeed Presbyterian in origin and in organization. But
it is hardly correct to say that the London Missionary Society
and the American Board are Congregational societies. From
its beginning in 1795 the London Missionary Society declared
that its fundamental principle was " not to send Presbyterianism, Independency, Episcopacy, or any other form of Church
Order and Government . . . but the glorious Gospel . . .
and that it shall be left (as it ought to be left) to the minds
of the persons whom God may call into the fellowship of
His Son to assume for themselves such form of Church

Government as to them shall appear most agreeable to the Word of God ". The American Board had a similar aim. It so happened that with the establishment of separate societies on denominational lines these two organizations were left mainly in the hands of Congregationalists ; and since churches which come into being on the mission field must have some organization for the development of their life, until they reach the stage of maturity which enables them to carry out the fundamental principle referred to, it was natural that the missionaries, of whom the majority were Congregationalists, should organize the new churches on Congregational lines. But in many cases strict Congregationalism was impossible. The groups of Christians in many villages were too small to perform all the functions of local churches, and the missionary had to exercise something like episcopal authority. As the community grew the tendency was to group the churches into unions, and to give to these certain of the functions of the Presbyteries. Thus the way was prepared for union with those of a more strictly Presbyterian type.

Yet the differences between the two types were considerable. If union was to be effected a good many questions must be left open and considerable difference in practice allowed. In the matter of Creed, for instance, Presbyterians were accustomed to having a Confession, and using it as a test for their ministers and office-bearers, while Congregationalists were in favour of only such declarations as one might be led to make in his own words. But the two sides had been drawing closer in this matter. The unions of 1901 and 1904 were on the basis of statements of doctrine much shorter than the Reformation standards of the home Churches, and on the other hand in the Union of 1905 the representatives of the London and American Board Missions, while " disavowing any thought of imposing a Creed upon the Churches " yet adopted a short Confession as an expression of their " common understanding as to the fundamental facts of the Christian religion ". The Confession included in the Basis of Union of the South India United Church is somewhat fuller, yet considerably shorter than those of the earlier (Presbyterian) unions ; and the relation of the Church to its Confession is defined in two notes, one of which declares that " as the Confession is a human instrument it is understood that persons assenting to it do not commit themselves to every word or phrase ", and the other reserves to the Church the right to revise its Confession when the consensus of opinion demands it.

So with the government of the Church. Presbyterianism is an organized system. The communicant members elect their elders, who with the minister as chairman form the session, and to the leadership of this body the members submit. The higher courts are the Presbytery and the General Synod or Assembly. Strict Congregationalism acknowledges no authority beyond the local church, which manages its affairs by meetings of communicants. In the Basis of Union the autonomy of the local church is recognized, but it is stated that it may " manage its own affairs either by the whole body of its members or through its session ". The Church Council takes the place of the Presbytery on the one side and the Church Union on the other. It consists of ministers and lay representatives of the churches, and has " the oversight and care of the churches ". With it lies the responsibility for the ordination of ministers. The General Assembly has less power than a strictly Presbyterian Assembly, but more than a Congregational Union.

The Basis of Union is thus a compromise. The experience of twenty years has shown that the compromise is one that works. The tendency as time goes on is to greater centralization, and a more authoritative General Assembly. Eleven meetings of that body have been held. Of its Presidents six have been foreign missionaries, and five, Indian ministers or laymen. But the membership is preponderatingly Indian. In the first eighteen years of the Church's history the Christian community grew from 142,000 to 224,000 (or 232,000 if the Malabar Council is added). But far more important than the growth in numbers is the growth in the spirit of unity. Differences of opinion have been manifested, but they have never gone along either racial or denominational lines. So with the capacity for self-government and administration. Of these there was little when the movement started. The uniting Churches contained many able men, and some who had a keen desire for union and for the development of the Church on lines suited to the genius of this country. Yet the rank and file were quite content to be led by foreigners, and even preferred to be so. Even in the matter of union it cannot be said that the first impulse came from Indians, or that the majority desired to unite with others. As we have seen, the first suggestion came from without, and in the earlier negotiations it fell to missionaries to take the lead. I do not think they can be blamed for this. If, by being the representatives of a divided Church in the West their predecessors had introduced divisions into the East—as was inevitable at first—it was natural that they should try to lead the Churches out of these divisions into real unity. The experience of these twenty years has justified their action. The missions still exist as separate organs of the Churches of the West, but the South India United Church is becoming more and more conscious of its independence, and for this development it owes much to the union that has been accomplished. No attempt at absolute uniformity has been made. The use of a partial liturgy is recommended but not enforced. Since each Church Council frames its own rules a large liberty in organization and practice is permitted.

Of plans for the further advance of the union movement there is not space to write. At its first Assembly the Church approved of the idea of federal union with Churches which might not yet be ready for organic union ; but while believing that much might be accomplished by such a plan it has never looked on it as more than a second best, and since 1919 it has taken part in the work of the Joint Committee which is seeking a wider incorporating union. Of this nothing need be said except this—that the experience of these twenty years encourages us to make a bold venture, believing that by the fellowship which a united Church makes possible many difficulties which seem to be insuperable may be overcome.

THE GENESIS OF THE UNITED CHURCH OF NORTHERN INDIA

The Rev. F. H. Russell, D.D., of the United Church of Canada Mission (Central India) has favoured me with the following account of the union of Churches

in the north which resulted in the United Church of
Northern India.

The first beginnings of Church Union in India originated
with the Presbyterian Missions of North India. To the
Synod of the American Presbyterian Church belongs the
honour of having initiated the negotiations which in 1875
led to the organizing of the Presbyterian Alliance of India,
in which five Presbyterian Churches were represented. The
Alliance had as its definite purpose, the promoting of mutual
sympathy and a sense of unity among the Presbyterian
Churches in India; of fostering the ideals of self-support
and of the evangelization of India by the Indian Church
among its congregations; and of stimulating co-operation
and work for organic union among the various branches of
the Indian Church.

After some years of correspondence and negotiations,
during which interest in union waned and was again revived,
the Alliance met at Allahabad in December 1901, and
accepted the report of the committee appointed to complete
the Basis of Union, in which the Confession of Faith, Constitution and Canons of the South India Synod (of which an
account appears elsewhere in this chapter), with a few
modifications, were recommended for adoption. The report
was sent down to the Presbyteries concerned, and also to the
home Churches. The General Assemblies of the Church of
Scotland, the United Free Church of Scotland, and the Irish,
American and Canadian Presbyterian Churches agreed to
permit their Indian Presbyteries to effect the union.

The eighth Council of the Alliance met at Allahabad in
December 1904, the delegates to which were empowered by
their Presbyteries to consummate union if mutual agreement
should be reached. Some time was spent in the consideration of proposed amendments to the Constitution and Canons,
special difficulty being found with the question of the relation
of foreign missionaries, both ministers and elders, to the
new Church, some of the home Churches having refused to
allow the connection of their missionaries with the Church
in India to in any way affect their relations with the Church
of which they were the missionaries. This difficulty was
finally got over by inserting in the Constitution a clause to

the effect that each Presbytery should, in conjunction with
the home Church or Churches concerned, determine the
relationship of missionaries to the Presbytery.   The Alliance
then adjourned *sine die*, after instructing its representatives
to meet two days later to constitute a provisional General
Assembly of the Presbyterian Church in India.   This meeting
took place, and the new Church was constituted, in the
Jumna Presbyterian Church, Allahabad, on December 19,
1904.

From this union the United Presbyterian Church of
America, the Reformed Presbyterian Church of America,
the Original Secession Church, Scotland, and the Welsh
Calvinistic Methodist Church held aloof, though the last-
named Church later joined the Presbyterian Church and is
now a part of the United Church.

The Church thus constituted consisted of 6 Synods, with
16 Presbyteries, 105 organized Churches, with 15,444 communicants, and a total Christian community of 49,022.

It had been one of the conditions of union that the South
India Synod should be permitted to continue negotiations
for a wider union in South India, so that, when three years
later the Synod asked for permission to withdraw from the
Presbyterian Church and unite with the Congregationalist
Churches of South India to form the South India United
Church, it received the very cordial consent and good wishes
of the Church.   The latter by this removal lost twenty-seven
of its organized congregations, and 12,399 of its Christian
community, but so rapid had been the growth of the Church
in the three years subsequent to union that the original
figures were practically maintained.

During the years that followed the Presbyterian Church
continued its efforts to bring into the union other Churches
in North India following the Presbyterian system, with a
view to a still wider union in the future.   As a result of these
efforts, a delegate from the Welsh Calvinistic Methodist
Church of Assam was present at the meeting of Assembly
at Nagpur in December 1917, and addressed the Assembly
on the question of the union of his Church with the united
Church.   The Assembly appointed a delegation to visit the
Assam Assembly, and at its next meeting at Calcutta in
1919 it welcomed the Welsh Church to its membership,

making a special concession, in view of the peculiar circumstances, which left the Assam Church free to continue its own rules as far as it might wish, and fixed a definite rate for its assessment and representation in the General Assembly.

By this further increase in its membership, added to its own growth during the preceding years, the Presbyterian Church now had a total of 702 organized churches, 36,816 communicants and a Christian community of 218,522.

At the Nagpur Assembly in 1917 there was also present a delegate from the American Marathi Mission, who, too, spoke on union. This was the Rev. Dr. R. A. Hume of Ahmednagar, whose name deserves special mention as one who played a prominent part in bringing about the union of the Presbyterian Church and the Congregational Churches of Western India. Negotiations were entered into with the General Aikya of the Congregational Churches, and the Assembly of 1921 sent down to Presbyteries a draft Constitution for the United Church, on which a report presented to the next Assembly in 1923 showed a two-thirds vote in favour of the Constitution. The Rev. Dr. Hume and Rev. Mr. Modak were present and addressed the Assembly on the position of the General Aikya with regard to union. The Committee on Church Union was instructed to carry on negotiations with a similar committee of the General Aikya, with a view to as speedy union as possible, and it presented a report to the Assembly of 1924 at Bombay, giving the various steps which had led to the unanimous decision of the General Aikya to unite with the Presbyterian Church to form what was later designated as the United Church of Northern India.

With a view to this union a new Confession had been prepared and submitted to Presbyteries for consideration. A number of amendments had been proposed, and the matter had not been finally issued when the proposal to consummate union was made. Any difficulty in this connection, however, was obviated by the decision of the General Aikya to unite on the basis of the new Constitution and, for substance of doctrine, of the existing Confession of the Presbyterian Church. After hearing and discussing the report of its Union Committee, the Assembly on the 30th December 1924 resolved immediately to proceed to union with the Con-

gregational Churches, and the representatives of the General
Aikya being present in Bombay for the purpose, the union
was effected the same afternoon, Dr. Hume being unanimously elected the first moderator of the new Assembly.

Some difficulty was still felt with regard to certain points
in the Constitution, and several other matters affecting the
union, and a special Commission of the Assembly was
appointed to consider in detail the Constitution, draft rules
and forms of procedure, and all other matters which in its
judgement might be necessary for bringing the union into
effective operation, and to convene a meeting of the General
Assembly when the Commission was ready to report. This
meeting was called in December 1926, at Ahmednagar, and
the report of the Special Commission submitted.

The chief modifications in the Constitution, as submitted
to and approved by the Assembly, were in the direction of
simplifying the carrying on of the work of the Church, while
guarding against anything that might impair the real unity
of the body. Church Councils or Presbyteries were empowered to frame their own rules, in accordance with the
Constitution for Church Councils adopted by the Assembly,
such rules to be sanctioned by the respective Synods. Similar
authority was given to Synods, their rules to be approved by
the Assembly. Large liberty was given to meet the varying
conditions throughout the area covered by the United Church,
and only such rules as were felt to be essential in the interests
of integral unity were made binding.

The relation of missionaries to the United Church was
defined. All references to missionaries, as such, were
omitted from the Constitution, but the presence of ordained
missionaries, as ministers, was taken for granted in the rule
determining the roll of Church Councils. As some doubt,
however, was felt by some Church Councils as to the precise
position of missionaries, the Assembly at Ahmednagar
passed a ruling to the effect that all ordained missionaries
whose names were on the rolls of the Presbyterian Church
in India or the General Aikya at the time of union were, by
virtue of this, members of the United Church. Ordained
missionaries coming to work within the field of the United
Church subsequent to the union may be admitted by the
Church Council concerned, with the consent of its Synod.

The statistical report submitted to the 1926 Assembly gave as constituting the membership of the United Church of Northern India 862 organized churches, 20,253 communicants, and a Christian community of 210,824.

It should be added that at the present time approaches are being made by several denominations in North India with a view to union with the United Church.

OBSERVATIONS ON THE UNIONS DESCRIBED ABOVE

There are a few observations which I desire to make on these two accomplished unions, as a spectator looking on from outside.

(1) *The Unions' Good Examples of Combination*

In all such unions as we hope to see gradually rebuilding the unity of the Church, one essential character must be that those bodies that come together will find that any permanently valuable characteristics which they had when separate have been preserved for the use of the universal Church. Thus, these unions will be essentially combinations of two or more principles of Church life and government. This is true both of the S.I.U.C. and of the United Church of Northern India. Neither of these Churches can now be called Presbyterian or Congregational. They have effected a genuine combination of the essential principles of both systems.

(2) *Constitutional Characteristics of the Combination*

From the point of view of a student of history and Church constitutions, it is obvious that the congregational system, so long as it insisted on the absolute autonomy of each congregation, was unable to build a Church of any great size, and incapable of suggesting the lines for a universal Church. The numerical

success of their Indian missions itself called attention
to this weakness of their system.   Many Congregationalist ministers in India felt the difficulty acutely.
This is well expressed by Mr. Maclean in a paper
written in 1908.

> As Church life developed, however, many missionaries
> felt that whatever might be said regarding the home Churches,
> it was desirable in India that the individual church should
> have the advice, and, even to some extent, be under the
> control of a larger body representative of a group of churches.

Consequently, both these united Churches take from
Presbyterianism the system of the presbytery, with its
control over all things appertaining to the ordination
of ministers, and many things concerning the life
of parishes (congregations). The internal affairs of
the local congregation, however, may in the united
Churches be managed either, as they are in Congregationalism, by the congregation as a whole, or, as they
are in Presbyterianism, by an elected body of elders or
deacons. This choice is one example of a principle of
union arrangements on which stress should be laid.
The older people will not change their minds, and only
with pain will change their ways. It is much better, if
it can be managed, that the two methods of doing
things should be left in the united Church, so that the
transition to union shall not be too painful to the old,
and the young will have before them examples of both
methods, from which freely to choose when their turn
comes to have authority in the Church.

But to return to the constitution, the Church Council,
as it is called, takes the place of the presbytery in Scotland. The presbytery itself had taken the place of the
Bishop, and essentially the great difference between the
Presbyterian system and that which preceded it was
that it accomplishes by means of a committee all the

things which in the diocese were in the hands of a
single officer. It is an interesting observation, therefore, to myself and my fellow churchmen, that the effect
of these unions is to return to the very ancient theory
of the autonomy of the diocese in certain defined
matters. There is also a return to the very ancient
notion that the diocese is the real unit of the Church,
not the parish or the congregation, nor any higher
combination of dioceses. Above the Church Councils
in the two united Churches are other Assemblies :
in the S.I.U.C. only one General Assembly ; in the
Church of Northern India, first of all, a series of Synods,
co-ordinating for certain purposes the local churches of
large areas, and above them the General Assembly.

The General Assembly in neither case appears to be
what it is in Scotland, the Supreme Court of Appeal
in the discipline of ministers. In neither case has it
absolute legislative authority. It can only legislate
with the consent of two-thirds of the Church Councils
in the Southern Church, and two-thirds of the votes
cast in the Church Councils in the Northern. It can
only accept appeals for decision if inferior bodies choose
to submit themselves to what is practically its arbitration. The General Assembly of the Northern Church
can entertain appeals from the decision of Synods on
matters which affect the Church as a whole. These
points sufficiently illustrate the powers of the General
Assembly. It is not, strictly speaking, the governing
body of the whole Church. It can only govern by
consent. The consent required is not a unanimous
consent, but the consent of some majority in the con-
stituent churches ; but that degree of consent is
required. Ultimately, consent is the only basis of any
Christian Church government, and the larger assemblies
of the Church, before they had placed at their disposal
the powers of the civil government for carrying out

their decrees, can have had no power of directing the Church, except through consent.   On the other hand, in modern days there are parts of the Church where the smaller units have voluntarily given their consent before-hand to be ruled by a central authority, and the advan-tage of this becomes very manifest, either when a great undertaking has to be conducted by the Church as a whole, or when it is remembered that small units are very apt to be defective in that wisdom and experience which the whole of the Church in a large country has at its command.

(3) *Confessions of Faith*

In the matter of Confessions of Faith, the problem of union was more difficult even than in that of government.   The Congregationalists started with an inherited objection to creeds in themselves, whereas the Presbyterians inherited long confessions (particularly the Second Helvetic Confession, and the Westminster Confession, the first of which declared adherence not only to the Œcumenical Creeds but to the Definitions of Faith of the four first General Councils, and to the so-called Creed of Athanasius, while the second incor-porates in its own articles all the technical terms with regard to the Person of our Lord, which are used in the Nicene Creed or the Chalcedonian Definition).   The solution in the S.I.U.C. has been to agree to a Confes-sion of Faith "as a basis of union, and as embodying substantially the vital truths held in common by the uniting Churches ".   In the North of India the Presby-terians had, in view of facilitating union with non-Presbyterians, prepared a similar (though much more elaborate) Confession of Faith, which, however, as Dr Russell has mentioned, was not adopted as the basis of union.

The principle on which the Confession of the S.I.U.C. and the rejected Northern Confession seem to have been based is that of stating the truths which all the ministers and thoughtful members of the uniting Churches agreed to regard as vital. They omit certain truths and certain well-known expressions which, presumably, did not command at the time of the union such universal consent. In the face of history it is impossible to affirm that because the Church or a Church omits from its creed or confession a certain truth, it may be assumed not to believe it. For instance, there is no mention of the Lord's Supper in the Œcumenical Creeds, but certainly the Catholic Church did not mean by that omission to express any doubt about its belief in either the necessity or the truth of that Sacrament. Still, there is a great difference when persons, or bodies of persons, who have previously affirmed a certain truth cease to affirm it. The least that *that* can mean is that they regard with equanimity the neglect or denial of that truth by their ministers. It would be out of place in this chapter to compare these Confessions of Faith either with the Œcumenical Creeds or with the Westminister Confession. I hope I am correct in understanding that each of them is of the nature of a creed of union. It aims at setting out those things which the uniting Churches at the time of their union considered necessary, on the one hand, to that life and preaching, and, on the other hand, to their mutual confidence, the one in the other, which justified their corporate union.

Quite another solution of the problem of a confession of faith for uniting Churches is illustrated by the Northern Union. Here the Congregationalists " offered to unite with the Presbyterian Church on the basis of the latter's New Constitution, adopted in 1923, and (for substance of doctrine) of its existing Confession of Faith ". This offer was accepted. Thus, the said existing Confession of Faith becomes the confession of the united Church, and at the same time it is permissible for anyone in the united Church to accept that confession only " for substance of doctrine ". This confession starts by explaining that it " does not reject any of the standards of the parent Churches, but, on the contrary, commends them—especially the Westminster Confession of Faith, the Welsh Calvinistic Confession of Faith and the Confession and Canons of the Synod of Dort—as worthy exponents of the Word of God, and as systems of doctrine to be taught in our churches and seminaries ". The confession itself includes the typical key-words and phrases of œcumenical Christianity and of Calvinism. Many of these—especially such as originated in the great ages of controversy —are absent from the Confession of the S.I.U.C., and still more had been removed from the rejected Northern Confession.

What, then, does the acceptance of this document " for substance of doctrine " mean ? I have not the information necessary for answering this question with regard to the United Church of Northern India. I therefore leave that aspect of the matter aside. For the purposes of this paper, it is important to recognize that this procedure of the Northern Union represents an alternative to the drawing up of a Creed of Union. That alternative is, that the uniting Churches should affirm some long-tried and universally or widely accepted standards, at the same time agreeing upon the sense in which the word affirmation is to be understood. I submit that two methods of affirmation of an ancient standard of faith are equally admissible and honest. One man may mean, by his affirmation, " I believe the truths stated in this standard, and I think the words in which they are stated are the best possible for the purpose ". Another man may mean, " I believe the truths stated in this standard, though I should not have chosen the words in which they are stated, and do not think them the best for the purpose ". Both of these states of mind constitute sincere acceptance. But there is a third state of mind, " I believe three-fourths of the propositions contained in this statement, and am willing that ministers and people of the Church to which I belong should preach and believe the remaining quarter, which I cannot believe ". Is that sincere acceptance of a standard ? Does it afford a basis for union ?

(4) *The Position of Missionaries in the United Churches*

Great difficulties appear to have been encountered on the subject of the position of missionaries in the united Churches. It was settled in general by allowing the different Church Councils to make what regulations they pleased on this subject. These regulations varied from giving the missionaries a place and vote on the Church courts as regular members, or giving them places as assessors, sometimes without vote, to demanding that they should renounce their membership of their home Churches if they desire to be members of the united Church. The home Churches in some cases insisted on retaining the discipline of the missionaries in their own hands. In other cases, they allowed them to pass under the discipline of the united Church. These variations are said to have been found no hindrance to unity.

These difficulties appear to a student of unity to indicate certain assumptions which are not without serious dangers.

(*a*) There seems to be a latent idea that the object of our efforts is an Indian Church, in the sense of a Church consisting of Indians. The common use amongst Protestants of the words " the Indian Church " to mean simply the sum total of Indian Christians shows the same deplorable tendency. So, again, does the sharp distinction between Church and Mission which is frequently made. All these ways of thinking are full of peril. A racial Church is not the Church of Christ. A Church in which Indians, as such, have exclusive rights is racial. In Christ's Church everyone, whether minister or lay member, has the rights of his status in the Church, whatever his race If in any Church a minister, because he is a foreign missionary, is disqualified from sitting on a Church court, that Church has taken a step towards becoming a racial Church.

(b) There seems to be a latent assumption that the united Church is a new Church, and that by joining it a man leaves his former Church. But this is only true if the common but false view is accepted that each Church necessarily represents a different brand of Christianity, to which its adherents hope to win over the rest of Christendom. The true path of unity is to go back to the territorialism which prevailed in the Early Church. We must have, once again, one Church in each village or town, and one Church, including all these, in each district, and one Church, including all these, in each country. The Churches of different countries must again recognize each other as parts of the one Holy Catholic and Apostolic Church. Towards this ideal we must build. We build amiss if we build on assumptions that traverse it. Thus, if it is allowable for a member of the Church of Scotland or the United Free Church of Scotland to live and work in the United Church of Northern India, that ought to imply that he will pass under the discipline of that Church while he is in India, but in Scotland will be under that of the Scottish Church to which he belongs. To adopt that theory is to take a step towards rebuilding the indispensable territorialism of primitive days.

NEGOTIATIONS FOR UNION BETWEEN THE S.I.U.C., THE ANGLICANS AND THE WESLEYANS IN SOUTH INDIA.

An attempt at a still more extended organic union is in process of negotiation in South India. It began with a meeting of Indian clergy at Tranquebar in 1919. This was followed by the appointment of a Joint Committee of the Anglican Church and the S.I.U.C., which met twice in 1920, and five times subsequently up to and including 1928. This Committee was joined by representatives of the Wesleyan Church in Southern India in 1925.

One is at a disadvantage in speaking of negotiations which are still pending. I may, perhaps, state one or two salient points about the agreements that have already been arrived at by the Committee—it must be remembered that the Churches have yet to consider these agreements, and may or may not ratify them :

(*a*) First of all we are agreed about the object of union:

That the only union which Christians should aim at is the union of all who acknowledge the name of Christ in the Universal Church, which is His Body : and that the test of all local schemes of union is that they should express locally the principles of the great Catholic unity of the Body of Christ. Our only desire, therefore, is so to organize the Church in India that it shall give the Indian expression of the spirit, the thought, and the life of the Church Universal.

(*b*) On the Scriptures it was agreed :

That the Holy Scriptures of the Old and New Testaments contain all things necessary to salvation and are the rule and ultimate standard of faith.

(*c*) With regard to creeds, it was agreed :

That we accept the Apostles' Creed and the Nicene Creed as containing a sufficient statement of the faith of the Church for a basis of fellowship.

(*d*) On the two Sacraments of the Gospel, the following was agreed :

That the two Sacraments, Baptism and the Supper of the Lord, are to be ministered with unfailing use of Christ's words of institution and of the elements ordained by Him.

(*e*) With regard to the acceptance of Episcopacy it was agreed :

(5) A. That believing that the historic episcopate in a constitutional form is the method of Church Government which is more likely than any other to promote and preserve the organic unity of the Church, we accept it as a basis of union without raising other questions about episcopacy.

B. That by a historic and constitutional episcopate we mean :

(*a*) That the bishops shall be elected. In the election both the diocese and the province shall have an effective voice.

(*b*) That the bishops shall perform their duties constitutionally in accordance with such customs of the Church as shall be defined in a written constitution ; and

(*c*) That continuity with the historic episcopate be effectively maintained, it being understood that no particular interpretation of the fact of the historic episcopate be demanded.

(6) 1. That after union all future ordinations to the presbyterate (ministry) would be performed by laying on of hands of the bishops and presbyters (ministers) ; and

2. That all consecrations of bishops would be performed by bishops, not less than three taking part in each consecration.

Further, on the nature of Ordination the whole Joint Committee agreed as follows :

In Ordination, God, in answer to the prayer of His Church, bestows on and assures to him whom He has called such grace as is appropriate and sufficient for that ministry, which grace, if humbly used, will enable the minister to perform the same.

It was further agreed that the existing ministers of the uniting Churches should be " accepted as Ministers of the Word and Sacraments in the Church after the union," with sundry regulations designed to guard against transfers of ministers which might cause distress or division. For the next thirty years ministers not episcopally ordained, from the founder Churches in the West, who may wish to come out as missionaries, should be allowed to officiate on declaring their consent to abide by the Faith and Constitution of the Church; but after that period " the Church will consider and decide the question of such exceptions to an episcopally ordained ministry ".

A great deal else was agreed with regard to Church Committees of Parishes or Congregations, and with regard to the Councils of the Church. Suggestions for solving questions about intercommunion have been adopted. The attempt is now (1928) being made to work out the implications of the theory which has been adopted, that none of the uniting Churches will be extinguished by union, but that each will live on with an unbroken but not separate life in the one body of the united Church. This leads to various decisions about preserving existing contacts with Churches outside India and other matters.

The general progress of these negotiations serves to show two things which are important in the theory of Church union :

(i) Every union which is negotiated depends upon local conditions. It should recognize those similarities of organization or belief which exist, and take full advantage of them. It will not, therefore, itself solve the universal problem of Church unity, but it must keep an eye on that problem, and endeavour to avoid any action which will make further and wider union more difficult.

(ii) With regard to the problems of organization involved in this union, they are still more difficult than those which have been solved in the Southern and Northern unions between Presbyterians and Congregationalists, but the negotiators have steadily taken the road which has been described above, and which met with the approval of the World Conference on Faith and Order at Lausanne. This approval was given in the following somewhat elaborate statement :

In view of (1) the place which the episcopate, the councils of presbyters, and the congregation of the faithful, respectively, had in the constitution of the Early Church ; and (2) the fact that episcopal, presbyteral and congregational systems of government are each to-day, and have been for centuries, accepted by great communions in Christendom ; and (3) the fact that episcopal, presbyteral and congregational systems are each believed by many to be essential to the good order of the Church, we therefore recognize that these several elements must all, under conditions which require further study, have an appropriate place in the order of life of a reunited Church, and that each separate communion, recalling the abundant blessing of God vouchsafed to its ministry in the past, should gladly bring to the common life of the united Church its own spiritual treasures.

This statement contemplates that the union of the whole Church would involve a recombination of the elements of system or government named in it. None of these are to be lost. The fact that in certain Churches one or other of them has been developed exclusively, has emphasized the meaning of each. Recombination must, however, involve a certain limitation in every case. Thus, Congregationalism cannot be represented by an absolute autonomy of every congregation, if there is to be any central government of the Church of whatever form. Presbyterianism cannot be represented by an absolute maintenance of the principle called the parity of ministers, if there are to be bishops who have

the duty of supervision over other ministers, and if
deacons are to be counted as ministers. Episcopacy
cannot be represented by an autocratic episcopate, if
the bishops have to obtain the consent of their synods
of clergy, or of clergy and laity combined, or of their
fellow bishops to most of their actions. Thus, recombination means a balance between the various elements
combined. It cannot mean the preservation of that
unrestricted exaggeration of the elements, which may
have taken place when a system of Church government
was founded on one of them only.

The required combination happens not to be very
difficult in South India—perhaps one might even say
in any part of India. There is first of all the very great
similarity between the organization of congregations or
pastorates or parishes, as they have grown up under
different missions. Some kind of management of the
affairs of the congregations either by the whole congregations or by elected members of them is fairly
general, especially in the south of India, amongst those
Churches which at present are negotiating for union.
If the Congregational spirit is satisfied by such a degree
of autonomy as the congregations have in the S.I.U.C.,
then the claims of that element have been met, except
so far as that spirit will also demand that the government exercised by the central authority must obtain to
a very large extent the consent of those who are governed. Then, again, there exists a system of assemblies
both in the S.I.U.C. and in the Anglican Church,
sometimes organized by missions, sometimes part of
the organization of the Church. In these Assemblies
ministers sit by right, and they take, together with
representatives of the laity, a real part in the government. The question which arises here, is whether such
assemblies adequately meet the demands of the spirit
of Presbyterianism.

Lastly, there exists in the Anglican Church a system of Episcopacy which has in India, as in all the sister Churches outside the British Isles, become constitutional, that is to say, the bishops require to gain the consent of their Synods or Councils in regard to a large number of matters, and in practice they take the opinion of such Synods or Councils in other matters as well. The conception that the bishop is not something by himself, but that the unit is the bishop and his diocese, is gaining ground, and in India is the principle of all our recent developments. Further, the bishops are constitutionally bound to act as a College, not every one at his own discretion, in matters of doctrine and worship. This conception of Episcopacy is not in any restricted sense Anglican. It is the conception of Episcopacy which existed in the undivided Church for centuries, and which carried the Early Church in the Roman Empire through the very same stages through which the Church in the Indian Empire is now passing. Thus Episcopacy as it now exists in the Anglican Church in India is capable of combination with the principles of the other systems. Further, the undoubted attraction which Episcopacy has for the Indian mind gives an additional reason why this combination should be effected.

THE HISTORIC AND CONSTITUTIONAL EPISCOPATE

The negotiators in South India have proposed to accept the principle of the historic episcopate in a constitutional form without raising other questions about Episcopacy. This is the acceptance of a fact, while men may hold and teach different theories about it. To some the theory of the apostolical succession is of great importance as true and as symbolizing spiritual truths. To others it is an erroneous bit of history, which has led to superstitions and abuses. A member of the Church will not be bound to either opinion ; a minister will not be condemned for teaching either. But the fact that all will accept is that the bishop, who has been set according to the historic custom over each convenient group of local Churches, does exercise all that he can of the authority which our Lord left to His Apostles, especially the oversight of the whole pastoral work of the Church ; and in this he has special responsibilities in accordance with the leading of the Spirit from the earliest times. These responsibilities concern the preservation of the purity of the faith, the direction of public worship, the ordination of ministers, the discipline of the Church, especially in excommunication and reconciliation of penitents. In all these duties he is bound in varying degrees to obtain the assistance and consent of his fellow-clergy and his lay people, and to act in accordance with the judgement of his fellow-bishops. But he has a special responsibility, a special gift of God for fulfilling it, and a special authority.

This subject is confused beyond bearing if political terms are introduced into it. The Church is not a democracy nor an oligarchy, and the only sense in which it is a monarchy is that Christ is its King. But, if one considers government among men, there is only one best form of government, and that is that a people should find its best men and make them its rulers and obey them. That is from the human side a good description of Episcopacy as it should be. But from the divine side the consecration (like the ordination of any minister) makes the bishop God's man more than the people's man. In all his work of oversight he should bring to the people that loving forbearance of God which wishes for nothing but willing compliance. He forgets that he is governing, and the people forget that they are obeying, because, like the Good Shepherd, he leads and they follow.

THE PRINCIPLES OF UNITY

Out of this fragment of contemporary history there emerge certain guiding principles of unity. As we get nearer to unity, we see them more clearly.

(1) The Church must be one, really one, visibly one, outwardly as well as inwardly one. This unity must be at hand ready to impress anyone who comes to the Church. Where is the Church of Christ ? That question ought to be easy to answer in any place. This condition is not satisfied by a partition of territories between different, separate and often competing Churches. The one Church in every place must be the one Church in every other place, that is the one Holy, Catholic and Apostolic Church.

(2) We believe that in spite of our differences and waywardness and sins, God sees what we do not see, one Church on earth at this present moment. We have to clear away all those things, both in our souls and in our organizations, in opinion and in practice, which hide from us and from all men the unity of the Church, which the all-seeing eye of God alone can perceive. Thus, we are not trying to invent yet another Church, we are trying to see the Church that God sees and to make it visible.

(3) This process will preserve and purify everything now to be found in the Churches that can really serve the Universal Church. Every union will be a process of combination, and at the same time a process of alteration and improvement.

(4) We may, in making a union, leave unresolved a good many questions of thought and even of practice. We may leave them to be decided by generations who

have lived together, prayed together, thought together, organized together, as one body, and those generations will be better able to make the choice between our differences than we. They will be qualified by unity to judge between those differences.

(5) God's purpose for unity holds. We go our various ways, we pursue sometimes one policy, sometimes another, we fail, we procrastinate, we succeed, we only make partial unions, we see but a few steps ahead, but all the time we know that we are working towards God's purpose, and that will not fail. The unity movement is assured of success, because God's purpose holds.

INDEX

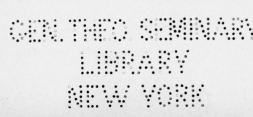

Printed in Great Britain by R. & R. CLARK, LIMITED, *Edinburgh*.

NEW AND RECENT WORKS ON RELIGION

The Primitive Church.

Studied with special reference to the Origins of the Christian Ministry. By BURNETT H. STREETER, M.A., D.D., F.B.A., Canon of Hereford. 8vo.

Adventure : The Faith of Science and The Science of Faith.

By BURNETT H. STREETER, M.A., D.D., F.B.A.; CATHERINE M. CHILCOTT, M.A.; JOHN MACMURRAY, M.C., M.A.; ALEXANDER S. RUSSELL, M.C., M.A., D.Sc. 8vo. 7s. 6d. net.

Christianity and the State.

By the Most Rev. WILLIAM TEMPLE, D.Litt., Archbishop of York. Crown 8vo. 4s. 6d. net.

Disestablishment.

The Charge delivered at the Second Quadrennial Visitation of his Diocese, together with an Introduction, by HERBERT HENSLEY HENSON, D.D., Lord Bishop of Durham. Crown 8vo.

A Christian State.

Reprinted, with a Preface, from "The Times." By Sir LEWIS DIBDIN, D.C.L., Dean of the Arches. 8vo. Paper Cover. 6d. net.

St. Paul's Epistle to the Ephesians.

A Revised Text and Translation, with Exposition and Notes. By J. ARMITAGE ROBINSON, D.D., Dean of Wells. *Cheaper Reissue.* 8vo. 12s. net.

Studies in Christian Philosophy.

Being the Boyle Lectures, 1920. By W. R. MATTHEWS, M.A., D.D., Dean of King's College, London. *Second Edition.* 8vo. 8s. 6d. net.

Human Values and Verities.

By HENRY OSBORN TAYLOR, author of "The Mediaeval Mind," etc. 8vo. 8s. 6d. net.

The New Quest.

By RUFUS M. JONES, D.D., Professor of Philosophy, Haverford College, U.S.A. Crown 8vo. 7s. 6d. net.

MACMILLAN AND CO., LTD., LONDON

NEW WORK ON BUDDHISM

The Pilgrimage of Buddhism and a Buddhist Pilgrimage.

By JAMES BISSETT PRATT, Ph.D., Professor of Philosophy in Williams College, U.S.A., author of "The Religious Consciousness." Medium 8vo. 15s. net.

"This is an attempt to give an account not only of the origins of Buddhism in India but of its spread throughout the East and its present status in all countries save Tibet, Nepal, and Mongolia. . . . Dr. Pratt's claim to our attention is his wide knowledge of Buddhism as it actually exists. . . . Concerning modern Buddhism in Ceylon, Burma, Siam, Indo-China, China, Korea, and Japan, he supplies much first-hand information that is of great interest and value."— *The Times Literary Supplement.*

"A long book, and more, a full book, one that most to whom the subject means much will buy (it is cheap) to have on shelf for reference. . . . It is eminently readable. . . . There is beauty and vividness in description, without the rattle of the globe-trotter. There is earnestness, appreciative sympathy, sincerity, yet withal ripples of humour. . . . A book good and useful in a big way."— *C. A. F. Rhys Davids in "The Journal of Philosophical Studies."*

WORKS BY SADHU SUNDAR SINGH

Reality and Religion: Meditations on God, Man, and Nature.
With an Introduction by Canon BURNETT H. STREETER. Crown 8vo. 2s. 6d. net.

The Search after Reality: Thoughts on Hinduism, Buddhism, Muhammadanism, and Christianity.
Crown 8vo. 3s. net.

Meditations on Various Aspects of the Spiritual Life.
Crown 8vo. 2s. 6d. net.

Visions of the Spiritual World: A Brief Description of the Spiritual Life, its Different States of Existence, and the Destiny of Good and Evil Men as seen in Visions.
Crown 8vo. 2s. 6d. net.

The Sadhu: a Study in Mysticism and Practical Religion.
By Canon BURNETT H. STREETER and A. J. APPASAMY, B.D. Crown 8vo. 5s. net.

MACMILLAN AND CO., LTD., LONDON